LEFT BEHIND:
Jesus

In the Age of the
American Empire

Brent Bourgeois

the apocryphile press
BERKELEY, CA
www.apocryphile.org

apocryphile press
BERKELEY, CA

Apocryphile Press
1700 Shattuck Ave #81
Berkeley, CA 94709
www.apocryphile.org

Printed in the United States of America
ISBN 1-933993-74-X

table of contents

foreword

I WAS IN LONDON IN LATE FALL of 2004 with a group of friends that were all in one way or another a part of a worship concert to be held at a church in Central London later that week. We had finished rehearsing for the day and had decided to all go out together for dinner that evening.

You went all the way to London to do a worship concert? And you're going to talk to me about starving kids in Malawi? How many Malawi meals could your plane ticket alone have bought?

Ummm...that's my conservative "friend," who sits on my right shoulder and will appear from time to time in this book to ask a question, make a point, or just generally give me a hard time. He really wasn't supposed to make an appearance *in the first paragraph.*

Anyway, there were seven of us in all at dinner: My son Adrian, who was seventeen years old at the time, and I, and five other people. These were people that I would consider good friends—either musicians, or business associates that I have known for quite some time and find the conversation with easy and fluid. We were well into the main course when someone made a comment about Iraq. I had learned through painful experience that to say anything at a time like this was to say too much. I knew that besides my son, I was sitting at a table of conservative Christians who most likely supported President Bush and the war in Iraq. We were having a nice, pleasant evening and I had had too many of these types of situations turn from nice to ice over politics, and anyways, I frankly didn't have the energy to debate the issue. So I kept my mouth shut between bites of pasta.

One of the people with us knew well my position on the war, and thought it would be good fun for me to "tell the table what I thought." I politely demurred, and then, when egged on further, I more strongly resisted. This in turn roused the person next to her, who also thought it would be "all in good fun" to hear what Brent, the village lefty, had to say. After even further baiting, I, weakly, took the bait, and fell into a debate with a guy that up until that point I thought I had a lot in common with. This debate got louder and louder, and shriller and shriller, until at one point this man, who I consider a friend, was turning a bright red and pointing his finger sharply at me, and yelling, "You don't know *what* you are talking about!! All the Iraqis that *I* know support this war, and until you have met as many Iraqis as I have, and you have asked them *how they feel about it*, you should just shut up about it!!"

Well...there it was, another good dinner spoiled. Believe me, it was longer and worse than I have described, but I remember my son on one side of the table calmly taking on two or three people while I was much less calmly trying to take on the rest. I went back to my hotel room that night deeply...disturbed. Disturbed, as in, "When I get in these debates, I almost immediately feel like I'm in over my head; I know *how* I feel, but I always feel like I'm grasping at straws for the nuts and bolts of *why*." Deeply *impressed*. Impressed, as in, "I can't get this feeling out of my head; why do I feel *so* strongly about this and so many other political things, and almost no one that I know that I share my faith with— with the exception of my poor son—feels anything close to the same way I do? We all love the same God, all believe Jesus is who

He said He is, and all read the same Bible, but we sure don't see the world the same way." Deeply challenged. Challenged, as in, "I've had it! I am not going to be one of these people any longer who purports to have strong political opinions and views but behind the opinions lies a shallow but wide puddle of knowledge; I know a little bit about a lot of things, but not enough about anything."

Over the next few weeks I wrestled with these feelings, and then one night I started to write. I was reading and writing and writing and reading. I had already accelerated my political science reading over the last several years, but now I had a purpose. So, a couple of years later and hundreds of books and websites later, here I am, feeling much better informed; there is every reason to fear me now around the dinner table. Actually, it has been the *process* of getting informed that has been so wonderfully enlightening to me and is really one of the main things that I hope to share with you; this is, in essence, what this book is about. I am excited about all of the things that I have learned; I am more than aware that there is so much information out there that I *haven't* read. It frankly makes me nervous to ever finish this book because I know that the day that I finally turn it in for the last time, I will read something else that will send me careening to my computer, sending revisions to my harried publisher.

This, then, is my declaration of political independence. I am no scholar; but then again, neither are many of the pundits that try to play one on TV or the radio. They are only one chapter ahead in the manual. Remember this when you are listening to them pontificate; remember this the next time your pastor goes off on some political diatribe—he's most likely just read this week's *U.S. News and World Report*, or a best-selling book. There is *no* substitute for doing your own research.

So go ahead, agree with me, or disagree with me—get angry, get insulted—as long as you get *engaged*, and then get *informed*. If you don't like what I am saying in this book, then you know *how* you feel. Try to find out *why* you disagree, and if these arguments are built on a strong foundation of facts. Test your arguments against *all* sides of an issue, not just the ones that support your side. Prove me wrong—please! That would mean that you took the time to read, or to research. And hopefully, that means that you are on your own road to political independence.

introduction

I LOVE MY COUNTRY. I THANK GOD that I was blessed with the good fortune to be born in the United States of America. Our Constitution has been the model for democratic movements throughout the world since it was first written over 200 years ago. The racial and ethnic diversity in our country, and the ability of these diverse people to coexist peacefully with one another is unmatched by any other nation, which is no small feat, as we have seen in other nations that have been cobbled together over the past two centuries across ethnic lines. The ability to stand up and criticize our government and its policies is something to be cherished; in too many places around the world, one can be thrown in jail for doing the same. We are allowed the freedom to worship in the manner of our own choosing, with Catholic churches, Jewish synagogues, Muslim mosques, Mormon temples, Protestant houses of worship, and many others lining our city and country roads. The individuality of our people, coupled with the entrepreneurial spirit encouraged by our leaders, has led to a myriad of advances in science, medicine, technology, and entertainment, unmatched in human history. Our people are loved and admired by most of the other people on the planet; the generosity of our charities and the good works of our missionaries have saved countless lives in virtually every country in the world. Plus, we invented jazz and baseball.

While not an overly patriotic person, I have a healthy sense of pride for many of the things that originate from American ingenuity. I don't want to tear down our government; it makes me sad to write some of what you are about to read. I also don't want this to seem like a left-wing rant, in spite of espousing positions that might appear radically left to most conservative Christians. While the secular left contains social and political positions that I tend to favor, I believe that they have made an almost fatal error in disavowing the spiritual and religious aspects that tend to be at the heart of many of these positions, ceding the field unnecessarily to the right. Most disturbingly to me, the left, by and large, has thrown the "baby" Jesus out with the "bathwater" of conservative evangelical ideology. I hope to show that the decisions made by the administrations of both political parties since the end of World War II have been equally damaging to our standing in the world, and more importantly, not in keeping with Christian principals, or more specifically, don't pass the "What would Jesus do?" test.

Why bother? Most people, Christians included, know that our government isn't, and has never been perfect. It has made some well-publicized mistakes; even the staunchest patriot would admit that. Our government has never been asked to pass the "What would Jesus do" test, anyways. It is secular, and despite having a born-again Christian in the White House for eight years, will remain secular. I know that polities are not bound by the morals of individuals. In the first fifty years of the twentieth century, our country was thrust into two world wars not of its making, and not of its choosing; however, as a nation we responded to both, and especially the second, with an astonishing vitality and strength that continues to be underestimated by our enemies. And it was out of those two wars, and especially the second, that the United States emerged, partially by default, as the dominant power in the world. The collapse of the Soviet Union in 1989 only confirmed that status.

So...why bother?

For starters, I've never been much of an activist. I would've gone to some of the peace marches before the beginning of the Iraq War, but I didn't want to deal with the traffic and the parking. Before starting this book, I had written exactly one letter of protest to the White House, concerning the above war, but I'm pretty sure that if it wasn't e-mail, and I would have had to find an envelope and a stamp, I wouldn't have done it. I'm a *song-writer*, hardly the credential for writing the kind of thing I'm attempting here (as I have subsequently found out!). I've always loved history, and have probably read more than my fair share. Reading a lot of history naturally led me to political science. Reading political science has left me with many more questions than answers, and a troubling view of our government. Frankly, the more I have read, the more disturbed I have become.

I'm bothering because I feel deeply at odds with how to reconcile my Christian faith with many of the actions over the last 60-plus years of a government that supposedly represents this nation of overwhelmingly Christian believers. There are several, if not many Christian and theological writers who have tackled this subject and who are more theologically equipped than I—the Reverend Jim Wallis and Rabbi Michael Lerner immediately come to mind.[1] One of the things I want to point out is that there is a large body of work available that presents a different view of the world than the rather narrow one that much of today's evangelical Christian leaders present. Many of these "evangelical" ideas are given as eternal truths, and are made out to have been around for as long as the Bible, yet have actually only been with us for a couple of hundred years or less. Evangelical Christians, especially through the vehicle of the Christian bookstore, are pointed away from most literature that doesn't bow to the conservative point of view of the mainstream Evangelical hierarchy. This "alternative" literature is painted as theologically unsound, even heretical, although the authors of these books oftentimes have considerably more Biblical knowledge and a more thorough theological background than those who question their veracity. (This battle over what constitutes heresy has been going on since the first generation after Jesus died.)[2] Another problem with finding any of this out, as well as being informed about other, alternative views of history seems to be that 21st century Americans live life on the run, and most people simply don't have the time to read anything close to the amount of books one would have to read to really get the whole picture. So, they get their information in little snippets, fifteen minutes of radio here, a headline or an article in the newspaper there, thirty minutes of TV news at night, and maybe an internet website or two. This information is a very narrow sliver of what is really going on in the world. It is made all the more narrow if all of the media that one watches, listens to, or reads is lined up to the same point of view.

I'm bothering because I feel compelled to get to the bottom of why it seems like 95 out of 100 evangelical Christians are conservative Republicans, and I'm not. I know that there are plenty of Christians out there who are not right-wing conservatives, but I'll be darned if I get to spend significant time around many of them. When I lived in Williamson County, Tennessee, the suburban area of choice for Nashville music types, I was playfully known as the county's only liberal. One of the main reasons for writing this book was that I frankly got tired of being the only person in the room who felt like I do about politics and I felt like I needed to equip myself better for the five-on-one or seven-on-one debates I constantly found myself in. The funny thing about those "debates?" It seemed to me to be like two drunks fighting in a bar; a lot of swinging and missing by both sides and no one really knowing what the heck they're talking about. "The little snippets of information *I've* heard about say *this*!" "Oh yeah, well the five minutes of spin I heard last night said *this*!" It's like a bad game of "telephone," with bits and pieces of out-of-context sound bites being regurgitated and passed on by people who put their own spin on the spin. This then is what often passes for political dialogue in our country. I got sick of it all, including the sound of my own miserable voice. Why *do* I believe what I believe? How *did I* get *here*, and *you're* over *there*? Where was that fork in the road? If considerably more credible information were easily available that refuted some long-held beliefs, would it have any effect on those beliefs?

I'm bothering because I want to know the answer to these questions:

- Why do a majority of people around the world like Americans, but hate the American government? There are a lot of conservatives out there who will either deny this, or will more likely counter that it doesn't matter what other people think. I think it is true, I think it does matter, and I'll tell you why.
- What would cause 19 middle-class Arab men, many of them well-educated, from countries that we call "friendly" to commit mass homicide, on a scale never before seen, against us? This is a crucial part of this book, and I have tried to present some history that shines some light on this question, in a form hopefully like *The Idiot's Guide to Wahhabism*, or *The Middle East for Dummies*. Just because I'm fascinated with history doesn't mean most people are, and this is part of our national problem: the lack of knowledge about most areas of the world not called America or Europe.
- Why do many American people, including many Christians, seem to think that any version of history that refutes the version of history they were taught in school is left-wing propaganda? If there's anything I hope you take from this book, it is to become curious about the world we live in, and how we got where we are as a nation; and *please*, try not to listen to people who say that anything that doesn't conform to their narrow point of view is unpatriotic, or just America-bashing, or radical. Actually, radical isn't bad. Jesus was a radical, and I hope to present the radical idea of following Jesus' lead when we're thinking about how our nation acts in the world.

I'm bothering because there were many things that I didn't know about our history and the actions of our government until I dug deeper to find them out. I am not talking about wacky "Who Shot Kennedy?" conspiracy-theory type of books. Our bookstores and libraries are teeming with well-researched, footnote-included, hard-to-refute books and publications from former government officers, retired CIA agents and military men, political scientists, foreign correspondents, research groups, man-on-the-street type compilations, timelines, Freedom of Information discoveries, theologians, histories of Congressional hearings, etc. A lot of these books are dry, and full of facts and figures. Many have decided points of view. The rant stuff is easily dismissible, on both sides. I tend to discount the Michael Moores, Bill O'Reillys, Al Frankens, and the Rush Limbaugh-type books. We spend way too much time on these...*entertainers*. In any statistical study a mathematician would tell you to throw away the "outliers," and in this discussion, these guys are the outliers.

I'm bothering because I've always felt out of step with *both* political parties, and frankly, have never known exactly where to place myself on the political spectrum. If pinned to the wall, I would have to say that I'm certainly more left than right (*oh really?*)—Yeah, I know that isn't a shock—but, what I've found in my research is that in the last 60 years, there hasn't been a lot of difference between either Republicans or Democrats when it comes to foreign policy, and both of them have acted in ways that leave me grappling with many questions.

In some ways, you could say that I am uniquely unqualified to be writing a book such as this. I had exactly one semester of college under my belt when I started writing. People that know me would readily agree that whatever else I may be, I am no theologian. These kinds of books are most often written from either the lofty perch of academia, or the wizened pen of the Biblical scholar. This, though, gives me the unique perspective of *everybody else*. Everything that I have learned is readily available to anybody and everybody.

I could say God laid it on my heart to say these things, but that would be heading down a path that I am always wary of. I've heard many self-righteous people say "God told me to tell you so-and-so," and "so-and-so" turned out to be really, blatantly, and loudly wrong. Oops! I do believe God is in the middle of this, as He is in all things. I also know that the truth, as versus Truth, is a slippery customer. Is truth objective, or subjective? In government and politics, it's most definitely the latter. You could sit three people down, present them with all of these facts, and one would call them black, another white, and the third would say they are all shades of gray. If one presents opinions, the question becomes, "where are the facts to support your opinions?" If one presents facts, the question becomes, "what are your sources for these facts?" If one presents data, the question then is, "where did you get the data, and is the data biased?" This type of skepticism, while healthy, stops many a discussion right in its tracks. As long as it is applied in every direction, and not just aimed at the side in which you disagree, skepticism can be a good thing. Skepticism unchecked can turn into cynicism, which is ultimately a dead-end street.

New advances in neuroscience have discovered that long-term concepts that structure the way that we think are embedded in our synapses. Someone telling us a fact cannot change long-term concepts such as these. Facts have to fit with the concepts already in our synapses. Otherwise, they go in one ear, and out the other. New facts aren't even heard, or if they are, they're labeled as irrational, or crazy.

I challenge anyone who reads this to indeed check the facts, do research of your own, come to your own educated conclusions. What concerns me the most are those who use our sound bite culture to determine their stance on the important issues that we face as a nation. This is whom I am aiming this book at. Am I right? Am I wrong? All I know for sure is that I am a Christian, and I am struggling with these things. This book presents what many people would call the "other" side of looking at government and its policies and actions. Why not present both sides? Until a couple of years ago I didn't really even know there was another side. We all hear about the left's side and the right's side, and media bias from both sides, but the popular, mainstream information available from textbooks in high school, to the news on TV, in magazines, newspapers, books, and in movies, is by and large telling the same story. That is the only story I had ever heard. I knew in the back of my mind that there was another version of the truth out there, but I had been so conditioned by my acculturation to treat it as a lunatic fringe, that I was almost frightened to approach it. What I found, much to my surprise, was a whole alternate universe full of intelligent, sensible, and moral people dedicated to trying to get the truth out over the din of the mainstream media. Is there a lunatic fringe? Of course there is, on the left, and on the right. They do nothing to further intelligent debate but clog up the drains. Try to keep in mind, though, that just because some opinion or piece of information is outside our normal realm of thinking, it does not *ipso facto* mean it came from the lunatic fringe. This is a crucial point to consider if one wants to get anything out of reading this book.

One problem for me with writing a book like this is that the very people that I would like to read it are also the very people, because of their own deeply embedded concepts, that are most likely to be turned off by its premise. For example, if I was to put the word "liberal" in the title, unless it was clear by the rest of the title that it was an indictment of liberalism, the book would almost certainly not be carried by Christian bookstores, no matter how much Christian content it contains. (If you have bought this book from a Christian bookstore, I stand pleasantly corrected.) On the other hand, to the extent that the book gets a readership, it is likely to be among people that already believe as I do, and you hence get the "preaching to the choir" effect. This, sadly, is not unusual, and is why there are parallel universes even amongst people who call themselves Christians.

If you consider yourself a conservative Christian and have stumbled upon this book, or if you are not religious at all but are intrigued by the premise, I urge you to put aside your presumptions and preconceptions for awhile and at least give a listen to an alternative point of view. For...

"To state the facts frankly is not to despair the future nor indict the past." —John F. Kennedy...and,

"Our lives begin to end the day we become silent about things that matter." —Martin Luther King

1 / how i got here

I GREW UP IN AN UPPER MIDDLE-CLASS Catholic home. I was not a particularly appealing boy; I was selfish, and dishonest when I had to be. As a youngster, I was all about baseball, but I was better at music. I was given the gift of musical ability, which, like sports, usually manifests itself in a public way. Religion was a thing that you had to do, God was a man to be feared because He could see what you were doing even when you were alone, and Jesus, well, He seemed nicer, and besides, I always felt sorry for Him because of the terrible Thing that happened to Him. I remember on Good Fridays (besides wondering why they called it "Good") trying to notice if it would actually get darker around the time that Jesus was supposed to have been crucified (and it always seemed like it did). Catholic Mass was always about screaming babies, old people who coughed a lot, priests who gave boring talks that echoed through the cavernous church, and endless standing, kneeling, and sitting. Time slowed to a crawl during that hour on Sunday mornings that we were in church.

I went to Catechism once a week, which is the closest thing a Catholic might get to Bible study, but we didn't study the Bible. I don't really remember what we did, but it no doubt had something to do with being Catholic. I do remember very well a time when I questioned my Catechism teacher about Africans in the jungle who may have never heard about Jesus. The teacher had claimed that no one would get to Heaven who didn't claim Jesus as their Savior, whether they had heard of Him or not, and everybody else was going to Hell. This didn't make sense to me. How could someone who never heard of Jesus be condemned to Hell just because they happened to be born in a particular place? This teacher, who was a neighbor and friend of my parents, got angry with me and said that this was just the way it was, and some bushman in Africa or nomad in Mongolia would just have to find a way to hear about Jesus or else they would be eternally condemned. I think I was ten or eleven years old at the time, and that marked my first serious break with Organized Religion. I honestly think that my view on Jesus or God hasn't changed much since then—I still don't believe that the God of my understanding would condemn whole swaths of people to the Lake of Fire because they happened to be born in a place where they hadn't heard of or been taught about Jesus.

My childhood was on balance a secular one. The closest thing to religious music that we ever had in the house, outside of Christmastime, was The Singing Nun singing "Dominique." I went to public schools in Morristown, New Jersey through the ninth grade. Though being a Catholic was definitely a part of my life, and if asked I would have called my family "religious," the church that we attended did nothing that I can remember to promote a faith community. In my experience, it is this, more than the doctrinal issues, that remains one of the main differences in the two faith traditions, Catholic and Protestant, that I have been a part of. Overall, evangelical Protestant churches do a much better job at creating communities. There's something going on every night of the week at these churches, and often multiple things. Nonetheless, my parents were not just nominal Catholics; they were true believers, and they tried to make sure that God was a part of our lives. I remember both of my parents loved Billy Graham, and would watch him every time he was on TV. I could never figure out what religion he was.

If you were a child in the Sixties, and a teenager in the
Seventies, it would have been hard not to be aware of or influenced by the political and cultural upheaval that bordered on revolution in America. Our household was not particularly political;
my father did not become overtly conservative until he retired. He
was too busy working to spend much time thinking about politics. I do remember the Goldwater bumper sticker on our 1964
Chevy, though. My dad took me to see a President Nixon drive-
by in 1968; he was standing up in the open limo giving that twin
"V" salute and grinning broadly. I don't remember feeling anything special about that; I was much more impressed with meeting Yankee great Whitey Ford in an elevator at a baseball banquet.
I was in my parent's bedroom saying goodnight to them when we
saw Robert Kennedy get shot. We all sat there in gloomy silence.
It was just before my tenth birthday.

I couldn't see much difference between Richard Nixon and
Lyndon Johnson. Accents aside, they seemed like the same kind
of person—remote, and not real. Robert Kennedy, though,
seemed different. With his murder, coming on top of Martin
Luther King's assassination and the riots that followed, I knew,
even at the age of almost ten, that we in America had lost something that we probably weren't going to get back. I clearly remember the imagery in my brain: one minute you had John
Kennedy—young, handsome, and eloquent; the next minute it
was Lyndon Johnson—old, homely and awfully Texan. One
minute you had Robert Kennedy—young, handsome, and articu-
late; the next minute you had Richard Nixon—older, homely, and
hard to believe. I remember seeing the brave speech Robert
Kennedy gave to a black community in Indianapolis the night
Martin Luther King was killed; it was an extraordinary moment I
will never forget. He had been scheduled on that evening to give
a talk before a group of black supporters in a poor section of
Indianapolis. To many in black America in 1968, Robert Kennedy
was the Great White Hope. Given the tragic circumstances, and
the raw racial emotions that Martin Luther King's assassination

was surely going to bring up, Kennedy's "handlers" tried to convince him to cancel the appearance. Instead, he gave the speech of his life, and it was largely improvised. First of all, *he* told the crowd that King had been shot and killed—the most of the people gathered there had not heard of it yet. And then he said this:

"Martin Luther King dedicated his life to love and to justice for his fellow human beings, and he died because of it.

In this day, in this difficult time for the United States, it is perhaps well to ask what kind of a nation we are and what direction we want to move in. For those of you who are black—considering the evidence there evidently is that there were white people who were responsible—you can be filled with bitterness, with hatred, and a desire for revenge. We can move in that direction as a country, in great polarization—black people amongst black, white people amongst white, filled with hatred toward one another.

Or we can make an effort, as Martin Luther King did, to understand and to comprehend, and to replace that violence, that stain of bloodshed that has spread across our land, with an effort to understand with compassion and love.

For those of you who are black and are tempted to be filled with hatred and distrust at the injustice of such an act, against all white people, I can only say that I feel in my heart the same kind of feeling. I had a member of my family killed, but he was killed by a white man. But we have to make an effort in the United States, an effort to understand, to go beyond these rather difficult times.

What we need in the United States is not division; what we need in the United States is not hatred; what we need in the United States is not violence or lawlessness; but love and wisdom, and compassion toward one another, and a feeling of justice toward those who still suffer within our country, whether they be white or they be black.

So I ask you to return home, to say a prayer for the family of Martin Luther King, that's true, but more importantly to say a prayer for our country, which all of us love—a prayer for understanding and that compassion of which I spoke.

The vast majority of white people and the vast majority of black peo-

ple in this country want to live together, want to improve the quality of our life, and want justice for all human beings who abide in our land.

Let us dedicate ourselves to what the Greeks wrote so many years ago: to tame the savageness of man and make gentle the life of this world.

Let us dedicate ourselves to that, and say a prayer for our country and for our people."

That speech, especially given the extraordinary circumstances, has to rank as one of the best ever given by a politician. I still get a lump in my throat reading it, all the more for knowing that in almost exactly two months from that night, he too would be dead at the hands of an assassin.

I believe it was that speech more than any other event that led me to the place I am today politically. I didn't know much about Robert Kennedy; only what a nine year-old boy would pick up in magazines or on TV. But in the same way that someone can be forever changed by seeing a brilliant musical or dance performance, hearing an inspired sermon, or seeing the green grass in Yankee Stadium for the first time, this beautiful eloquence coming from a *politician* made a big impression on me and stayed with me as I grew up. No politician since has touched me in the same way. Indeed, only the filmed sermons of Martin Luther King have ever matched that moment for me in emotional eloquence.

In the same way that having a great history teacher in college informed my love of history, a few years later when we lived in Dallas, Texas, there was a Catholic priest whose gentle sermons focusing on Jesus' love gave me a perspective on my Savior that I carry with me to this day. I would actually look forward to going to church if Father Don Fisher were saying mass. This is no small thing; at a time in my teens when many of my friends were dropping out of religion, I had stuck my foot back in. The love of almost *anything* can be obtained through a loving and inspired teacher. The love of Jesus and Jesus' love for us, in particular, has often been made more complicated by organized religion than it ever needed to be. I feel that the legalism that Jesus fought so hard to abolish in His lifetime has, slowly but surely, come back to dominate many Christian denominations in direct proportion to the amount of time they *don't* spend talking about Jesus. Father Fisher made it simple; in almost every sermon there was a direct link to the principles of Jesus and the love that surpasses all others. His Jesus was all about the goodness that would come into your heart and your soul and your mind if you simply called on His name, rather than all of the evil that would happen to you if you didn't believe all of the peripheral doctrine. For Father Fisher, doctrine boiled down to The Great Commandment. Some would call this a version of the Church of Love, as opposed to the Church of Law.[3] I have always been partial to the Church of Love, and I have Father Don Fisher to thank for that.

My development as a musician and songwriter was way ahead of my development as a positive human being when I headed out to Northern California in 1976 with a band to make it big. For the next eleven years, all I did was use up brain cells and take up space, while coasting ever so slowly downhill with the gifts that God had given me. I pretty much abandoned organized religion during this time, although I never stopped believing in God. As for politics, there wasn't much depth behind any of my feelings. I was interested, I suppose, but more so because of my interest in history than anything else. I can't really say that I was deeply interested in anything during those years other than climbing the ladder of success, and then shooting myself in the foot every chance I could. I always read lot of history; that was one positive thing. Religion lost its grip on me for a while, but history never did.

I voted for Jimmy Carter in my first election as a voter because I thought he was a breath of fresh air. He seemed honest and candid. Gerald Ford seemed honest, too, but he was too boring, in my opinion, to be the president. By 1980, America seemed at its lowest point in my memory, and Ronald Reagan made even me *feel* better about my country's future. I felt this from a place of almost complete political naïvety, for almost everything I know about those years politically, I learned later. So there it is; I voted for Ronald Reagan not only in 1980, but also in 1984, I believe. A true measure of how much it really meant to me is that I'm not 100% sure about 1984.

In June of 1987, with a child on the way, I surrendered to my inability to control the substances controlling me, and I entered a 12-step program. I had watched a good friend of mine go through the doors of "the program" a year or so before me, and he now seemed like a completely different person. He had also become a "born again" Christian, and through him, I had my first exposure to what that was. Until that point, I honestly hadn't given it much thought. Before I had gotten sober, I had gone to my friend's church a few times for Christian concerts and for a couple of services. The services were on Sunday mornings and for me Saturday nights were always the...*most potent.* I distinctly remember showing up at church after having stayed up the whole night before, smelling like *God only knows what* (obviously there was a tug-of-war going on inside me) and I was received with nothing but kindness. The music was good, the pastor was humorous and made sense, and I was drawn to come back. When I got sober, it was as if I had never left church. What I realized was God hadn't gone anywhere, I had. I had put a cloud of guilt and shame between God and me that was lifted the day I got sober. And there He was, where He had always been, patiently waiting for my return.

There is a saying in 12-step programs that they are programs of *attraction*, not *promotion*. It was, indeed, through attraction, not promotion, that I was led to Christ. Being a selfish person, I wanted what other people had, and I wasn't shy about taking it. I saw through my friend's story a life that had been in as bad, if not worse shape, than mine; and this life was transformed through knowing Jesus Christ. His future looked very attractive to me. I believe that many well-intentioned Christians convey evangelism through an array of promotional ideas, almost like they are marketing a product, rather than through the attraction of their lives in Christ. Far be it for me to say that promotion doesn't work—I know personally of a Calvary Chapel pastor who was saved by a Christian tract or pamphlet. It is my personal opinion that the attraction of a person's life made whole in Jesus is more powerful than promotional materials with pleasant graphics and catchy slogans. Any way a life can be saved, though, is the right way.

2 / the fork in the road

MY EXPERIENCE IN THE EVANGELICAL Protestant community has been that there are two main ways people find themselves
becoming evangelical Protestants. The first is they are born into it,
grow up in it, and know no other reality. I met a lot of this type
of person in Nashville, where I lived and worked for eight years.
Theirs was a whole different life experience than mine. I have met
quite a few people who were never allowed to listen to "secular"
music in their homes until they were out of high school. My
household never had religious music on except at Christmas. I
took a popular Christian singing group to Abbey Road Studios in
London one time to record the orchestra for their record, and the
entire "Beatleness" of the experience was completely lost on them.
I brought them into Studio Two, a shrine if there ever was one in
pop musicdom, where the Beatles recorded almost everything
they ever did, and they just stood there befuddled, humoring me,
wondering what the big deal was. When I pleaded for them to
sing a Beatles song, *any* Beatles song, if for no other reason than
they could someday tell their kids or grandkids that they had
done it *there*, in *Studio Two*, they shuffled their feet and looked at
each other and one of them finally asked politely, "Was *Yesterday*
a Beatles song?"

I point this out not to embarrass them, but merely to illuminate the cultural gap that exists between many people brought up in the "Christian bubble," and most of the rest of American society. It is absolutely not surprising to me how this particular type of Christian votes, or what they believe. Indeed, it is most surprising to ever meet anyone born, raised, and still nourished in the evangelical bubble who does not conform to the stereotypical political norms that their faith and their acculturation inscribes into them.

The second way a person often becomes an evangelical Protestant Christian is through variations on the way that I did. It usually involves a conclusion made at some point in the early to middle stages of adulthood that one's life, for any of a million reasons, is in need of spiritual renewal or intervention. Sometimes a person simply feels a hole in their life, and material things aren't filling it. Sometimes this need for renewal comes about because of having children, and feeling the need to connect those children to a moral foundation to counter the values being promulgated all around them. For others, it comes after reaching the end of one's rope which has been fashioned by their own strong will, and finally surrendering to the idea that they simply can't live any semblance of a decent or valuable life powered by their own stubbornness. In many cases, these are people who are returning to faith on some level; either they were brought up in another faith tradition (say, Catholic) and had fallen away, or they had been Protestants as children and had let go of their faith, as so many do, around college age.

Surely there are more ways than these to find yourself a member of an evangelical Protestant church, but I would imagine that a majority of people fit one of these two models. I relate to the second group of folks the most, being one of them myself. And I find myself struggling to understand how it is that, when faced with the ideological fork in the road, most of this second group went right, and I went left.

I've heard it postulated that many of these people might have looked at the values of the left as the very ideas that they needed to leave behind if they wanted to start anew. There is probably some truth to this, as we tend to think of the left as less disciplined, more likely to live and let live, and certainly less associated with organized religion than their counterparts on the right. It is also probable that conservative Christians got to them first. This is not a bad thing; on the contrary it is the very sense of belonging to a community of good, solid, moral people that is attractive to someone facing a deep hole in their heart. I know—it was very attractive to me. The congregations at today's evangelical churches are, by and large, very welcoming people. For the most part, they show a great deal of patience and empathy with people in various stages of alcohol and drug abuse.

What began to happen was, as I gained more and more understanding of who Jesus was and what His teachings were all about, and at the same time accelerated my studies of history and political science, I found myself more and more at odds with the conservative positions that many of my Christian friends were taking. The Jesus that I had begun to know and had grown to love seemed to me to have almost nothing in common with right-wing Republicanism. Most of my Christian friends, however, were either staunch, long-time Republicans, or had become Republicans almost immediately upon conversion. I'm pretty sure it wasn't a qualification of converting. No one asked me, and there wasn't a Republican voter registration card shoved in my face when I accepted Christ as my personal Savior. No one at the different churches that I have attended has ever said that you couldn't be a Democrat and come to that church, although in most of them you probably want to keep that fact to yourself unless you are very comfortable and confident in expressing your political views.

So, then, why is it? Why does my understanding of Jesus cause me to go left when so many of my friends and fellow Christians who worship the same man are swayed to the right? Why is it that I could listen to my former pastor's sermons and be in almost total harmony with what he was saying, but when we had a political discussion we found ourselves ideologically180° apart? He's a nice man and I like and love him, and I'm an okay guy and he likes and loves me. We both share a desire for the unsaved to know Jesus and to accept Him as their personal Savior. Yet with the exception of the act of abortion, I can't think of one thing that we would politically agree on. What, if anything, does Jesus have to do with this? In the last ten years the more that I have studied, the more I have read, the deeper I have gone—the further and further "left" I have strayed. People tend to think of this in almost exclusively economic lingo. When one says, "further left," most people think reflexively, "communist," or "socialist." While I do have some serious issues with the unregulated capitalism as it is being perpetrated by the United States and its Western allies, my "leftness" has much less to do with macro-economic systems than it does with the simple way that the American government treats less fortunate people both in our own country, and around the world. My "leftness" has a lot to do with my love for and understanding of Jesus Christ and His teachings. I wish there was a better way to describe my political state of mind, because the terminologies of "left" and "right" and "liberal" and "conservative" really belong to another era, and carry around so much baggage as to render these words meaningless, at least to me. Heck, when *I* think of a word like "leftist," it conjures up images that scare *me.* It makes me think of being hauled before the McCarthy Committee in the early '50s and having to deny that I am a Soviet spy. And yet, the way the rules in the manual have been written, I can't see where else I fit. It is the conservatives, by and large, over the past twenty-five years who have determined where the center is, and the rules governing what determines where one fits on the spectrum. And by their reckoning, I'm left. Way left. Way, way left. That's fine with me—I'm comfortable where I am on that spectrum, and confident in expressing why. In fact, I've never been so sure of where I am politically and what I believe spiritually as I am today.

The fact remained, though, that I sat out there on the left end of that spectrum pretty much alone in the evangelical world in which I lived and worked. I moved with my family to Nashville, Tennessee in 1994, and worked for eight years in the Christian music industry doing all kinds of things, from being an artist, to being a producer, to writing songs, to finally working at a Christian record company. I would have to say that 90 to 95% of the people I worked with were Republicans. I may be way off on that, but if there were more Democrats, they knew better than to tell anyone. The Christian Democrats that I *knew* about were the drinkers and smokers, the crazy fringe people that most people liked, but wouldn't want their daughters to marry. It would be easy to assume that because it was Nashville, that meant we were in the South, so it was inherently conservative. The fact is most of the people in the Christian music business in Nashville have come there from all over the country, with the largest contingents from California and New York, Florida and Michigan, Massachusetts and Texas. Okay, Texas, I understand. I would say that the percentage of people born and raised in the Christian bubble, as opposed to coming to it later in life, was about fifty-fifty. So what I have yet to figure out is, why or how did most of those latter fifty percent of people, many of whom were artists and musicians, individualistic and not prone to following too closely to the rules, become card-carrying conservative Republicans?

For starters, I think abortion has *a lot* to do with it. Most Christians I know think that you can't be a Democrat and be pro-life. While it is true that more Democratic politicians are pro-choice than not, there are both Republican politicians who are pro-choice, and Democratic politicians who are pro-life. In my opinion, being pro-life is about much more than abortion. I will have more to say about this topic in Chapter Five. Abortion is a very important issue for Christians, and it should be a factor in choosing politicians. It shouldn't be the only one. It shouldn't even be the only pro-life issue when choosing a politician. What is their view on the death penalty? What is their position on war? How about gun control? How do they plan on addressing the issue of poverty in our country and around the world? What is their plan for the environment? To me, these are *all* issues of life; every one of these issues is vital to saving lives, or taking lives. The Bible teaches us that *every* life is sacred—not just the ones that we're personally attached to. I think many Christians simply haven't thought this issue completely through. They just stop at abortion, and that's it.

Randall Terry has probably been the most visible anti-abortion activist in the country. He is the founder of Operation Rescue, a militant Christian pro-life group. He said this: "Who can imagine that a God on the pro-life side might be willing to overlook 'a little bit of murder' or take no offense at the murder of babies as long the concerned parties are given ample notice that it is to occur?" He was talking about abortion, and I agree. I would then presume that Mr. Terry would have been picketing outside the White House to get the Bush administration to stop dropping bombs on innocent babies in Afghanistan and Iraq, but I never saw him out there.

Another thing I often hear is that many Christians vote Republican because they don't like the government intruding in their families' lives. Along side of that is the idea that they want less government in general. You can also throw in there that they want to pay fewer taxes. To take the last thing first, I don't know a single person out there who *wants* to pay more taxes. *Everybody* wants to pay fewer taxes. Some people want *other people* to pay more taxes, but nobody *wants* to pay Uncle Sam more money. Citizens expect their roads to stay paved, their sewer systems to function properly, their police and fire departments to be timely and efficient, and their libraries to stay open, but they never seem to want to pay for these things. They also talk of patriotism out of one side of their mouths, but don't want to pay for our foreign adventures out of the other. Many Christians also tithe, which means systematically giving 10% of your income to the Church, which is a biblical principal. This means that for the faithful Christian, they are already in a higher tax bracket before they start.

As for more or less government, this is a big myth brought to us by the right-wing propaganda time machine. There was a time, forty, fifty, or sixty years ago when true Conservatives wanted less government—less agencies, less bureaucracy, no deficit spending, less social programs, even less Defense spending because many Conservatives were also isolationists. This was also during the time that the Democrats were introducing a plethora of government interventions to pull the country out of the Depression, and these government interventions continued into the Sixties with the Great Society programs of Lyndon Johnson. This has all changed. The election of Richard Nixon in 1968 ended most of these distinctions, and since then, from a spending and bureaucracy point of view, the only differences are those of emphasis, not of size. The people who control the Republican Party today are not our fathers' or certainly not our grandfathers' conservatives. In fact, they are not really even conservatives. They have created more government agencies, with more bureaucracy. They have certainly embraced deficit spending, and have gone crazy with Defense spending. The only thing today's Republicans are in favor of cutting back on are social programs for the poor, even though Jesus said, "Whatever you did not do for the least of these, my brothers and sisters, you do not for me" (Matt. 25:45).

Concerning the subject of government intrusion into our lives, the Patriot Act is the single most intrusive government document ever written. Created in an amazing six weeks after the 9/11 attacks with little Congressional debate, the Patriot Act significantly increases the surveillance and investigative powers of law enforcement agencies in the United States. Simply stated, this act allows law enforcement and intelligence agencies much easier access to monitor private communications and access personal information. The Act does not provide, however, for the system of checks and balances that traditionally safeguard the civil liberties that are so important to our freedom. There is no question that the inability to gather intelligence and share it with other intelligence agencies in a timely manner was a major failing in the run-up to 9/11. I happen to think, though, that much of what is contained in the Patriot Act is an unfortunate but necessary byproduct of the *blowback* from fifty years of questionable foreign policy decisions. To the extent that they know what is in the Patriot Act, many people probably feel, with some justification, that the Act is only intrusive to the extent that one has anything to hide. In a perfect world, law enforcement agencies would only use their expanded powers to catch the bad guys that these provisions were created for. What I fear is that this has given our government unprecedented powers to silence dissent if it so chooses. Remember back to the Sixties, when the FBI had wiretaps on Martin Luther King's phone lines, and had infiltrated anti-war organizations for the purposes of disrupting them.[4] The road to a repressive state begins much like this.

My goal here is not to debate the relative merits of the Patriot Act. I am only pointing out for those who have long lamented the intrusion of the government into their lives, this massive piece of legislation has invited the government into our computer, into our mail, into our local library, into our answering machine, our cell phone, and any and all of our personal and heretofore private information and transactions with banks, our doctors, cable companies, schools—basically you name it, they can see it without asking us. This will help them catch bad guys, but it's extremely intrusive.

Understand—this is not a long-winded plea to join the Democratic Party. Most of my Christian friends assume that because I lean heavily the way that I do politically, I am a member of the Democratic Party. I am, in fact, a registered Independent. The Democrats, as seems typical for the party that until recently has not been in power, are mostly long on criticism and short on solutions. I would merely hope that this might cause open-minded Christians to pause and think about our political decisions more deeply, or *holistically*, to use an apolitical term. Once again, my greatest joy would be that more Christians would become true Independents, and vote in each election for the candidates that truly represent the closest thing to "WWJD" on all of the issues taken as a whole, not on just a few hot-button topics. My road, after much reading, investigating, prayer, and meditation, has led me much of the time to the left. Your road may well lead to different destinations, which is great, as long as we all take the time to pause and ask for directions along the way.

My Family

I come from a politically and religiously interesting and diverse family. My father is an almost Libertarian-style conservative Republican.

Just keep the government off his back and out of his life and he's happy. He thinks George Bush Sr. is a liberal. He's a devout Catholic and was a high-ranking executive at General Electric for many years until he retired. My mother, a college math professor, was not particularly vocal about politics, but tended to vote with my father. My oldest brother is a staunch Rush Limbaugh Conservative—a classic "angry white male," who absolutely hates anything that smells like a Democrat or a big "L" liberal. He is also a devout Catholic and has raised three lovely children with tolerance and grace. The tragic loss of his oldest child, Sean, in a car accident two years ago has seemed to soften his anger. My "younger" older brother is a quiet Libertarian—an economic conservative and a social liberal. He is an atheist and a quantum physicist who works for NASA, and is married with one stepchild. My older sister is an artist who lives in the Northeast. She is not particularly political, but is a nominal Democrat in most ways. I think she would find it easier to talk about what and who she doesn't like, rather than define a political philosophy of her own. She is agnostic, but is attempting to instill some religious values in her children by taking them to church on a semi-regular basis. My younger sister is a far-left liberal, almost leftist. She is politically active, puts her walk with her talk, and generally espouses the kinds of causes that drive people like my oldest brother crazy.

She and her husband are Baha'i. She has one child from a previous marriage.

The talk is lively and interesting at family reunions. My dad always said, "If you're not a liberal at twenty-five and a conservative at fifty, there's something wrong with you." I think that there are many people in this country that would agree with him, but unfortunately, his youngest son is not one of them.

3 / lib·er·al

From Dictionary.com:
lib·er·al   *adj.*

1. a. Not limited to or by established, traditional, orthodox, or authoritarian attitudes, views, or dogmas; free from bigotry.

   b. Favoring proposals for reform, open to new ideas for progress, and tolerant of the ideas and behavior of others; broad-minded.

   c. Of, relating to, or characteristic of liberalism.

   d. Liberal of, designating, or characteristic of a political party founded on or associated with principles of social and political liberalism, especially in Great Britain, Canada, and the United States.

2. a. Tending to give freely; generous: a liberal benefactor.

   b. Generous in amount; ample: a liberal serving of potatoes.

3. Not strict or literal; loose or approximate: a liberal translation.

4. Of, relating to, or based on the traditional arts and sciences of a college or university curriculum: a liberal education.

Synonyms: bounteous, bountiful, freehanded, generous, handsome, munificent, openhanded; a willingness to give unstintingly: a liberal backer of the arts; a bounteous feast; bountiful compliments; a freehanded host; a generous donation.

Liberal

adj 1: showing or characterized by broad-mindedness; "a broad political stance"; "generous and broad sympathies"; "a liberal newspaper"; "tolerant of his opponent's opinions" [syn: broad, large-minded, tolerant] 2: having political or social views favoring reform and progress 3: tolerant of change; not bound by authoritarianism, orthodoxy, or tradition [ant: conservative] 4: given or giving freely; "was a big tipper"; "the bounteous goodness of God"; "bountiful compliments"; "a freehanded host"; "a handsome allowance"; "Saturday's child is loving and giving"; "a liberal backer of the arts"; "a munificent gift"; "her fond and openhanded grandfather" [syn: big, bighearted, bounteous, bountiful, freehanded, handsome, giving, openhanded] 5: not literal; "a loose interpretation of what she had been told"; "a free translation of the poem" [syn: free, loose] n 1: a person who favors a political philosophy of progress and reform and the protection of civil liberties [syn: progressive] [ant: conservative] 2: a person who favors an economic theory of *laissez-faire* and self-regulating markets.

From Merriam-Webster:

Main Entry: 1 **lib·er·al**

Function: *adjective*

Etymology: Middle English, from Middle French, from Latin *liberalis* suitable for a freeman, generous, from liber free; perhaps akin to Old English l Eodan to grow,

1. a: marked by generosity: openhanded.

    b: given or provided in a generous and openhanded way

    c: ample, full

2: broad-minded; especially: not bound by authoritarianism, orthodoxy, or traditional forms

3. a: of, favoring, or based upon the principles of liberalism.

   b: of or constituting a political party advocating or associated with the principles of political liberalism; especially: of or constituting a political party in the United Kingdom associated with ideals of individual especially economic freedom, greater individual participation in government, and constitutional, political, and administrative reforms designed to secure these objectives

Synonyms: generous, bountiful, munificent, mean giving or given freely and unstintingly. LIBERAL suggests openhandedness in the giver and largeness in the thing or amount given (a teacher liberal with her praise). GENEROUS stresses warmhearted readiness to give more than size or importance of the gift (a generous offer of help). BOUNTIFUL suggests lavish, unremitting giving or providing (children spoiled by bountiful presents). MUNIFICENT suggests a scale of giving appropriate to lords or princes (a munificent foundation grant).

And, from Merriam-Webster's Thesaurus:

Entry Word: **liberal**

Function: *adjective*

Text: marked by generosity and openhandedness

Synonyms: bounteous, bountiful, free, freehanded, generous, handsome, munificent, openhanded, unsparing

Related Words: exuberant, lavish, prodigal, profuse; benevolent, charitable, eleemosynary, philanthropic

Contrasted Words: closefisted, miserly, niggardly, parsimonious, penurious, stingy, tight, tightfisted; meager, scanty

Synonyms: plentiful, abundant, ample, bounteous, bountiful, copious, generous, plenteous, plenty, not bound by authoritarianism, orthodoxy, or traditional forms

Synonyms: advanced, broad, broad-minded, progressive, tolerant, wide

Related Word: forbearing, indulgent, lenient

Contrasted Words: rigid, rigorous, strict, stringent; dictatorial, doctrinaire, dogmatic, oracular; conservative, reactionary

Antonyms: authoritarian

From the Cambridge dictionary:
liberal (POLITICS)

adjective

(of a political party or a country) believing in or allowing more personal freedom and a development towards a fairer sharing of wealth and power within society

Definition

liberal (SOCIETY) *adj.*

respecting and allowing many different types of beliefs or behavior: a liberal society/attitude

NOTE: The opposite is illiberal or intolerant.

From Roget's thesaurus:
Main Entry: **liberal**

Part of Speech: *adjective*

Definition: giving

Synonyms: altruistic, beneficent, benevolent, big, bighearted, bounteous, bountiful, casual, charitable, eleemosynary, exuberant, free, generous, good Joe, handsome, kind, lavish, loose, munificent, open-handed, open-hearted, philanthropic, prince, prodigal, profuse, Santa Claus, soft touch, softie, unselfish, unsparing.

Word Association
I aspire to be a true liberal someday; I'm nowhere near it yet. You might, too, but you wouldn't know it because the word has been so distorted by people too arrogant or ignorant to look it up in a dictionary. As a follower of Jesus Christ, the definitions and

synonyms of this word describe in a secular way the kind of person I would most like to be. Nowhere on this list do I see "alcoholic Senator from Massachusetts," just like under the definition of Christian you won't see "boorish President of a Christian college in Virginia." Do your own word search—look up as many definitions and synonyms for the words "conservative" and "liberal" as you can find and ask yourself honestly as a believer in Jesus which word most describes you. The word "liberal" has been perverted almost as much as the word "Christian."

If you did a man-on-the-street random sampling of the first word that pops in your head when you hear the word "Christian," what do you think the answer would be? How far down the list would Jesus be? Probably somewhere behind the President of a Christian college in Virginia. Quick—Christian? Conservative. Christian? Republican. Christian? Right-wing. Christian? Fundamentalist. Christian? Intolerant. Christian? Fish on the back of a car. Christian? That Tammy Faye lady. Christian? James Dobson, Pat Robertson, and Jerry Falwell. Jesus would probably make an appearance right about here. This is unbelievably sad. Doesn't it make you want to say, "People! You've got it all wrong! Being a Christian is all about love, and humility, and giving, and self-sacrifice, and *Jesus!*" Unfortunately, people who, for the most part, have only a passing and incomplete knowledge of what it really means, have perverted the word. The people who have gotten the most national exposure representing you and I have, with a few exceptions, been pretty embarrassing characters. You want to reach through the TV sometimes and say, "That's not me! That self-righteous pompadour does not represent me!" But to many unbelievers, he does.

Now, let's do a word association with the average conservative Christian on the word "liberal." Liberal? Left-wing. Liberal? Environmentalist wacko. Liberal? Democrat. Liberal? Socialist or communist. Liberal? Tree-hugger. Liberal? Jessie Jackson. Liberal? Al Sharpton. Liberal? Feminazi. Liberal? Northeastern elitist, intellectual snobs. Liberal? The media. Liberal? Un-American. Am I making my point?

How would you like for Howard Stern, Michael Moore, or Bill Maher to define the word "Christian" on your behalf? Five days a week, fifty-two weeks a year, these guys would be out there defining what the word "Christian" means. And millions and millions of people are buying it! That's what has happened to the word "liberal." Starting with Rush Limbaugh, the word has been successfully re-defined by the very people who seem to understand its real definition the least and misuse that definition the most. The outer wing of each political party has loud-mouthed camera hogs who most sensible people are loathe to have speak for them, much less define them. I'm sure, no matter which side of the aisle you're on, you can think of a few.

There was a woman at my former church, a conservative Republican political lobbyist—obviously intelligent, and very well respected. I mentioned the book I was writing to her and what it was about, and she commented, in an almost off-hand way, "Well, you know, Jesus was a liberal," as if it was a universally understood thing. I honestly didn't know what to say. This represented a snapshot of the disconnect that I have with much of the evangelical Christian community. Somewhere in the back of this woman's mind is the image of our Lord and Savior as a liberal human being, probably of the sort in the definitions that I so over-did in the preceding pages. Yet this same woman was taking a group of conservative talk-show hosts to Baghdad to broadcast their shows from there.[5] (To which I heard from another member of my church, "Great! We'll finally hear some *truth* from Iraq!" as if everything we know and hear about from over there isn't strictly controlled by our government). The word "liberal" is the most dirty word one could speak or hear from this group. In fact, it would not be unreasonable to assume that this same woman spends most of her professional life doing battle with some definition of the word "liberal" that I can't find. And yet, for some mystical reason, it was extremely easy for her to say, "Jesus was a liberal," as if everybody knows that. Maybe she was just being polite, and didn't want to hurt my feelings.

The word "liberal" has been so demonized by the Right that even liberals aren't using the word "liberal" anymore. The more common word today is "progressive." That's fine with me. It's another word for the same thing.

I think author Joe Conason says it best in defining what a liberal *is*:

"If your workplace is safe; if your children go to school rather than being forced into labor; if you are paid a living wage, including overtime; if you enjoy a forty-hour work week and you are allowed to join a union to protect your rights—you can thank liberals. If your food is not poisoned and your water is drinkable—you can thank liberals. If your parents are eligible for Medicare and Social Security, so they can grow old with dignity without bankrupting your family—you can thank liberals. If our rivers are getting cleaner and our air isn't black with pollution; if our wilderness is protected and our countryside is still green—you can thank liberals. If people of all races can share the same facilities; if everyone has the right to vote; if couples fall in love and marry regardless of race; if we have finally begun to transcend a segregated society—you can thank liberals." I would add that if you appreciate the safety of seat belts in your car, or the fact that people can't smoke at the table next to you in restaurants, or in your office space, elevators, or airplanes, you can also thank liberals.

What I am proposing is no less heretical than the marrying of the words "liberal" and "Christian." I am trying to be a liberal, or progressive Christian. Not the Rush Limbaugh-defined liberal, and not the Howard Stern-defined Christian. If you re-read the definitions and synonyms of the word "liberal," you'll see that they go quite nicely with the definition of "Christian" that most Christians would agree on. Two words, both misunderstood, both poorly defined by the last people who should be doing so: two words, the meanings of which have strayed a long way from where they ought to be.

4 / the good guys

THE MORE I LEARN ABOUT THE WORLD that I live in, the
more I am convinced that there is a deep disconnect between the
real world and many of the people that I work with, go to church
with, and consider my closest friends. I become more concerned
every day that the vast majority of people in our nation, left, right
and in between, have become either blinded to the truth by par-
tisanship, or have buried their head in the sand like ostriches.
This "blinding" didn't by any means start with the election of
George Bush, nor is it confined to a particular political party. It is
far too easy to revert to partisan mud slinging, and catchy sound-
bite "gotchas!" when the truth, as I see it, is far more complicated
and beyond the petty differences of what passes for a two-party
system in this country.

I'm speaking of the role of our nation in the world, and how
each of us has been taught a particular *version* of the history of our
country. Most of us have grown up unquestioningly believing the
vast majority of this history, never stopping to think that it may
have been fed through a prism, or a strainer; the same prism that
all Great Nations have used throughout their own histories to justify their actions. But ours is different; we've been taught endless-
ly in books, comics, on television, and in the movies that we're

the Good Guys. We're a kind, generous, compassionate people, a nation of immigrants, and a vast congregation of every other nation on earth—"the bastion of freedom." There is a great deal of truth in this thought. But this idea is so ingrained in the American psyche, drilled into us from birth, that to think that anyone from almost anywhere else on this earth would not want what we have, or would not change places with most of us in a heartbeat, is beyond our comprehension. The entire "America-bashing" we hear of from overseas is chalked up largely to jealousy and envy, but I believe this is simplistic and arrogant.

While there is no doubting that jealousy and envy of America and Americans does exist, much in the same way that I sometimes envy the bigger house, or the higher salary of my neighbor, it is this idea that we are viewed as Good, or the Good Guys, by the rest of the people in the world, and they all want the thing or essence of what makes us Good—this is where our lack of intellectual curiosity and our national deficit in history have led us sadly down the wrong path. Our view of what "they" want and what "they" *really* want is often quite different. Meic Pearse writes in the introduction to his book, *Why the Rest Hates the West*: "Westerners can no longer act on the bland assumption that their ideas about what constitutes common sense are universal or beyond examination." He also quotes the author Patricia Crone, "We all take the world in which we were born for granted and think of the human condition as ours. This is a mistake. The vast masses of human experience have been made under quite different conditions."

I believe that it is entirely possible to be a nation of mostly good people, without necessarily being a good nation. Does that make sense? The idea that we are a Good Nation is one of the most deeply embedded concepts in our brain. We have been fed the idea for so long, reinforced lately by anniversaries of pivotal moments of World War II and the resultant media barrage about "The Greatest Generation," that we *still* think we are the Good Guys.

Amongst nations, these things do change. Just think about who the Bad Guys were in World War II. Germany and Japan, former Bad Guys, are now Good Guys. Italy switched from a Bad Guy to Good Guy *during* the war. The Soviet Union was a Bad Guy until Germany attacked her and then she became a Good Guy until the end of the war when she not only became *a* Bad Guy, but became *the* Bad Guy. Now, Russia is sort of a Good Guy on the way to being a Bad Guy at some point again in the near future. You could say the same thing about China, a Good Guy with Bad Guy potential. Look at Israel. We as a nation would call them Good Guys, while 90% of the other nations on the planet would call them Bad Guys. Israel is a good example of a nation full of people who are passionately convinced that they are the Good Guys, based on their actual history before 1948, and the version of history that has been fed to them after that. The French? You tell me. It seems to be a day-to-day thing with France.

There is even an accepted phrase for this "Good Guy" feeling: American Exceptionalism. American Exceptionalism also means that when we as a nation do something that the rest of the world thinks is illegal, immoral or short-sightedly dangerous, most Americans can't wrap their brains around the fact that our country, which promotes "Freedom and Liberty and Democracy," could be capable of such things. The films of Hollywood have had as much to do as anything else with mythologizing the image of the United States as the Good Guys.

We are exceptional! We were the first Republic in a thousand years. American ingenuity and hard work saved the world from being overrun by fascism and then communism. We rescued Europe twice and helped Germany and Japan become thriving democracies. We put a man on the moon! How do you define exceptional?

The Chinese and Japanese have thought of themselves as exceptional for thousands of years. The Romans had to have thought of themselves as exceptional. The Jews certainly think of themselves as exceptional—they're God's "Chosen People." The British thought they were the exceptional ones for over two hundred years. The French think they're exceptional yesterday, today, and tomorrow. With the possible exception of the Jews (and that is certainly debatable in Israel's case), all of these nations took the idea of their own exceptionalism too far and were ultimately done in by their own arrogance.

I think we *are* an exceptional people, and an exceptional nation. But this doesn't mean that we have the right to impose our way of life, or our economic or political systems on other nations. The more that we impose, the less attractive our ways become. When this secular idea of exceptionalism is coupled with religious fervor, it becomes downright dangerous. This would seem to me to be a very obvious idea, and yet to the Bush Administration and the people that voted for them twice, I get the feeling that they don't buy into this thought one bit.

It goes against every fiber of our national being to think of ourselves as anything but a Good Nation. That is why one can present fact after fact of instances of American foreign policy not living up to its lofty rhetoric, and these facts seem to bounce off the psyche of the American people. It's similar to not wanting to know that your parents are capable of wrongdoing. It took me long enough to figure out that my father wasn't always right about everything. The last thing I would ever want to hear is that my mother or father committed a crime. It is very similar to what might happen if you opened up a locked chest in your parent's attic and found information that seemed to implicate them in all sorts of questionable activities. There would be the temptation to lock the chest right back up and forget you ever saw what you saw.

The war in Iraq was viewed initially by many Americans, and indeed, a sizable minority of people around the world, as a humanitarian intervention, with the United States one of the Good Guys, and Britain, another self-seen Good Guy, liberating the oppressed people of Iraq from the clutches of the murderous Baathist regime led by the brutal dictator Saddam Hussein. This position was not without merit; in fact, in its purest sense, it could very well have been the right position. One could make the case that less lives will ultimately have been lost in the intervention than would have been lost had Saddam stayed in power, especially if you factor in that his two sons, murderers in their own right, were poised to carry on his brutal legacy for years to come.

Unfortunately, our record of interventions over the past sixty years (and more in Latin America) has not been a good, or noble one. With the Cold War as a backdrop, the record is clear that we supported many heinous dictators as long as they weren't communist. People in the Middle East have a hard time forgetting that up until eighteen years ago, the United States supported Saddam Hussein and supplied him with some of the very chemicals and technology that we have accused him of possessing. Our double standards have been long, and wide. Since the end of the Cold War, we have imposed our version of globalization on the world, mainly through international institutions that we largely control, whether countries like it or not. Add to this the circuitous route of obfuscation that the Bush administration took to arrive in Iraq, in which "humanitarian intervention," if mentioned at all, was buried in the muck meant to bind Saddam Hussein, WMDs, and Osama bin-Laden together. The White Horse on which the Americans saw themselves riding into Iraq has taken on a dull, sickly, grayish hue.

This is why there were millions of people demonstrating in the streets of cities all across the world, from across the political spectrum, to try and prevent the liberation of the people of Iraq by the overthrow of a fascist dictator who had murdered up to 300,000 of his own people. The people of the world knew what kind of a rotten fellow Saddam Hussein was. We may still be the Good Guys in our own eyes, but this doesn't appear to be the perception of a majority of people around the world.

5 / to be truly pro-life

We are separated by time and distance from the evil that we create.
— Andrew Kimbrell, author of *Fatal Harvest*

A PARTICULAR QUESTION HAS BEEN bothering me for a long time. Why are almost *all* evangelical Christians Republicans? Conservative Republicans? It can't be solely about abortion, can it? Gay marriage? I understand why a Christian would be pro-life, as I am, too. It seems, though, that the Religious Right has narrowed down the entire moral values field to two issues: abortion and gay marriage. While both of these issues are important, especially the abortion issue, there is *so much more* to discuss and be passionate about in the vast arena of moral or family values.

More importantly, though, is the idea that if one claims to be truly pro-life, then that person must take a hard look at how our nation is treating innocent people around the world. If you are truly pro-life, how can you justify the bombing and killing of innocent Afghan and Iraqi civilians in pursuit of our enemies? High-altitude bombing is much like our view of it; too far away to really see the effects of what we're doing, it enters an almost surreal realm. This is referred to as "The Pilot's Dilemma." Disconnected from the actual killing by the enormous distance created by altitude, this sort of bombing loses its meaning that one is actually killing another God-created human being. It is easier to call these killings by their euphemisms, such as "collateral damage." How is the killing of some poor Afghan or Iraqi mother and her children any less of a murder than the killing of a stockbroker in the Twin Towers? Intent? Is this the way God sees it? Are their lives any less valuable in God's eyes? "But," it might be claimed, "we don't *intend* for innocent civilians to die in these bombings. These are the unintended consequences of war—a war that we did not want to fight but were forced to in self-defense." Mahatma Gandhi said, "What difference does it make to the dead, the orphans and the homeless, whether mad destruction is wrought under the name of totalitarianism or the holy name of liberty or democracy?"

Let's take a look at intent for a moment. What if our government, with no consent from us, harbors murderous war criminals for whatever reason; let's say that these war criminals might help our country gain an advantage of some kind over one of our nation's enemies. Our government knows the whereabouts of these war criminals, but for security reasons refuses to divulge their location to anyone. Let us then say that the country that was initially harmed by the war criminals finds out that these bad people are in our country. A diplomatic fight ensues over whether the criminals are to be extradited to the wronged country. Our government, for whatever reason, (sovereignty?) refuses to turn the war criminals over. After a quick ultimatum, the wronged country then proceeds to invade our country, but not before it drops the equivalent of the total amount of TNT dropped on Germany in WWII on towns, suburbs, cities and farms, killing thousands of people who were only vaguely aware that these war criminals were even in our country, much less had a voice in their being there. The wronged country justifies the killing of our children and friends by calling it collateral damage in the act of self-defense; after all, these war criminals were responsible for the killing of thousands in their country. This sounds like a specious argument, but is it? What if the wronged country was Israel, and the war criminals were German scientists and SS military officers brought into the U.S. after World War II to help us in our fight against the Soviet Union? I know that on the face of it, this couldn't have happened, but that is only because we were much stronger than Israel was then. Israel had as much of a moral reason to go after these guys, certainly, as our country did in going after bin-Laden. So, in reality, the only thing that makes the bombing of Afghan or Iraqi civilians justifiable is that we're more powerful than they are. Or is it justifiable because of revenge? Is revenge a Christian concept? What did Jesus say about revenge? He said something about turning the other cheek. Gandhi also said, "An eye for an eye soon makes the whole world blind."

This, however, goes beyond revenge, because simple revenge would be the actual killing or capturing of bin Laden and his associates. We have entered into the realm of indiscriminate killing, because we know without question that innocent people are going to die when we drop high explosives from 35,000 feet. As much as we try to mitigate the circumstances with "precision, laser-guided munitions," civilians who have nothing to do with what we are angry about are going to die. They always do. This also enters into a concept that is ugly to even bring up. This is that somehow the life of a human being born in Afghanistan, or Iraq, or Rwanda, or Darfur, does not possess the *value* of the life of a human being born in the United States, or Great Britain, or Canada, or Italy. This is an idea as quickly denied as it is spoken, but the *facts* speak much louder than the denials.

What then? Are we better than they? Not at all. For we have previously charged both Jews and Greeks that they are all under sin. As it is written: "There is none righteous, no, not one."
—Romans 3:9-10, Ps. 14:3

There comes a moment in a nation's history, especially a strong nation like the United States, where it becomes inevitable that in order to satisfy its own citizens, and show the rest of the world that it will not stand by idly while it is brutally attacked, that it embarks on a violent act of retribution. After September 11th, we had to do *something*. The nature of the attacks in New York and Washington and the elusiveness of the perpetrators of these acts were both entirely new paradigms for our government. Was this a *war* or a *crime*? Attacking Afghanistan was as inevitable as the leaves changing in October. As an American, it was hard not to have a feeling of solidarity with the victims of 9/11 and with the Bush administration as it struck out at the perpetrators of this horrible crime. As a Christian, my feelings became conflicted and confused. Justice is one thing, revenge, another. The bombing of innocent civilians, no matter what strategic purpose it may serve, is simply not something that we, as Christians, should tacitly condone under any circumstances. It is hard to maintain this position in the face of our own feelings of revenge, and surrounded by the sounds of fear, anger, and the lust for blood.

I'm afraid that if we are *truly* pro-life, then we have to care about the sanctity of *all* human life, not just the unborn children. It's unfortunate, in a way, that abortion gets 95% of the ink in the Christian pro-life discussion. It would seem to me to be a wonderful opportunity to turn the tables on Christian labels by pronouncing abortion to be just one of the many ways that we are pro-life. We should also be against indiscriminate killing of all civilians in military operations, and should stand ready to *hold our elected leaders accountable* for these kinds of murders. After all, a life is a life is a life. We should also stand in the front lines fighting world hunger, poverty, and disease, the triple killers of millions of children *and babies* every year, and thus support politicians who make this issue a priority. Being truly pro-life, we should oppose the death penalty because only God has the power to decide to take a life, and as much as it might quench a deep desire for revenge to see a murderer put to death, no human form of investigative justice is infallible. Therefore, we should leave the "ultimate" penalty in God's hands. For, as it says in 1st Peter 3:9, "Do not repay evil with evil."

What non-Christians see is our passion about abortion, which is justified, but then they don't see a similar passion when it comes to the sanctity of other kinds of human life. This appears hypocritical.

If we are truly pro-life, then we should care about the violence that Hollywood feeds our kids in movies and TV shows, and *especially* the video game market, but we should also care about gun control. The argument over guns in our country is probably second only to abortion in the degree of passion on both sides. The concept of "The Right To Bear Arms" is a deeply embedded one, particularly immune to any recitation of facts. The United States regularly ranks right up with the most violent nations on earth in gun-related deaths per year. The statistics relating to violence committed by gun use from nations with strict gun control laws are overwhelmingly lower than ours. I urge you, though, to look at the facts. Look at the raw statistics. Many conservatives do support some level of gun control, mainly centered around who can own a gun and the consequences of allowing kids access to the guns. The *fact* remains, though, that since 1963, more Americans have died from gunshot wounds *at home* than died in all the wars of the 20th century.

Being pro-life is a wonderful, Christian concept. It can't be applied discriminately. I would hope as Christians we might take a closer look at the politicians that we support and just what their positions are concerning *all* of these pro-life issues.

6 / social studies

DID YOU LIKE OR DISLIKE SOCIAL STUDIES in school when you were growing up? Did countries, and dynasties and eras, and the history of this and the history of that, and the location of the Volga River (or was it the Danube?), and the Monroe Doctrine excite your imagination with visions of a far-off time and place, or did they stay in your brain long enough to be answers on a test, and then mercifully were deleted the moment the test was over? Did the thought ever cross your mind, "When in my entire life am I ever going to need to *use* any of this?" I had the same thoughts when I was forced to learn the Elemental Tables in Science against my will. Don't worry—you're certainly not alone if you see yourself here. In my own family, despite my love for history, geography, and political science, the entire set of subjects elicit a yawn and a groan from all but my son. My wife would admit that she still gets Austria and Australia confused, and has to think really hard about whether World War I came before or after the Civil War. While this might seem laughable to some, I suspect that in some form or permutation, in this country it is more common than not. The facts would seem to indicate that we as a nation are not very educated about the world that we inhabit, the history of it, the geography of it, and the people who live in it. This has huge ramifications in how we perceive the events we hear about happening "over there somewhere," and more tragically, how we react to the news of disasters taking place in areas of which we are only dimly aware.

Author Tariq Ali makes the point that the way many Americans learn geography is by bombing countries. "You don't know where Afghanistan is? It's here, look, we're bombing it. You don't know where Iraq is? It's here. We're going to bomb it, and then you'll know where it is." Or as the curmudgeonly journalist Ambrose Bierce said a hundred years before that, "War is God's way of teaching Americans geography." Nobody had any idea where Vietnam was until we started to bomb it. We only found out where Laos and Cambodia were because it was discovered that we were secretly bombing them, too. Not many people know the locations of most of the countries in Africa because we've never militarily intervened there. This is a very unusual way to learn geography.

One of the critical factors in the dearth of our knowledge in that bundled group known as Social Studies is the way that they are taught in school. This is true of any subject; a great teacher doesn't just race through a series of facts for the sole reason that they will be on an end-of-the-week test. The first mark of a such a teacher is that they are genuinely in love with the subject that they are teaching, and they do everything they can to transfer the love of that subject to their students. A great teacher will try to explain *why* a certain thing is important to know, and how knowing about this thing might be important in the student's post-educational life. Such a teacher as this might have explained the Table of Elements to me in a way that fired my imagination in science and all of the wonders of the building blocks of nature. Instead, it was just a list of symbols that I needed to memorize long enough to try and pass the science test. In today's teach-to-the-test, No Child Left Behind, school-achievement-scores-are-everything, gotta-beat-the-Japanese mode of educating, it is the rare teacher who can pause long enough in the blitz of facts in any subject to give their students a *why*.

In my first semester in college many a moon ago, I had an incredible teacher in American History. I can't even remember his name, or I would give him his *props* here. The class was mainly concerned with the American Revolution and the years immediately before and after. This fellow wove such a great story, and made all of the characters come so alive, that I couldn't wait until the next class to find out what happened next. This is history at its best—the finest writers and teachers tell stories like the great novelists; only for me, the added bonus is that these things *actually happened.* My love of history really took off from that one class, and it's no coincidence that my son's love of this subject is directly the result of having fantastic history teachers in each of his last two years of high school.

I think the first non-fiction history book I read for enjoyment was *The Guns of August*, by Barbara Tuchman. *The Guns of August* is a fascinating description of the events and personalities that led to the awful culmination of World War I. Her narrative of these events concerning the crumbling monarchies and empires at the turn of the twentieth century, their dynasties intertwined by marriage, bristles with the energy of a great novel. I immediately read through her collected works. Other historians who captured my attention during this time were Robert Massie, Stephen Ambrose, David McCullough, and Alison Weir.[6] Each of these writers shares the gift of making history jump off the page with the same flair of a great novelist.

For most students, though, Social Studies is taught as another list of facts that need to be memorized to take the unit test. There is no context to the information, no *why.* Unless we take it upon ourselves to get educated about these things, this deficit follows us around for the rest of our lives. This is one of the main reasons for the disconnect that Americans display concerning the actions of our government towards the rest of the world. Our lack of knowledge about the world we live in is what can lead us to a general lack of compassion about the dire predicament that so many millions of people now find themselves in. It is in large part what compels us to expect condolences from around the world when we lose 3000 civilians to a terrorist attack, while we hardly blink an eye at numbers much higher than that caused either by a natural disaster, or by our own military in what is unemotionally termed "collateral damage."

During the Vietnam War, how many Americans were aware that a young Ho Chi Minh, an admirer of the American Revolution, had sought Woodrow Wilson's help in 1919 at the Versailles Conference to end French rule in Indochina and help establish an independent Vietnam? He was rebuffed, even though President Wilson had staked his claim on self-determination for all peoples, and Ho soon found open arms in the French Communist Party. He returned to Vietnam in 1941 to lead the Viet Minh independence movement, and fought the Japanese and then the French before eventually taking on the Americans in what we know of as the Vietnam War, but what most Vietnamese call their Thirty Year War of Independence. Seen in this context, as a war of independence, with Ho Chi Minh as the Vietnamese George Washington, it becomes all too easy to see why the South Vietnamese never had their heart in the fight. The point here is not whether Ho was a good guy or not, but rather the way he was viewed by the majority of the Vietnamese people. This information would have been valuable for Americans to understand as they tried to grasp the complexities of the situation in Vietnam.

In the same vein, the Islamist Revolution in Iran in 1979 following the overthrow of the Shah is much more easily understood if it is seen as the *blowback*, or unintended consequence, of the CIA-engineered coup in 1953 that overthrew the elected Prime Minister Mohammed Mossedegh and installed the Shah in the first place. It's the knowledge of the latter that puts the former into a more rounded perspective. Once again, it's not passing judgment on the Ayatollah Khomeini or his revolution to simply be in possession of the knowledge of the circumstances that preceded such an important event.

Similarly, understanding how the countries of Yugoslavia and

Iraq were cobbled together by British diplomats in a room in Versailles in 1919 makes the ethnic and religious tensions in both nations much easier to comprehend. In the case of Yugoslavia, the diplomats somehow figured that the dominant Serbs, and their long time rivals the Croats, along with rivals of both, the Slovenians, and the Bosnian Muslims, and the Kosovan Albanians, and the Montenegrins, along with the Greek Macedonians and Albanian Macedonians, would all suddenly come together as a national entity. During the Cold War, the authoritarian hand of the communist Josef Tito held these disparate groups together. Tito was a World War II war hero and a strong enough leader to keep the tenuous bonds together. Following his death in 1980, the various ethnic factions fell upon each other in a vicious internecine struggle that tore the artificial structure apart.

Likewise, in Iraq, British imperialists made one country where three would have probably been better, and this at a time when the emerging country of Turkey would have been in less of a position to argue about losing another chunk of their land in their east to the Kurds. The three would have been an independent Kurdistan in the north, with a capital in Kirkuk; a Sunni entity in the center, with Baghdad as its capital, and a Shia nation in the south, with Basra the main city. It has taken authoritarian rule, either civilian or military, to keep the three factions from fighting each other. When one takes away the authoritarian rule, the gates open to sectarian violence. The idea that these three groups are going to live in democratic harmony is fanciful, at best. There's no history of it. Of course the Shias like the idea in theory, because they are the majority faction who has been ruled by minority Sunnis for a long time. The Kurds like it as well, because they get to have a voice in a government of which they have been virtually shut out. They are also, in the main, still fighting for as much autonomy in their region that they can possibly get away with, and will most certainly in the future become an independent state. It is the Sunnis, however, that are going to fight this democracy idea to the bitter end. They find themselves suddenly on the bottom looking up, after many years of privilege as the ruling elite.

This is all crucial knowledge if we hope to fully understand the mess that we find ourselves in in Iraq. It is also important to understand that the government plays upon—in fact, counts on—our lack of knowledge about Islam, Iraq, Afghanistan, and before that Vietnam, Latin America, and Iran, because that is how they can do what they do with such little dissent from their citizens. How can you argue or protest something that you know so little about? The problem with Vietnam was that those pesky pinko journalists started nosing around there, and started writing about what they *actually saw*, instead of what the government was telling "we, the people." It was this knowledge, along with the photographs and film shot by courageous photographers that turned the nation against the war. The American government and its military have since gotten wise to this, and now restricts access to the battlefield in the interest of...whatever excuse they've cooked up. In Iraq, this led to the sad irony that al-Jazeera, the Arabian CNN, was providing the only real pictures of what was going on there, before they were kicked out of the country by the Americans for being too partisan.

The advent of the Internet has provided an amazing amount of information at our fingertips. There are historical documents sitting out there in cyberspace that one would, at the very least, have had to travel to some far-flung university library and go through all sorts of procedures to view. There are political speeches, biographies on obscure but important historical players, any kind of international, national, state, or local law or statute you can think of, and facts, figures, and opinions pertaining to people and places about which only the most miniscule public information was ever before available. The great search engines like Google are treasure troves. The importance of the Internet cannot be overstated, because as traditional media outlets have been consolidated and corporatized, journalistic standards have taken a back seat to corporate profits. There is a kind of one-size-fits-all mentality in mainstream American media today, which makes it almost impossible to get in-depth information on anything except celebrity relationships and scandals. The Internet is filled with billions of bytes of mindless blather (and worse), but you don't have to go there. I can't speak for the other academic disciplines, but in my opinion, the Internet is the best thing that's happened to the learning of history and political science since the invention of the printing press. It's now remarkably easy to call bull-headed politicians on their lies. It's also much easier to give those same politicians your opinion.

It is fascinating to take a subject like the Israeli-Palestinian conflict and browse around a search engine. You will find a staggeringly vast array of insights, opinions, facts, interviews, official documents, and maps from every conceivable angle. It becomes all too clear that two peoples are looking at the same picture and one sees black and the other sees white. Mixed into the kaleidoscope are Israelis who attempt to understand the Palestinian cause, and Palestinians who are attempting to see the Israeli's point of view.

I suppose at the bottom of this has to be a desire to want to learn about these things. I'm not inherently curious about trying to understand how strontium helps or hinders the world that I live in. When my brother wrote his dissertation on quantum physics, I couldn't make it past the title. My wife, whom I have already embarrassed about her lack of knowledge in Social Studies, is extremely knowledgeable in Child Psychology, and while I have more than a passing interest in the major points of this discipline due to the fact that we have four children, if she attempts to explain anything to me past the *USA Today* version my eyes begin to glaze and my mind begins to wander. While all educational subjects are important in the interconnectedness of living things and their relationships with one another, there is this crucial difference: it is through the study of history, political science, and current events that we can equip ourselves with the knowledge to make sensible and thoughtful choices about the events and people that shape the fate of our planet.

The majority of people in this country cast their ballots for national leaders based on domestic issues because it is domestic issues that are going to have a greater short-term impact on their lives. Because Americans, by and large, have such an incomplete picture of the rest of the world, it becomes relatively easy for politicians to speak in broad terms about foreign policy; all Americans want to know is that they're going to be safe and secure. Look at 9/11, for example. After the initial shock wore off, many Americans had their sporting instincts kick in. They just wanted the American military to go "kick some ass," and it didn't really matter whose ass it was. It seems incomprehensible to think that a majority of Americans *still* believe Saddam Hussein had something to do with the attacks on the World Trade Center and the Pentagon until our nation's history deficit is dropped into the equation. Once it is realized that most Americans have no idea that Saddam's regime was 1) secular, and 2), Osama bin-Laden is fighting just as much or more against secular Arab governments as he is against America, then we can see how easy it is for the Bush administration to put this story over on its citizens. To most people, Iraq, Iran, Syria, Afghanistan, Egypt, Jordan, Pakistan, Libya, Yemen, Turkmenistan, Kyrgyzstan, Sudan, the UAE, Kazakhstan, and Uzbekistan all melt together into a great big Muslim soup and therefore an unintentional monolithic haze develops when any of them are mentioned.

Most people in those countries probably don't know that much about the obscure places in the rest of the world, either. Why in the world do I need to know anything about Turkmenistan, or any other "stan?" Are we getting ready to bomb them?

The guy does have a sense of humor. The answer is we are the only country in the world that is trying to run the rest of the world. We have all but stopped denying that we are a full-fledged empire, and our country answers to no one, not even the UN. As such, we have a vested interest in the affairs of almost all of the countries in the world. They either represent emerging markets for our products, or they have commodities (oil) that we need to keep the great engine of capitalism humming, or they might make a good geographical location for an Army or Air Force base so that we can protect the flow of our products into and the flow of commodities (oil) out of these countries. That is why it behooves us as citizens and voters to have at least a rudimentary knowledge of these places because they are not a monolithic entity, and they figure to play an increasingly important role in the unending War on Terror (*Pre-emptive Struggle for Control of Commodities*©). For starters, while all of these countries are majority Muslim, some are Arab, some are not; some are predominately Shia, but most are mainly Sunnis. Some are secular, others bow more or less to the Muslim faith and the influence of the *imams* and *mullahs*. Some are family-run kingdoms and sheikdoms, and some are run overtly or covertly by their military.

Conversely, the less we know about the people of Turkmenistan, or anybody else that isn't European or doesn't speak English as a first language, the less we have to humanize them in our minds and the easier it is to psychologically deal with whatever we have to do to them to get what we need from them. Or in the case of Africa, the easier it is to put them out of our minds because we *don't* need anything from them. Over five hundred pro-democracy demonstrators killed by government troops in our new buddy nation of Uzbekistan? Don't even know where it is. Hey, the Uzbeks just kicked the U.S. military out of their country! Still don't have the slightest idea where it is. Two-and-a-half million people on the verge of starvation in Niger? Rings a bell, but maybe I'm thinking of Nigeria. They aren't the same thing, are they? And where, exactly, is Darfur?

A big part of being able to make informed, independent judgments on whether or not the government that we voted for is doing what they said they were going to do is *getting informed* and then *thinking independently*. I feel so much better about actually having an opinion on the government and its policies because I have taken the time to start getting informed. I no longer feel like a drunk brawler in a bar, swinging wildly at my opponent while he swings wildly at me. It's like self-defense, really. I feel like I can sit in a room with a half-dozen people with whom I disagree and more than hold my own. And this, in turn, has led me to start to get involved in political solutions to the problems I might have heretofore just griped about. Knowledge is indeed empowering. I also feel like I can make independent decisions on the issues of the day because by being informed on my own, I don't have to rely on the spin or the party line of the day from either political party or their mouthpieces to tell me what is going on in the world. When you get your information from Fox, or Air America, or the EIB Network, you are not getting news—you are getting spin.

7 / history lessons

"New opinions are always suspected, and usually opposed, without any other reason but because they are not already common."
—John Locke (1632-1704)

"The great enemy of the truth is very often not the lie, deliberate, contrived and dishonest, but the myth, persistent, persuasive and unrealistic."
—John F. Kennedy

MAYBE BECAUSE WE SEE OURSELVES as a Good People, we inherently attach noble motives to some of the most violent and barbarous acts of our government. This is where we have to read alternative history, not just the history of our high school textbooks, or our patriotic apologists. Howard Zinn's *A People's History of the United States* is as good a place as any to begin our search. Mr. Zinn presents a well-researched, sober view of the history of our country that focuses on the "others" in the story. For example, he explores the settling of Plymouth Rock and Jamestown from the point of view of the displaced natives. Along the way, he dispenses with many of the myths surrounding the coming of age of the United States. Some people would rather not know the truth about these things; others simply refuse to believe that some important parts of what they've "known" all their lives could possibly be wrong. The default defense in both of these cases is to then label books like *A People's History* un-American, or unpatriotic, or liberal hogwash, when all Mr. Zinn is trying to do is his job as a historian: getting closer to the historical truth, which includes seeing the picture from the point-of-view of all who were involved, not just the white Euro-settlers. This point-of-view seems radical because it is so far removed from what we have been taught for the better part of our lives. It may be a little more painful, but it doesn't make it any less true. Should Mr. Zinn's be the only book we read about American History? Certainly not, but this book, or one like it, should be *one* of the books we read to help us see the whole picture.

All countries, all empires, have their birthing myths, and their tall heroes striding across the pages of their history books; our history is really not that much better or worse than any other. Like most countries and empires, we are fed a version of this history designed to foster patriotism, loyalty, and the readiness to serve one's country in time of need. There's nothing unexpected or necessarily wrong about this. The interesting thing about it to me is that the citizens of our country are among the last to understand our own truth.

To use but one example, we've been told all of our lives that Christopher Columbus "discovered" America. Of course there are those who have said for a long time that Columbus couldn't have possibly discovered a place that already had a teeming population in the tens of millions; but it has recently become fairly common and public knowledge that the Chinese made all of these voyages and many, many more, seventy years before Columbus ever thought about his voyage; that they discovered and mapped the "Magellan Straits" almost one hundred years before Magellan; that they knew the benefits of fruit as a preventative for scurvy hundreds of years before the "Limeys" did; this list could go on. What I find interesting is that this has been known by those that make it their profession to know such things (mapmakers, historians, professors, anthropologists, etc.) for hundreds of years, but the Columbus "concept" has been a hard one to unhitch with "facts."[7] Christopher Columbus was a brave, intelligent, deeply-flawed sailor who, to put it gently, almost certainly did as much harm as he ever did good, and whose claim to fame should be limited to being probably (but not necessarily) the first European to sail to the Caribbean. Instead, he's a city in Ohio, with his own national holiday, and, well, you know the rest.

The entire history of the European settlers' dealings with the Native, or Aboriginal Americans has been subject to one long revision, almost in inverse proportion to the receding "threat"; once the settlers had safely corralled what was left of the natives into their "pens," or reservations, they began to examine their consciences and methods, and more critical views of their own behavior were advanced.

Even Benjamin Franklin, one of the greatest Americans of all, has a confession to make from beyond the grave. Of all of the things that he is justifiably famous for, the one thing that he is probably most famous for is the kite and the lightning in the bottle. It seems to have never happened. He wrote about *trying* it, but it has lately come to light that he didn't actually *do* it.

Karl Marx is famous for a quote, "Religion is the opiate of the masses." This quote has been used over and over again, and has in many ways defined what many in the West know about Karl Marx. In fact, the full quote is this: "Religious suffering is at one and the same time the expression of real suffering and a protest against real suffering. Religion is the sigh of the oppressed culture, the heart of a heartless world, and the soul of soulless conditions. It is the opium of the people." That middle sentence is beautiful; how many times have we ever heard *that* one attributed to Karl Marx? Does this quote alone mean therefore that Karl Marx was a great guy and we should adopt all of his theories? Certainly not, but reading the whole quote does put the most famous part of it in a different light.

These can be described as "alternative histories." They are neither "left" nor "right," although some historians indeed have a pointed story to tell. They are well-researched, well-documented versions of events that long ago passed into an almost unchallenged rite of passage for schoolchildren in the Western World: learning about the Great Discoverers, the Founding Fathers, the taming of the Wild West, and Manifest Destiny. More and more of these alternative histories have come to light—many simply because the science and technology have gotten better, many because diligent and sometimes courageous historical detectives have challenged the myths. Since these more recent findings challenge some of our most dearly held concepts about Who We Are, they tend to be dismissed, or ignored, or even demonized.

Much of what is embedded in our collective psyches about the settling of the western frontier has come from a form of cinema known as the Western. The great Hollywood director John Ford is more responsible for what Americans know about their relentless push across the continent in pursuit of *lebensraum* than any historian.[8] The myths of the Wild West are many, while the true story is harder to come by. Many Americans would just as soon leave it that way.

I think that most citizens tend to swallow the myths of their own country, while having a much more jaundiced opinion of the myths of other countries. This is why people from other parts of the world sometimes look at our foreign policy decisions with such scorn: they often know us better than we know ourselves. We have a particularly bad case of myth believing in our country, partially because we are still quite young. Nobody has ever stuffed our myths down our throats...yet. Most other countries and empires at some point in their histories were forced at the point of a gun (or a spear, or flaming arrow, or nuclear bomb) to confront their myths. Not us...not yet. Vietnam, I suppose, is where we lost our "myth virginity." We were made to realize, as many a child does at some point early in their teens, that we were not invincible. One doesn't win every single game. We found out, via the attacks of 9/11, that we aren't invulnerable, either. This is a hard fact for most Americans to swallow, and it has led to the desire for revenge.

We're still a nation in our adolescence—gullible, volatile, vain, stubborn, and self-absorbed. A rich teenager. A rich teenager with no guardians—rich enough to say to hell with parents, teachers, relatives, or anyone. We can do what we please when we please because...who's gonna stop us? There's no doubt that every empire at the top of their game has echoed these sentiments. And every last one of them has come tumbling down.

8 / "love the people..."

We are never deceived; we deceive ourselves.　　　　—Goethe

THE GENERAL CONSENSUS FROM PEOPLE around the world when asked their opinion of America is roughly this: "Love the people, hate the government." If we are a government of the people, and by the people, have you ever wondered why this is? Why are Americans viewed so positively, when their government is hated so widely? It would seem to me that if the "jealousy and envy" argument held water, then American people would be hated in the same way that our government is. It is assumed by a majority of the people in our country that because of who we are—the Good Guys—then the things that have been done by our government, on behalf of "we the people," to other nations and peoples around the world, are Just and Good for those nations as well as our own. This is one of the biggest myths of all, or at best a half-truth. We are still living under the illusion of who we were as a nation during WWII, when we actually *were* the Good Guys, at least relatively speaking. This is still our self-image, coming to the rescue of poor nations who can't defend themselves, can't think for themselves, and can't run their own economies. Respect for American values, such as freedom and democracy, persists, as does admiration of our entrepreneurial ingenuity and prosperity. Not to be dismissed as well is the large amount of foreign aid that emanates from our government's coffers. But because of the way the U.S. has thrown around its military, economic, and political clout, especially lately, this admiration is being diminished by mistrust, resentment, and hostility across a wide spectrum of countries and peoples.

"I'm amazed...that people would hate us," President Bush said last October. "Like most Americans I just can't believe it. Because I know how good we are." They don't hate *us*, Mr. President.

Here are some numbers:[9]

Overall, strongest negative views of U.S. foreign policy were expressed in Germany (83% said "worse than before 2000"), France (81%), Mexico (78%), China (72%), Canada (71%), Netherlands (70%), Spain (67%), Brazil (66%), Italy (66%), Argentina (65%), and the UK (64%).

Favorable views of the U.S. have declined over this time in countries such as Great Britain (83% favorable in 1999-2000 to 40% in 2004), Germany (78% to 38%), France (62% to 37%), Morocco (77% to 27%), and Turkey (52% to 30%). These are our *allies*.

Other countries with strong majorities saying our policies had made them feel worse were Norway (74%-3%), Japan (52% to 9%), Zimbabwe (62% to 9%), Kenya (56% to 23%), the Czech Republic (60% to 14%), and South Africa (48% to 26%).

The nerve of these people after all we've done for them. And why does it matter whether people from other countries like us? This isn't a popularity contest, and our government can't do what's right for the American people based on polls from other countries.

That's absolutely right. Sometimes our leaders have to make choices that may not be popular in other peoples' eyes. But the breadth and the depth of the dislike for our policies is pretty staggering. The point behind these numbers that jumps out at me is that these are supposed to be our *friends*. Most, but not all of these countries are democracies, inspired in many instances by our form of government to be so. A good portion of these governments are center-right in ideology, as the pendulum swung during the Reagan/Thatcher years from Social Democracies to more conservative-leaning forms of government. Keep in mind, though, that this is a pendulum. As discontent with policies of the United States (by no means confined to Iraq) rises and festers in these countries, the pendulum is starting to swing back to the left. Recent elections in Venezuela, Brazil, Bolivia, Uruguay and Argentina bear this out. Voters in these countries are starting to elect governments that won't necessarily fall in lockstep with American policies.

Take a look at what John Madison, one of our Founding Fathers, had to say about what *they* think:

Attention to the judgment of other nations is important to every government, for two reasons—the one is that, independently of the merits of a particular plan or measure, it is desirable on various accounts that it should appear to other nations as the offspring of a wise and honorable policy; the second that, in doubtful cases, particularly where the national councils may be warped by some passion or momentary interest, the presumed or known opinion of the impartial world may be the best guide that can be followed.

There was a funny (or sad, depending on how one looks at it) political cartoon that appeared at the height of the maniacal run-up to the war in Iraq that sums up the arrogance of the "'who cares what *they* think" crowd. It showed Defense Secretary Donald Rumsfeld standing in front of a map of the world. Our country had the "US" marked on it, and every other country that was visible had "THEM" marked on it. With the exception of Israel and the government of Great Britain, this cartoon is beginning to come true. It *is* important what *they* think because we need *them* right now to help *us* in our fight against terrorism. John F. Kennedy said, "Our most basic common link is that we all inhabit this planet. We all breathe the same air. We all cherish our children's future. And we are all mortal." The planet is shrinking.

With the coming of great advances in technology and communications, we are more linked to all of the people on this planet than we ever have been before. As has been proven so horribly, our mighty military seems helpless against determined and cunning foes willing to lose their own lives. More importantly, there are other ways than just militarily to bring down an out-of-control empire. Our economy is heavily dependent on the investments of many of the nations in the above surveys through the carrying of our national debt. Make no mistake about it; we are heavily in debt, some $8 trillion at last count, a number that is all but incomprehensible. A withdrawal or selling off of this debt would mean economic disaster for our country. We are more vulnerable than we think. I know that most people think this economic disaster could, or would never happen. History has shown us a lot of things most people thought would never happen. As this book is being finished, it *is* happening.

The people of the world constantly hear our leaders speak of democracy and freedom, and then watch as we topple democratically elected governments overtly or covertly because they didn't jibe with our foreign policy. They hear our leaders speak of democracy and freedom, and they watch as we coddle dictators, corrupt monarchies, and military juntas because they have something we want, or they will do our dirty work for us. Some would say this is the way the world works. Fine, but let's quit pretending that our nation's morals are the envy of the earth. Again, people in other parts of the world understand the ramifications of our government's actions more clearly than most American citizens do.

Along the way, our Goodness as a nation has been flaked off bit by bit like cheap paint on a nice car. The problem is, everybody driving by us can see that, but we who are in the car cannot, and we keep driving along assuming that our car still looks shiny and new.

A majority of Americans think of ourselves as a Christian nation. Statistics at least marginally bear this out. Polls taken

immediately following the 2004 election showed that "moral values" were the overriding issue that re-elected our president. The
overwhelming support of evangelical Christians is credited with
the margin of George Bush's victory. We have an evangelical
Christian for a president. How is it, then, that we don't hold our
elected leaders to a higher moral standard?

> *"Politics have no relation to morals."*
> —Niccolo Machiavelli (1469-1527)

Well, he got me there.

But Why Do They Hate Us?

Many people in the U.S. assume that the hatred of the American
government around the world is for basically two reasons: one,
our unflagging support for Israel, and two, because they are jeal-
ous of our prosperity and of our freedoms. While there is validi-
ty to both of these claims, especially the first (and especially
among Muslims), I believe that the number one reason for the
negative feelings is that the actions of our government don't come
close to matching its rhetoric. While our actions have by no
means been unique, it is our self-righteous proclamations of "freedom," "liberty," and "democracy," that have burned in the ears of
the nations of the former Third World, especially those in Latin
America, Southeast Asia, and the Middle East.

While American leader after American leader speaks of "self-
determination" for all, the following are just some of the actions
our government took to the contrary:

• The overthrow in 1953 of Mohammed Mossedegh, the elected
  Prime Minister of Iran, in favor of the previously deposed Shah;
  the British and the Americans were not amused that Mossedegh
  nationalized the oil industry, so they put a more pliant "leader"
  in charge. (*The New York Times* ran an editorial on August 6th,
  1954 that said this: "Underdeveloped nations with rich
  resources now have an object lesson in the heavy cost that must
  be paid by one of their number which goes berserk with fanat-
  ical nationalism.")

- The supporting, along with the British, of the overthrow in 1953 of the first democratically elected Prime Minister of Guyana, Cheddi Jagan, who lasted 133 days.

- The overthrow in 1954 of Jacobo Arbenz Guzman, President of Guatemala, because he angered the United Fruit Company, Guatemala's largest landowner, by re-distributing some of the 70% of the land owned by 2% of the population to peasant farmers. (There is a fine book on this unpleasant episode entitled *Bitter Fruit*, by Stephen Schlesinger and Stephen Kinzer.)

- The two assassination attempts in 1959 and 1963 on Iraqi President Abdul Karim Qassim, who was subsequently executed in a coup in February of 1963. (Tariq Ali writes about this and much more Iraqi history in his book, *Bush In Babylon*.)

- The involvement, along with the Belgian government, in the overthrow and assassination in 1961 of Patrice Lumumba, the first Prime Minister of the newly created country of The Congo.

- The alleged involvement in the overthrow in 1961 of Dictator Rafael Trujillo of the Dominican Republic, which continued a disturbing pattern of interventions in that sovereign nation; our government subsequently overthrew Juan Bosch, the first democratically elected President in the Dominican Republic's history, in 1962.

- In Haiti, we have since been involved in the overthrow of President Jean-Bertrand Aristide, not once, but twice, in 1991 and in 2004.

- The backing of the military coup in 1963 against Ngo Dinh Diem, President of South Vietnam, who was murdered along with his brother.

- The supporting of a military coup in 1964 against João Goulart, President of Brazil, because of his support of left-wing causes;

- The overthrow in 1965 of Sukarno in Indonesia and the installing of Suharto. This was one of the bloodiest coups of the 20th century.

• The backing by the CIA of the military coup of Greece in 1967. (This coup was the subject of the Constantine Gravis film *X.*)

• Our government's involvement, specifically Henry Kissinger, in the overthrow and murder of Chilean President Salvador Allende in 1973, and the subsequent backing of one of the most brutal military regimes in modern times, led by General Augustus Pinochet.

• The support for Cambodia's Khmer Rouge from 1979–1983 in their struggle against the North Vietnamese; this was five years after the end of the Vietnam war. The Khmer Rouge, led by Pol Pot, made Pinochet look like a Boy Scout.

• The support for Iraqi leader Saddam Hussein in the 1980s, selling him a huge amount of weapons, conventional, and otherwise, before subsequently calling him the next Adolph Hitler.

• The support of brutal and repressive right-wing dictatorships in South Korea, Guatemala, El Salvador, Nicaragua, and Panama; the latter was our buddy Manuel Noreiga, who was an ally until he suddenly turned into a corrupt drug-runner.

• The support of the mujahedin fighters in Afghanistan, including Osama bin-Laden, in their struggle against the communist regime backed by the Soviet Union; we're finding out right now how that turned out.

This list is by no means comprehensive; on the other hand, I know there are reasons for these actions that I will never be fully aware of, or never completely understand. Many of these actions by our post-World War II governments were taken under the backdrop of the Cold War, and should be viewed with that lens. The aim here is not to present the United States as the Great Satan; these type of actions are all too typical of Great Powers throughout history, and certainly the Soviet Union was guilty of more than their fair share, along with being incredibly cruel to their own people. The point here is what people around the world are thinking when they hear our president talk about freedom, and liberty, and self-determination. They've seen all too many times that these wonderful words are backed up by our government only when it is in our best interests to do so. This is not America-bashing; this is telling the truth, and as sad as it is, it is necessary to know these things in order to put the feelings and actions against us in context. There is precious little in our schools' history books about any of these events, obviously because they don't paint a pretty picture of the role of our government in them. What happens as a result, though, is that we raise a nation of citizens in profound ignorance of the untidy things that our own representatives did on our behalf, even though they are common knowledge in much of the rest of the world. We then act with righteous indignation when confronted with polls showing how deeply resentful the rest of the world is towards our government, because we naively maintain that if we are a nation of Good People, we must be acting as a nation for the General Good of All.

Why teach high-school kids about these negative moments in our history?

You took the words right out of my mouth. You really want to raise a whole new generation of America-bashing One-worlders?

Actually, I'd rather not raise another generation of ignorant cheerleaders for American exceptionalism. A citizenry that is well informed about the good *and* the bad that their government has done in the past is better able to have informed opinions about the ramifications of the actions of the present, and the future. For example, the kind of information presented here might make it easier to understand why more nations didn't rush to our side to topple Saddam Hussein.

There is also a love/hate tug-of-war going on in many parts of the Developing World over what is sometimes referred to as our "cultural imperialism." While there is nothing unusual in seeing young Arabs or Asians in Gap jeans drinking a Coke, listening on their iPods to Usher on their way to see Lindsay Lohan's latest movie, this is a very disturbing set of conditions for many traditional tribal societies, especially the more conservative religious ones. We are viewed from afar by such peoples as a degenerate society, rich and indolent. Our sexual freedoms are watched with particular horror, while nonetheless offering the same temptations for Developing World men that they do in the West. We see the covering up of women in the Muslim World as a lack of freedom for women; they see the complete uncovering of women in the West as barbarous perversion.

Furthermore, many of the people in these societies are rightfully confused when they see Christian missionaries get off the boat with a Bible in hand, preaching the righteousness of a Christian life, and then they see American businessmen get off of the same boat trying to sell them the cigarettes that they can't sell in America, Jack Daniels bourbon, pornographic and violent movies, and other decadent products. To the people of these countries, our products represent the United States far more powerfully than Christian missionaries ever can.

Geez, we might as well drink the Jim Jones Kool-Aid as a nation right now!

I realize that this sounds like doom and gloom negativity, but I feel it is vitally important for those that haven't considered these issues to understand the possible perspective of the average citizen from the other side of the world. You don't hear much about this for the simple reason that no one likes to be the bearer of bad news, especially politicians of any stripe. But as Christians, we must remember that in order to be equipped with the whole armor of God, as Paul urges in Ephesians 6:10-20, we must know the truth, even if the truth runs counter to the official story. This is the only way we will truly be ambassadors of the gospel of peace.

9 / buddy, could you
spare a bomber?

CONSIDER THE COUNTRY OF MALAWI. This landlocked African nation has the dubious distinction of being one of the poorest of the poor countries on this earth. Malawi has recently suffered through the perfect storm of maladies: drought, floods, crop failures, famine, malaria, and AIDS. This is a predominately Christian country, 55% Protestant, and 20% Catholic. The average life expectancy in Malawi is 37.8 years. The average person in Malawi lives on $210 *a year*. The infant mortality rate is one in ten. AIDS has absolutely ravaged this already destitute country. Despite experiencing these crises, Malawi is expected to pay $66 million a year, mainly to wealthy countries and the IMF, to service their debt.[10] There was an economics guru on the radio who was talking about world poverty. He was speaking about the "ladder" a country needs to get on to start escaping poverty. He mentioned Bangladesh as a good example of a country that has placed itself on the first rung of the ladder. He said Malawi is not even near the ladder.

Maybe what we ought to be more concerned about when we talk about "moral values" as American Christians is the extreme and dire situation in sub-Saharan Africa. Instead, we crucify Bill Clinton over his sophomoric sexual behavior, or go apoplectic

over Fred and Fred tying the knot. In any event, we failed to rec-
ognize Clinton's bigger moral crime: building over twenty B2
bombers at a cost of $1.2 billion apiece! One point two *billion* dol-
lars *per plane*. Now these planes, nice as they must be, can only
do a little bit better the job our other ridiculously expensive
planes *that we have hundreds of* can already do. The thinking here,
I believe, is that since we usually sell last year's super-duper hi-
tech killing machines to countries who might be next year's enemies, we have to keep building killing machines that are one
chapter ahead in the technology manual. This has led to the un-
peaceful fact that the United States is by far the largest arms deal-
er on the planet.

For the cost of two of these B2 bombers, we could supply every
man, woman and child in Malawi with a year's worth of income.

What about the next year, and the year after that?
That's a valid question. What Malawi really needs is an education. They need a generation of engineers, scientists, computer
programmers, and civil servants to help build an infrastructure to
begin to dig themselves out of this deep, deep hole. They need
tractors and modern farm equipment, doctors and teachers. For
the price of one B2 bomber, we could send 500,000 Malawi students to almost any university in the world for one year, or
125,000 students for four years. This is what I don't understand.
Wouldn't the world be more inclined to follow our leading/like
us/stop blowing up our buildings if we sent 125,000 Malawi kids
to four years of college so that they could go back to their country with some practical skills instead of buying another $1.2 bil-
lion dollar high-altitude killing machine?

*Why would we spend all that money to send Malawians to college
when there are lots of kids in our own country who can't afford to go to
college and there aren't enough scholarships or grants?*
That's a fair point, and if we decided to send 125,000 more poor

Americans to college rather than build another B2 bomber, I wouldn't complain.

This raises the issue of how we can help the children of Malawi make it into their late teens so they might have a chance at this mythical college education. This is no easy matter. According to the World Health Organization, 500 million people each year are infected with mosquito-borne illnesses: dengue, malaria, yellow fever, and various forms of encephalitis, including West Nile virus. More than 2.5 million die, many of them children, most of them in the poorest equatorial regions. For around $5 apiece, a treated mosquito net can cut the chances of contracting one of these diseases by fifty percent. It sounds ridiculous, but for the price of one B-2 bomber, we could provide the continent of Africa with 240 million mosquito nets! How do we want *our* money spent, on bombers or mosquito nets? After all, it's *our* money that the government is spending. We elected them, and we have more to do than we think in deciding what they're going to spend our money on. Obviously, we have to have enough modern military hardware to defend ourselves. Just as obviously, it's not as simple as mosquito nets versus B2 bombers. It's more the basic philosophy behind each of these items. Personally, I have to separate myself as a Christian from being an American.

How can you do that?!?

I am a Christian *first*. As a Christian, I would rather my tax dollars go towards relieving poverty and disease than towards being the policeman of the world. As an American, I realize that there are global responsibilities that a nation of our size and strength has to bear, but I also think that if we as a country acted more like followers of Jesus, and less like policemen, we would probably have less *need* to act like policemen.

If certain Christian communities vote as a bloc for a particular party, that's fine, but our responsibility doesn't end there. Christians are still a powerful bloc between elections. It's really dangerous for politicians to assume that because we voted for them, that this gives them the right to do whatever they want, and we will meekly assent to whatever they do. It's hard for me to see how putting massive resources to work solving hunger and disease is not as important an issue for Christians as whether Mike and Mike get married. How much did we hear about *that* in the last election, and how much did we hear about hunger, poverty, and disease? What's also interesting is that when the election is over, we stop hearing about Mike and Mike.

Hey Mother Theresa, in 2004 the United States spent some $3.2 BIL-LION dollars in aid to Sub-Saharan Africa. By your calculations that would buy around 640 million mosquito nets, or almost enough to cover the whole continent in a Christo-type wrapping.

That's very funny. It is true that the U.S. gives billions of dollars in foreign aid each year. This would also be a good time to point out that President Bush pledged an unprecedented fifteen billion dollars towards combating the AIDS virus in sub-Saharan Africa. However, numbers are tricky things. You can find a set of numbers that will support almost any idea, cause, or ideology that you can dream up. Here are some more numbers:

Among the twenty-two richest nations in the world, in 2004, the United States ranked first in total amount of dollars spent on foreign aid. That should warm the cockles of any liberal's heart, shouldn't it? However, as a percentage of GDP, which is the percentage of foreign aid compared to the size of our economy, the United Stated ranked twenty-first out of the twenty-two, barely nudging out Italy for the first time in several years in 2004. Keep in mind that the U.S. considers reconstruction money in Iraq part of its foreign aid, as well as money given to Pakistan for its assistance in the War on Terror.

Another factor, which is dealt with in greater detail elsewhere, is that most poor nations spend a large percentage of their current foreign aid paying down their previous debts. The G-8 Summit in Scotland in 2005 made some strides in beginning to eliminate these crushing burdens. The fact remains that almost none of the

22 wealthiest nations are living up to the targets on Official Development Assistance that they set in 1970 at the United Nations General Assembly. It was there that the donor governments pledged to spend 0.7% of their GDP per year on poverty reduction. In 2004, only five nations reached that goal: Norway, Luxembourg, Denmark, Sweden, and The Netherlands, with Portugal coming close. Aid flows are largely dictated by geostrategic concerns rather than efforts to reduce poverty, as the seven largest recipients of ODA in 2004 were: Egypt, Russia(!), Iraq, Congo, Israel(?!?), Pakistan, and Jordan.

Those Europeans nations can spend that much on foreign aid because they know that we are largely providing for their defense.

A good point. Wouldn't we all agree that with a population of 460 million, and a GDP that is equitable to the United States, the European Union should be capable of managing its own defense? The idea that we have to watch Europe's back seems born of another era.

Wacky Thinking

Did you know, by the way, that the average subsidy of a European cow is more than the median income of the average Sub-Saharan African? Or that we spend more on dog and cat food each year in America than it would take to eliminate the worst of the world's poverty? I don't place too much stock in anecdotal statistics like these, because as stated earlier, one can find statistics that will make almost any point that one chooses to make. Factoids like these do tend to linger in your brain longer than dry statistics.

Here's a really wacky idea. Our "Defense" budgets are generally around seven times larger than the next largest country's. That figure is close to $400 billion a year, sometimes more, sometimes less (lately more). This, as most people probably know, is not primarily spent on "defense," unless you subscribe to the saying that "the best defense is a good offense." This figure does *not* include paying for the wars in Iraq and Afghanistan; those funds are included in a separate Supplemental Spending bill. I realize that to propose a one-year moratorium on "defense" spending would be heretical lunacy, not to mention un-American, but let's say for the sake of argument that for just one year, all we spent on "defense" was as much as the country that spent the 2nd most spent, or around $50 to 60 billion. Now I know that a billion dollars isn't what it used to be, but $60 billion dollars is still nothing to sneeze at, and probably would be at least enough money for salaries and maintenance.

What to do with $350 billion? Since we don't seem as a nation or a government to be all that concerned with our own budget deficit, we'll forget about that. What used to be called the Third World, and is now better known as the Developing World, or the South, (as opposed to the affluent North) is suffocating under a massive debt load. These debts were brought on by huge loans from the International Monetary Fund and various Western and oil-producing nations in the 1970s and '80s, and often taken on by prior military rulers and dictators which Western countries put into power as a bulwark against communism.

Here are some facts about this debt: the forty-seven countries most in debt have a debt load of $422 billion as of 2001 (this figure is certainly higher now). The Developing World spends thirteen dollars servicing this debt for every dollar it receives in foreign aid. Sub-Saharan Africa spends over $10 billion a year servicing their debt—four times the amount that is spent on healthcare and education combined. (Keep in mind that these figures are constantly changing estimates, and even then vary from source to source.) Along with these loans, the IMF and the World Trade Organization have imposed stringent economic guidelines and crushing shock therapies on nations already in too much poverty and disarray.

What might have worked in the defeated nations of Germany and Japan, two countries with well-educated populations, a history of industrialization, and a civil service long in place, has not worked in these poorer underdeveloped places. Japan was given the advantage as well of being able to impose trade barriers on imports coming into their country while flooding our market with their goods in exchange for allowing American bases in their country in perpetuity.

Imposing our version of capitalism, free trade, and privatization on these developing countries has been mostly a disaster. Privatizing basic industries formerly owned by the state, where there isn't enough homegrown wealth or capital to buy these industries, has opened the door (actually the door was opened by "free" trade) for multinational corporations to swoop in and gobble them up. "Free" trade, on a level playing field and with semi-equal trading partners, is not a bad concept. There is nothing level or equal about the version of free trade the wealthy North imposes on the poor South. It's like having a ten-lane superhighway going in, and a dirt road coming out. There is the now-infamous example of the region in Bolivia known as Cochabamba, which was forced by the IMF to privatize their water utilities. The price of water, determined then by a subsidiary of the American giant corporation Bechtel, became so steep that almost no one in the region could afford water.

Poor countries can't dig themselves out of their deep holes because so much of their money goes to servicing previous debts. Undoubtedly, mismanagement and corruption of the original loans played a key part in most of these countries being in the position they are today.

So let's just throw more billions of dollars down the same rat-hole and hope for a better result. Isn't that the definition of insanity?

Yes, it is. But imposing harsh conditions is making a bad situation worse. According to the group *Christian Aid*, sub-Saharan Africa is a massive $272 billion worse off because of "free" trade policies forced on them as a condition of receiving aid and debt relief. "The reforms that rich countries forced upon Africa were supposed to boost economic growth. However, the reality is that imports increased massively while exports went up only slightly. The growth in exports only partially compensated African producers for the loss of local markets and they were left worse off."

I don't believe that our road into these countries has been deliberately paved with bad intentions. The greedy leaders of these sub-Saharan nations deserve a hefty amount of the blame for their countries' dire predicaments.[11] I think, rather, that it is more likely the stubborn one-size-fits-all mentality of those who preach the gospel of Free Trade. What if we took the $350 billion dollars from the one-time moratorium on Defense spending and applied it to Developing World debt? There would be no strings attached. This is what Bono has been running around the world trying to get the Western politicians to do. The money would go back into the coffers of the institutions that originally made the loans (meaning that U.S. banks would get a large percentage of it). Combined with similar gestures from other prosperous Western nations and Japan, we could erase this crushing burden entirely. This would be a huge step towards beginning to level the playing field for the type of capitalism that we would like to see these nations embrace. The goodwill that this gesture would create is incalculable, and would make it less likely that we would be targets of the hatred that spawns terrorism. It also seems to me to be the Christian thing to do. After all, we are supposed to speak for the last, the least, and the lost.

I know this little fantasy will never happen, Republican, Democrat, or Martian in the White House. The arms industry has become too vital a part of our economy, and that is sad. Guns and movies are our two greatest exports. Ironically, in this most capitalistic of all countries, the arms industry operates for all practical purposes as a state-run operation. It has basically one client—the Pentagon, which operates as a built-in, fail-safe market. The arms industry knows that year after year, through the ups and downs of our economy, the Pentagon is going to be buying their wares at almost whatever cost they put on these items. If they don't buy, the excess or the old inventory is simply sold to the highest bidder on the Pentagon's list of countries in need of more weapons.

It doesn't matter who is in the White House; the Defense budget is only going to vary by a small degree, because no administration wants to be known as being "soft on Defense." The whole idea of calling it the Department of Defense is kind of nutty, anyway. They used to call it the Department of War, which is a more appropriate nomenclature. We've actually had more wars since it's been called the Department of Defense. When it was the Department of War, we didn't have an industry devoted entirely to the tools of war. If a war arose, the country would have to retool some of its industries to produce armaments, i.e., the automobile industry into tank production. After World War II, however, the industry was just too much a part of the U.S. economy and made too much money to stop. We have been on a perpetual war footing ever since. President Eisenhower warned us about this in his farewell address to the nation.[12] There was a time, not too long before that, when people might have actually listened to him.

With Germany and Japan becoming among our closest allies, one might wonder why we're still maintaining an almost occupying-size army in each country. Oh, for the Cold War? The struggle that ended *seventeen* years ago?? What are we still doing with over 60,000 troops in Okinawa? If the Chinese want to take Taiwan by force, 60,000 American troops aren't going to stop them, anyway. I thought that's what our over 10,000 nuclear weapons were for. What if the Chinese were to put 60,000 troops on Bermuda? That would add to world peace and stability, I'm sure. The sad fact is our overseas troops aren't going anywhere. Oh, they might shift around, as some troops have finally left Germany. But guess where one of the newest, biggest, most expensive bases is? It's called Camp Bondsteel, and it cost over one billion dollars to build and it's in...Kosovo. We helped drive the Serbians out of Kosovo and we decided to...stay. We drove the Taliban out of Kabul and we've decided to stay in...Uzbekistan, where we've built a new base that rivals Camp Bondsteel. This is but two examples of a trend that is repeating itself all over the globe. So, for those of you who think we're going to leave Iraq anytime soon, like in the next fifty years, think Kosovo, think Uzbekistan. (*UPDATE—the Uzbekistan government asked us to leave.* Oh well, there's always Kyrgyzstan, next door.)

President Bush spoke famously of the Axis of Evil, which was supposed to be Iran, Iraq, and North Korea. The Military-Industrial Complex, which is another name for the Pentagon/Arms Industry partnership, is always in need of enemies to slay. There will always be someone. You can count on that. China is looming large over the horizon, and if I may try my hand at predictions, this relationship will become testier and testier over the next ten years until it becomes a crisis. The partnership is counting on it.

Meanwhile, the real Axis of Evil in this world is environmental degradation, pandemic poverty, and a world awash in weapons. We as Christians need to wake up to this reality, and lead the chorus calling for solutions to these most moral of problems, rather than submitting meekly to the call for more bombs and more bloodshed in the name of "freedom" and "democracy."

10 / the coming struggle over oil[13]

WHAT THE UNITED STATES HAS BEEN DOING, and it can be easily seen on a map of U.S. bases around the world (this is no secret), is throwing a ring around the Persian Gulf and Central Asia to protect the supply of oil for now and for the coming economic struggle with China, and to a lesser extent, India. China is the fastest growing industrial economy in the world, and is lapping up oil at a rate that would even make us blush. There is a finite amount of fossil fuel left under the earth, and a large portion of it that we know about is under the Persian Gulf and Central Asian regions. Nobody knows this more than the former Oil CEO's that have run our country for eight years, and as a result, we will do whatever is necessary, bear any burden, and pay any price, to insure the continuous flow of oil.

The China of Mao Tse Tung and the Great Leap Forward was a much easier foe to control than the China that has started to beat us at our own game. A capitalist-economy China with a billion low-cost yet efficient workers is a nightmare to the West. Add India to the equation, with another billion low-cost workers, and the problem doubles. The coming battle will be over oil, because it is a finite resource, and because all three of these countries need lots of it to grease the wheels of their economies.

It boggles the mind that our country, with such immense achievements in science and technology, and with the creative minds that brought us such rapid advancements in communications and medicine, is still fighting a battle to the death costing hundreds of billions of dollars over such a Flinstone-esque commodity like fossil fuel. Does it really make sense that we can't find a better way to make our engines go putt-putt? The fact is, we have the technology, but it is an extremely expensive proposition to retool the huge infrastructure that undergirds the procurement, supplying, refining, and consuming of oil. It is also a fact that no one is sure enough of what the next big energy source is going to be, whether hydrogen, biomass, wind, solar, or something else, to invest the hundreds of billions of dollars it would take to ramp it up, only to find out twenty years from now that they bet on the wrong horse. Add to this that the Big Oil corporations are not about to let their grip on world transportation go easily. If we spent one-hundredth the amount of money on developing alternative solutions to fossil fuels as we do defending them, we would probably already have an industry devoted to this problem and its solution. Instead, we get a lot of talk about it, and very little action.

In fairness to the former Bush administration, this was a problem that they inherited, and one that has been a long time coming. The problem is multi-faceted, but has two main components. One is, the substance(s) that we use to make the world go 'round are going to run out. Not tomorrow, but soon enough that there is a vital need to consider the alternatives today. The other problem that goes hand-in-hand with #1 is that the energy that the earth uses today is already causing major environmental damage and will cause even greater damage in the near future.

The legacy of energy in the Modern World has gone from wood, to coal, to oil and natural gas, to nuclear, and then there are the "others," like hydroelectric, hydrogen, solar, and wind. There have been energy crises before: in medieval times, the forests were so denuded for firewood that a kind of state of emergency had to be declared in some places to allow the forests to replenish themselves. Coal became the energy of choice for about three hundred years, but it was a dirty, dangerous business that blackened the skies of the major cities of the Industrial world, and caused innumerable health problems.

The Age of Oil was ushered in on January 10th, 1901, when the massive geyser of black gold known as Spindletop erupted for the first time just outside of Beaumont, Texas. Oil had been a relatively minor energy substance up until then, and although it was known to burn more cleanly and more efficiently than coal, no one had drilled down far enough to locate the massive amounts of the stuff that would be necessary to seriously compete with coal. The United States (largely Texas and Oklahoma) quickly became the center of the oil universe, as huge amounts were found with better drilling techniques. The invention of the gasoline-powered internal combustion engine sealed the dominance of oil as the energy of the future, and changed the way modern societies live.

World War II was fought in part over the struggle for access to and dominance over oil, as the have-nots, Japan and Germany, fought to seize control over the energy-producing areas of Southeast Asia and the Caucasus Mountains, respectively. The United States played a huge role in the Allied victory by supplying oil to Great Britain throughout the war.

By 1946, however, despite pumping one out of every three barrels of oil in existence, the United States had become a net oil importer. The reason for this is that the U.S. was using one third of all of the energy in the world. From that moment until today, our very prosperity would come to haunt us and hold us hostage to the vagaries of dependence upon a product controlled in other parts of the world.

The largest reservoirs of oil were found under the desert sands of Saudi Arabia, along with huge amounts in such places as Venezuela, Iran, Iraq, Nigeria, the Soviet Union, Mexico, and Norway, among others. The Western industrial nations possessed the technology and the money to drill and pump the oil out of these places, many which were still rather primitive backwater states, and they scrambled to procure the rights to as much oil drilling as they could; in the United States' case, they agreed to provide security to the king of Saudi Arabia in return for the rights to drill for oil in the king's desert, as we shall see later on.

One by one, these oil-rich nations realized just how much more money was to be had if they actually asserted their sovereign rights to the land providing all of this oil. Mexico nationalized its oil industry in 1938, Iran in 1951, and step-by-step, all of the oil-producing countries in turn nationalized their oil. On top of that, realizing that there was even more power in numbers, in 1961 a group of key oil states banded together to form the Organization of Petroleum Exporting Countries, or OPEC. In a matter of just a few years, a global industry that had been largely controlled by a few multinational oil companies was now in the hands of a new kind of entity, the petrostate, as Saudi Arabia, Venezuela, and other oil-rich countries were now labeled. To add insult to injury, in 1970, the United States hit its oil peak, which meant that from then on, oil production in the U.S. would decline.

It is only a matter of when, not if, the rest of the oil-producing areas of the world are going to hit their peaks. Although there are more than a few estimates floating around (and as one might imagine, these estimates are not immune to politics), the general consensus is that worldwide oil production will peak out around 2035. That means around that time, the world's glass of gas will be less than half-full. Add to that, much of the oil still in the ground (or under the sea) is harder and harder to get to, and the new strikes are smaller and smaller, making them more expensive to capture. All of the "easy" oil has been gotten.

You want some more bad news? World energy consumption is growing by leaps and bounds, meaning that we're using this finite product at a greater and faster rate than ever. It's not just gasoline for the cars; oil and natural gas (and coal, to a lesser extent) are the energy behind electricity, and electricity is one thing that everybody wants and everybody cannot get enough of. The main measuring stick that a developing nation uses to judge "progress" is how much energy their country is consuming. China's economy is growing at a terrific pace, and right along with it is their energy consumption. India is on much the same road. This is almost one third of the world population, and they want to be just like us...in many of the wrong ways.

Americans are the kings and queens of consumption. When politicians talk about preserving our way of life, they are to a large degree talking about our energy consumption. It is our larger and larger houses, and the two air conditioners it takes to cool them, and the *extra* refrigerator or freezer in the garage, and the electric *everythings* in our houses, and the SUVs in the garage—this is what we're fighting in Iraq and Afghanistan to preserve. This is what we as a society have decided that we can't do without, and we're willing to send our soldiers to die for it.

The war in Iraq *is* about oil, but it isn't as simple as that. No one knows the truth about what I've just written better than the Bush administration—they're oilmen. The fact that they came up with every angle that they can think of to sell the Iraq war to the American people affirms my theory that telling Americans the truth about the looming energy crisis and especially telling them what they might have to give up is absolutely the closest thing to political suicide. Much of this information has been known since the 1970s, and Carter didn't tell (well, he actually did, but in such a somber, negative way that he became the model of how *not* to do it, and future politicians saw what happened to *him*), Reagan didn't say anything, Bush Sr. was quiet, Bill Clinton was mum, and now George W. said anything but what was happening. The person in the best position to level with the American people would be a president in his second term, like Ronald Reagan was, like Bill Clinton was, or like George W. was. President Bush did say in his 2006 State of the Union address that America is "addicted to oil." At the end of the day it's just lip service, because there was too much riding on the 2008 election to expend the political capital it would take to make the hard choices that we must make. So, it gets put off, and put off, and it will probably get put off until we are at an absolute moment of truth; what that looks like, I don't want to speculate. Suffice to say, it works just like nature; any repair you put off and put off gets worse and worse until you have to fix it, when it would have been much less painful to have just fixed it when the problem first arose. At some point, it's going to start to hurt, but unfortunately this will just be the tip of the iceberg.

It is very easy for me to point the finger of blame at the Bush administration; unfortunately, in this case there are four fingers pointing right back at me. We have to wake up. This is our problem, and it won't even begin to get solved until a large number of Americans realize what is going on. Any electable politician will never have the *cajones* to do what has to be done about energy until it is far too late. The truth starts in my home, today, not tomorrow, and I must admit that I am really embarrassed by what I see when I look around my own house.

I'll leave former Vice President and oil executive Dick Cheney with the last word about this, because, in fact, simply stated, frankly speaking, no one tops the VP in timely quotes. "We all remember the energy crisis of the 1970s, when people in positions of responsibility complained that Americans just used too much energy. Even now, environmentalists are demanding that the government step in and force Americans to consume less energy; as if we could simply conserve or ration our way out of the situation we're in. Conservation *might be a sign of personal virtue, but is not a sufficient basis for a sound, comprehensive energy policy.*" (Italics added.) Spoken like a true, capitalist oilman.

Not mentioned here is the environmental calamity that goes part and parcel with our energy addiction. That is for another chapter of the book. There is, however, a real piece of irony. Russia is fully aware of the global warming problem and the greenhouse effect that goes along with it. For Russia, however, a little global warming is not such a bad thing. There is a large amount of oil and natural gas in and around the Russian area of the Arctic Circle, but it has historically been very hard to get to because of the severe conditions and the miles upon miles of frozen ice that it is trapped underneath. Global warming is doing for the Russians what they can't do for themselves—melting the ice and warming the surface, making it easier to get at the oil, therefore putting more oil into the marketplace, which adds a little more money to their bank accounts, which puts off the problem a little bit longer, all the while adding more hydrocarbons into the atmosphere, further exacerbating the problem.

OK, Imagine You're China

This is Secretary of Defense Donald Rumsfeld, speaking to the International Institute of Strategic Studies in Singapore on June 5th, 2005:

"Among other things, the report concludes that China's defense expenditures are much higher than Chinese officials have published. It is estimated that China's is the third largest military budget in the world, and clearly the largest in Asia."

(And...your point was...? China *is* the largest country in Asia, and unless I'm mistaken our "defense" budget was something like *seven* times theirs!)

"China appears to be expanding its missile forces, allowing them to reach targets in many areas of the world, not just the Pacific region, while also expanding its missile capabilities within this region. China also is improving its ability to project power, and developing advanced systems of military technology."

(Ummmm...why wouldn't a country like China—soon-to-be-if-not-already the biggest rival of the U.S. economically and then militarily—not begin to set up some sort of missile capabilities when the United States has missiles pointing at them and every other potential rival around the world?? Did Rumsfeld really think the U.S. could have a monopoly over these things?)

"Since no nation threatens China, one must wonder: Why this growing investment? Why these continuing large and expanding arms purchases? Why these continuing robust deployments?"

(The United States military, the United States military, and...the United States military.)

I mean, c'mon! This was the height of American arrogance. Imagine that we were the leaders of China, staring at this enormous colossus called the American Empire, with military bases in over 90 countries, including a ring of them around your country. This American Empire has almost outspent the rest of the world combined in yearly military spending, and this guy was pointing the finger at us for increasing our military budget? For developing advanced systems of military technology? Nah, let's just roll over and let them rule the entire world....

Of course China is going to beef their military up. What does any rational person think they're going to do? China is the only country in the world with the potential to be our serious rival, unless you include the EU, and they are stagnant right now.

Again, on October 17th, 2005, Rumsfeld, speaking at a school in China that grooms future Communist Party leaders, said this: "Many countries have questions about the pace and the scope of China's military expansion. A growth in China's power projection understandably leads other nations to question China's intentions, and to adjust their behavior in some fashion. The rapid, and—from our perspective at least—non-transparent nature of this buildup contributes to their uncertainty."

(Mr. Pot, meet Mr. Kettle.)

Rumsfeld went on: "China's efforts to form regional institutions *that exclude the U.S. also has raised doubts about its intentions*, and whether it will make the right choices—choices that will serve the world's real interests in regional peace and security." (Italics added.)

This is like one fox telling another fox to stay out of the henhouse, while the first fox is spitting feathers out of his mouth. I have to wonder if the Chinese students were sitting there trying not to laugh, or were they so stunned by the hubris of this guy that they sat there gaping, mouths wide open, casting sideways glances at one another. This would have to be very similar to the Chinese Minister of Information lecturing students at Harvard's Kennedy School of Business on breaches of freedom of the press in America and unfair business practices at Wal-Mart.

In the fall of 2002, lost in the hoopla over the National Security Strategy document that basically laid out the neoconservative plan for pre-emptive war and unilateral decision-making was the release of the Air Force Space Command's projection for the next several years. It said that the United States would move from "control" to "ownership" of space. Let the words "ownership of space" sink in for a minute. Beyond the question of how a nation can decide that it can "own" space, how do we think that China, or Russia, or the European Union, or anyone else is going to react to this? It seems completely logical to me, a songwriter, for gosh sakes, that we are fast approaching the not-so-funny reality of that cartoon that I was talking about in chapter eight, the one where Rumsfeld is standing in front of the map with "US" labeled on our country, and "THEM" on every other country. The only way that China or anybody else is going to have half a chance against this runaway train called the United States is to band together in a super alliance to stop us. This has happened over and over again in history, every time one single entity has gotten—or is perceived to have gotten—too big for its boots. I don't pretend to know what the straw will be that breaks the rest of the world's back, but the phrase "ownership of space" has got to be a fairly scary gauntlet thrown down by the Americans.

So, once again, when Donald Rumsfeld lectured the Chinese on building up their military, or chided them for forming strategic alliances that didn't include the U.S. (the current leaders in unilateralism), I seriously have to wonder whether he was really talking to the conservative base in this country, because I can't for a minute think that he was so delusional as to actually believe that China, or anyone else was going to buy what he's selling. This is not to say that the Chinese government is anything but the authoritarian Communist regime that it is. The point here is not to make China look good at our expense, although Rumsfeld seemed hell-bent on doing just that. I simply don't understand how the United States government thinks it could lecture anybody on military spending and unilateralism at a time when we were the poster child for both.

11 / saudi arabia

THE "ANCIENT" KINGDOM OF SAUDI ARABIA has only been a kingdom for around seventy years, coincidentally about as long as it's been since oil was discovered under its desert sands. Before that, it was a poor land of many small Bedouin tribes.

In the mid-18th century, a man from the Arabian plain of Najd named Muhammad ibn Abdul Wahhab developed a strict new approach to Islam, stressing a highly conservative and militant version of the faith. He found a political partner in Muhammad ibn Saud, the ruler of the tribe of Diriyah. Together, through ruthless conquest backed by a questionable interpretation of the faith, which soon became known as *Wahhabism*, they conquered large parts of the Arabian peninsula and created, through marriage, the dynastic family that rules Saudi Arabia to this day.

This is extremely important, because Wahhabism is the form of Islam most practiced in Saudi Arabia today, and is officially sanctioned and approved of by the Saudi royal family. It is Wahhabism that turned the word "jihad" from a meaning of "struggle," somewhat akin to "self-mastery," into the phrase "holy war," which is what most Westerners think it means. It is Wahhabism that preaches militant intolerance of other faiths, such as Christianity and Judaism. Most Muslim sects throughout history protected

Christians and Jews as "people of the book." It is also Wahhabism that finds other Muslims who don't believe as they do to be *kafir*, or infidels, and subject to the same brutal penalties (or worse) as non-Muslims. It should be noted that *jihad* is not one of the Five Pillars of Islamic faith, but under Wahhabism it has been elevated to a central obligation of Islam.

In 1933, a giant oil concession of 360,000 square miles was granted to Standard Oil of California by the new king, Ibn Saud, even though it angered many of his followers to be dealing with the infidels. When oil was struck in 1938, serious money started flowing as well, overpowering the arguments of the *ulamas*, or religious leaders, and the "special relationship" between the United States and Saudi Arabia began to take shape. However, herein lay the seeds of the divide between the royal desire to make billions of dollars, the need to have a powerful nation provide security, and the religious *ulama's* insistence on Wahhabi principles. Thus, for example, the U.S. was allowed to maintain an airbase in Dhahran, but was not permitted to undertake Christian religious services on the base, or anywhere in Saudi Arabia, for that matter.

In 1962, in an effort to curb the spread of secular Arab nationalism of the kind made popular by Egypt's President Nasser, the Saudi government hosted an Islamic Conference in Mecca out of which the Muslim World League was formed. The ultimate goal of the league was the spread of Wahhabism to the rest of the Muslim world. The Saudi government, awash in petrodollars, provided 99% of the financing for the Muslim World League. In 1963, the entire education system in Saudi Arabia was turned over to the Wahhabi *ulamas*, including the Islamic University of Medina and the King Abdul Aziz University. This meant that the entire generation born from the late 1950's on grew up with the doctrine of Wahhabism. Add to this the fact that many leading members of the militant Islamic group Muslim Brotherhood began teaching at these universities and gathering recruits for their coming jihad. The Muslim Brotherhood, which created havoc in Nasser's Egypt,

Jordan and Syria, and sought refuge in Saudi Arabia after being run out of their native countries, got its original inspiration from the teachings of Muhammad ibn Wahhab.

In the 1980s, the Saudi government gave billions of dollars to the Pakistani Intelligence Service, or ISI, to teach, train and equip young militant *mujahedin* fighters in their battle against the Soviet-backed Afghan government. Along with this came further billions in private Saudi money to further the Wahhabist cause. The Pakistanis spent much of this money opening *madrassahs*, or fundamentalist Islamic schools, where the most conservative Muslim theology was taught. It was out of these schools that the Taliban was born. It was also here that the rich Saudi, Osama bin-Laden, with the help of his own country's Intelligence Service, created an organization to funnel money to the *mujahedin* and train and equip Arabs from across the Middle East to become *jihadists*, or warriors.

The United States, in its zeal to stop the spread of communism to Afghanistan by any means, funded many of these same militant Islamic fighters to the tune of billions of more dollars. With all of these billions upon billions of dollars of support coming in, it's no wonder that the Islamic rebels eventually prevailed. It was to be a Pyrrhic victory for the U.S., however. The end result was the Taliban in power in Afghanistan, thousands of trained Arab radicals itching to export their jihad, and an organization swimming in money called al-Qaeda, run by Osama bin-Laden and given shelter by the Taliban.

With this bit of Saudi history, it becomes all too easy to understand how fifteen of the nineteen hijackers on 9/11 came from Saudi Arabia, funded and masterminded by the Saudi bin-Laden. The Saudi royals play a brilliant game of both-ends-against-the-middle, allowing militant Islamic teaching in their schools and universities, funding radical Islamic terrorist organizations that have been a major part of the worst terrorist actions of the last 30 years, all the while somehow managing to convince the U.S. to provide a shield of defense against these same radicals. Pretty nifty stuff. Meanwhile, we oil-aholic Americans belly up to the bar for another barrel of the hard stuff, shelling out billions upon billions of dollars that pass through the hands of our Big Oil companies, then go straight into the Saudi coffers to be distributed to the very Islamic terrorist organizations that we are trying to defeat. If this all wasn't so sadly true, you couldn't make it up.

Sunni vs. Shia = Catholic vs. Protestant?

There are two main sects of Muslims, Sunnis and Shias. At the beginning, in the 8th century, there was a dispute over who would succeed the Prophet Muhammad. Most Muslims accepted Muhammad's right-hand man, Abu Bakr, as his successor, or the first Caliph. A smaller group thought it should be his son-in-law, Ali. Ali did eventually become the fourth Caliph, but was quickly overthrown by descendants of Bakr, or the Umayyad Dynasty. At this point, the Sunnis followed the Umayyad line, and the Shias followed Ali's descendants, who were called Imams. Most of the basic tenets of Islam are the same in both sects. The majority of Muslims are Sunnis, but Iran is a majority Shi'ite nation, as is Iraq. The thought struck me that there sure have been a lot of bad feelings over the centuries between these two sects who, in most respects, believe the same things. So many people have died over the details.

Then I started thinking about Catholics and Protestants. I grew up in the Catholic faith. Both my mother and father were born and raised Catholic. All five of us kids were baptized Catholic, took our first Holy Communion at age seven, and were all Confirmed at thirteen. My older brothers and my older sister went to Catholic schools, but my younger sister and I, for the most part, didn't. I don't really know why. There were a lot of Catholic families in my neighborhood, families with lots of children.

I'm not sure where I learned this (probably Catechism), but I distinctly remember believing that Catholics were the only ones who were really serious about getting to Heaven because we *had* to go to church and we took Holy Communion every Sunday.

Those other people, the Protestants (whatever that was), were a kind of Catholic *lite*. The way I understood it was that they didn't *have* to go to church, and they didn't take Communion every Sunday, and they didn't go to Confession, and they didn't believe in *Mary*! Saying "Hail Marys" were second in importance only to the "Our Father" in important prayers. I remember sitting in the back of my parent's car on Sunday morning as we would pass a non-Catholic's house, and I would think, "I wonder what those people *do* on Sunday mornings?"

Fast-forward about twenty years. After a time away from any organized religion, I was brought back into the Faith through an evangelical non-denominational Protestant church. I realized that most of the things that I thought about Protestants when I was a child were either wrong, or misunderstood. But one day, something disturbing happened to me. Someone, knowing that I was brought up in the Catholic Church, asked me, "When did you become a Christian?" I came to realize soon enough that many Protestants don't really think being a Catholic qualifies as truly being a Christian.

When I worked at a Christian record company, which really means a Protestant Christian record company, there was a problem when I wanted to sign a very talented Catholic singer. It was agreed that she would need to be "indoctrinated" in the Protestant lingo, and that she would play down her Catholicism as much as possible. I heard many times that Catholics were a kind of Christian *lite*.

Having spent a considerable amount of time in both faith groups, I'm confident about a couple of things. There are both Catholics and Protestants who talk a lot about being religious, but there isn't a lot of heart in it. There are also a lot of Catholics and Protestants who make it their life's goal to know Jesus Christ, and to try and walk in His footsteps. There sure have been a lot of bad feelings over the centuries between these two sects who, for the most part, believe the same things. So much blood has been spilled over the details.

12 / the toughest issue of all[14]

The Origins of the Israeli-Palestinian Problem

What can I possibly add to the debate that festers in the Middle East concerning Israel's place amongst a hostile and unforgiving Arab majority? I read a parable about the dilemma that spoke to the heart of the matter:

A man was standing on top of a burning building, in which many members of his family had already perished, when the flames became so intense that he had to jump. He managed to save his own life, but as he was about to hit the ground, he struck a man standing below him, breaking the man's arms and crushing his legs. Ironically, the terribly hurt man on the ground had saved the falling man's life. Unfortunately, neither man saw this tragic situation through the other's eyes. The injured man, extremely angry with the falling man, accusing him of deliberately hurting him, and failing to see that the tragedy that had occurred was a horrible accident, swears revenge. The falling man, for his part, instead of apologizing for the grievous injury caused to the man on the ground and thanking the man for saving his life, became incensed at the man's anger, insults him, kicks him, and beats him every time he sees him. The kicked man again swears revenge and again is punched and punished. The bitter enmity hardens and comes to overshadow the whole existence of both men and to poison their minds. —Isaac Deutscher

To try and sort out this complicated mess requires a brief history lesson as free from bias as possible. The problem one encounters when trying to be unbiased is the charge of anti-Semitism whenever the sorting out starts to be critical of Israel or Zionism. The other problem is trying to have a historical discussion about Palestine/Israel without just ceding the field to the Jews on the basis that the land was given to them by God. This argument is like the person that tells you, in the course of a debate, that "God told them such and such," which effectively ends the debate. If one is to have a reasonable chance of untangling the complexities of the Israeli-Arab problem, this Biblical Manifest Destiny can only be a part of the picture as it historically fits in, not the end of the story. Where I would like to pick up the narrative is in the 19th century.

There is no doubt that throughout history, the Jewish people have been one of the world's most oppressed minorities, no matter where they ended up settling. Periodically, Jews would be blamed for whatever ills had befallen a particular kingdom or country, though they rarely had little or anything to do with the problems. They would often be given jobs that no one else wanted, like tax collecting and money changing. Despite being in the minority, Jews would often represent a disproportionate percentage of the well-educated and wealthy in their given areas of settlement. Being outsiders, they provided a convenient scapegoat for the ruler to rally the masses around in common hatred, to deflect them from the real ineptitude or corruption, and there would be *pogroms*, or periods of intense, violent repression aimed at the Jewish people.

Enter Theodor Herzl, a Viennese journalist and founder of modern political Zionism. Born in Budapest, Hungary, in 1860, Herzl was deeply affected by the anti-Semitism he saw in supposedly liberal late-19th century Western Europe. His pamphlet, entitled "The Jewish State," called for the immediate exodus of Jews from Europe. Originally Herzl, who was a secularist, had several places in mind as a homeland for the Jews, including

Uganda, Angola, and Argentina, before settling on Palestine. He died in 1904 before achieving his goal, but is generally recognized as the father of Zionism.

Followers of Zionism believed the Jewish people had an inherent and inalienable right to Palestine. Religious Zionists referred to God's promise of the land to the tribes of Israel. Secular Zionists thought of Palestine as the one and only answer to the worldwide problem of anti-Semitism. In formulating this plan, the Zionists had some pretty strange allies: the anti-Semites in many European governments, not the least of which was Great Britain.

Meanwhile, at the turn of the 20th century, there were around one million Palestinian Arabs living in Palestine, which is slightly smaller in size than the state of New Hampshire, and the Jewish population living there numbered less than 10% of the whole. Contrary to popular belief, these were not simply nomadic tribes or Bedouins, but farmers and villagers just like other parts of the settled Arab world. They were ruled nominally by the Ottoman Empire, which was in the final years of decay. Theirs was a feudal society of landowners, shopkeepers and peasant-farmers, basically unchanged over many hundreds of years. The city of Jerusalem had been in Arab hands for much of the past millennium, and was home to one of the holiest sites in Islam, the Dome of the Rock, or the el-Aqsa Mosque, where Mohammed was said to have ascended into heaven. The el-Aqsa Mosque is built on the site of Solomon's Temple, which was said to have housed the Ark of the Covenant, and which is one of the holiest sites in Judaism. This situation was treacherous before it started.

In 1917, the British government, with their backs to the wall in World War I and desperate for help, produced the Balfour Declaration, which opened the way to widespread Jewish immigration to Palestine. Many credit the Balfour Declaration with clearing the way internationally for what was to be the state of Israel. This agreement seemed aimed at two main groups, the Jews in revolutionary Russia, who had just dropped out of the war, and more importantly, the Jews in America, who were an influential minority in a country just deciding to go to war on behalf of the Allies. The Brits, in fact, were talking out of three sides of their mouths. In 1915 they agreed to include Palestine in a zone of independence for Arabs in return for an Arab revolt against their Ottoman masters (led by T.E. Lawrence, better known as Lawrence of Arabia), and then in 1916 agreed via the Sykes-Picot Agreement with the French and Russian governments to place Palestine under international supervision. The British were to pay a heavy price for the next thirty years of conflict-ridden rule over Palestine.

Each side took these agreements for what they wished them to mean. The World Zionist Organization was better organized and financed than any comparable Arab group, and had been making plans for some time for a democratic Jewish state in which Arabs would have minority rights. The problem with this plan was that even with a large influx of immigration in the 1920s and '30s, the Jewish population in Palestine comprised only 28 percent of the total in 1936, and 32 percent by 1947. Obviously, the Zionists were not going to have a democratic Jewish state in which they were the minority. However, the well-financed WZO had a further plan to buy large tracts of land in Palestine from absentee landowners and "transfer" the indigenous population that lived and worked on this land to other surrounding Arab countries. Once this land was bought, it could never be sold to anyone that wasn't Jewish. This amounted to nothing less than systematic ethnic cleansing. From the point of view of Chaim Weizmann, president of the WZO, speaking in 1930, the needs of 16 million Jews of the Diaspora had to be balanced against those of one million Palestinian Arabs.

The Palestinian Arabs revolted no less than three times in these years, aiming their anger mainly at the British Colonial government, whom they thought had lied to them about their own political aspirations and had sold them out to the Jews.

"For the last two and a half years there has been war in Palestine, a war waged by an oppressor against a colonial people. All the devasta-

tion measures employed by the oppressor, the aerial bombardments, the razing of villages to the ground, the imposition of fines, the taking of hostages, the enactment of martial law, the establishment of concentration camps, along with old-time methods of bribery, intrigue, corruption, all these failed to break the determined will of a united Palestinian people to attain national liberation."

This familiar-sounding quote was from a writer in 1938, speaking of Palestinian resistance to British Imperialism.

Meanwhile, hardworking Jewish settlers tilled the soil, built Jewish schools, towns, and a civic infrastructure, and started arming themselves for the inevitable confrontation with their reluctant and angry cohabitants and neighbors.

The Holocaust, in which six million Jews from all over Europe and Russia were systematically massacred during World War II by Hitler's Nazi killing machine, changed the moral equation in the Jewish/Arab debate over Palestine. The inability or unwillingness of the Western Allies to do anything about the slaughter was a dark stain on the governments of Great Britain and the United States. The U.S. government turned away a large ship of Jewish refugees in 1939 and sent the passengers back to almost certain death in concentration camps. The British, tired of fighting the Arabs and gearing up for a fight with Germany, severely restricted Jewish immigration to Palestine in 1939 just when the Jews needed to flee the most. The Allies' strategy of winning the war before doing anything about the Jewish tragedy (when from 1942 on they knew what was going on in the death camps), led to feelings of collective guilt that paved the way for the United Nations in 1947 to agree to a partition of Palestine into two states: a Jewish state, and a Palestinian Arab state.

This is where it gets tricky again. The Arabs were unhappy because the Jews got 55% of the new state although they constituted only a third of the population. The Jewish leaders claimed that the new state of Jordan (or Transjordan as it was known then), granted independence in 1946 by Britain, was actually part of Greater Palestine and constituted almost 70% of the land promised by the League of Nations as a Jewish National Home. Plus, the city of Jerusalem was to be an international city (which may have been the smartest part of the plan). With the annexing of the West Bank by Jordan in 1950, the Jewish leaders could claim that they actually only controlled 17.5% of the original land promised to them. There was enough fuzzy math to go around for everybody.

What's In a Phrase?

I wanted to pause for a moment and look at some of the ways that we are taught our history as we are growing up. What got me thinking about this was the way that the Zionists (and many Westerners, too) felt that it was their "right" or their destiny to have a homeland in Palestine. Because of the religious overtones, this would be understandable, except for one thing: people already lived there. The idea that they could eventually outnumber and then ethnically cleanse the area of the indigenous population reminded me of the European settler's position on the people who lived in America before they did.

More significantly, I was focusing on the types of language that we use when describing these great movements of peoples. When it is the large migration of European immigrants crossing the Mississippi River to settle the West, this is referred to as our "Manifest Destiny." This is an elegant turn of phrase that I always thought was some sort of law when I was in grade school; it was presented in Social Studies as a sort of inevitable right of the Euro-settlers; a foregone conclusion that the indigenous population would move out of the way or be moved out of the way for the superior race. Because the native population had no concept of "ownership of land"—the idea was absurd to them, that you could "own" the earth—the settlers simply "bought" or were given the land from the U.S. government, who "claimed" it, and then moved the natives out. It's interesting to ponder some of the words used to describe the various movements and migrations of peoples around the world. When it's Central Asians moving west, then it's the "Mongol barbarian hordes" brutally invading. (It's telling that the word "barbarian" has been used by peoples all over the world to describe foreigners—including us—that are different from themselves.) When it's the U.S. government moving west, it's Manifest Destiny, and it is the native population that is "heathen." Ah, but we were bringing *civilization* to the natives. What we brought them was gunpowder and disease. At least fifty million natives, and probably many more, up and down the Americas were killed as a result of disease brought upon them by the Europeans. All the while, it was just assumed that it was our inalienable right to govern them, to teach them our ways, whether they wanted to know them or not, and most of all, to "civilize" them.

It was a selling point of the Zionists to recalcitrant European governments that the Jewish settlers would be bringing civilization to the East; an outpost of European and Western intelligentsia and values in a sea of Arab nomads. The invading Ottomans of the Middle Ages similarly thought it their spiritual duty to bring Islam to the "infidels" and "polytheists" of Europe, and got as far as the gates of Vienna before finally being rebuffed.

Israel-Palestine 1948-1973: Jews 4, Arabs Nil

The British, having won the war (WWII) but lost their Empire, were bailing out of positions all around the globe. They simply didn't have either the money or the manpower to keep or administer their far-flung possessions. Besides, they had made all kinds of desperate deals regarding independence when their backs were to the wall during the war, and now the bill was due. The British turned over the impossible problem of Palestine to the new United Nations, and the fledgling Jewish Nation turned to the United States, home of the largest and wealthiest remaining Jewish population in the world, to be their new benefactor and protector.

Although anti-Semitism wasn't unknown in America, it was a less significant factor than, for example, prejudice against blacks. In fact, the Jewish minority maintained a political position in the Democratic Party that far outweighed their numbers. There were many influential and wealthy Jews, especially on the East Coast, who carried great sway with the powers in Washington. This, added to the fact that there was no such comparable Arab lobby, made it inevitable that the United States would become Israel's "special friend." The major counterweight to this scenario was that oil was being uncovered in Arab-controlled Middle Eastern lands at an astonishing rate. The United States had to walk a tight rope to keep its hands on the gas pump while still appeasing the powerful Jewish lobby at home.

The UN Partition of 1947 left all sides feeling like their glass was half-empty. The day after the Jews declared independence in May of 1948, they were attacked on all sides by a coalition of Arab states that included Egypt, Lebanon, Syria, Jordan, and Iraq. Just about everything that happened during this war is a matter of dispute. The Arabs claimed that the Israeli Army had already taken up positions inside the Palestinian sector and so the Arabs were defending the Palestinian land. The Israelis, obviously, say they were attacked. Both sides accused the other of horrible civilian massacres.

The Israelis claimed the huge masses of Palestinian refugees that went streaming into Gaza, Lebanon, and Jordan were the result of an overconfident Arab military, who urged the Arab populations to remove themselves for a short period of time until they defeated the Jews, and then they could return. The Arabs say that this is nonsense, and point to the Arab exodus as the ultimate goal of Zionism—a pure Jewish State. It is safe to say that no one's hands were clean in this mess. In the end, after initial setbacks, the feisty Israeli Army defeated the Arab coalition and ended up with a much larger piece of territory than they started with. When the cease-fire was declared, the only parts of the original whole Israel didn't control was a strip of land in Gaza, and what the Jewish people knew of as the lands of Judea and Samarra, which the Jordanians controlled and renamed the West Bank.

Between the establishment of Israel in 1948, the conclusion of the 1973 war, and the disengagement agreements in 1975, Israel's borders did not see even one day of quiet. The years from 1948 to 1973 can be regarded as a twenty-five year war between Israel and its neighbors—one war, with five rounds, taking place over one generation. Israel's border wars with its neighbors during the years 1949–1956, which began as actions attempting to prevent Palestinian refugees from returning to their homes, quickly evolved into days of limited warfare between the Israeli Defense Force and the Egyptian, Jordanian, and Syrian armies respectively. These years were marked by repeated attacks on Israeli settlers by Arab *fedayeen*, which means both "sacrifice," and "commando" in Arabic. These attacks killed over four hundred settlers during this period, and were countered by vicious retaliatory raids into Palestinian refugee camps in the Gaza Strip led by the recent Prime Minister of Israel Ariel Sharon, killing 20 people, mostly women and children. This raid was followed up by a nighttime attack on the Jordanian village of Qibya, killing 70 villagers inside their homes. It is telling that many of the pivotal political leaders of later years—Menachim Begin, Yitzhak Shamir, Moshe Dayan, Yitzhak Rabin, Ehud Barak, and Ariel Sharon—were all either underground resistance fighters (some would call them terrorists), or major military figures in the middle of the action against the Arabs in the years preceding their political careers.

It was also during this period that the Cold War came to the Middle East. The Soviet Union, which had supported the creation of Israel and had sold arms to it, switched sides and began supporting Arab interests and selling them arms. Included in this were $200 million worth of Soviet made weapons purchased by Egypt from Czechoslovakia in 1955, after the West had turned down President Nasser. The United States, angered over the purchase, reversed a decision to loan Egypt a large amount of money to build the Aswan Dam on the Upper Nile River. Nasser responded by nationalizing the Suez Canal on July 26, 1956, hoping to use its profits to pay for the dam. This was one of the high points of the new Arab nationalism, and made Nasser a huge hero in Arab countries throughout the Middle East.

The British and the French, two colonial powers on the wane, and the two biggest users of the canal, plotted with Israel to regain control of the Suez Canal and open the Straits of Tiran in the Gulf of Aqaba, which was Israel's only outlet to the Red Sea and points beyond. This led to the second Arab-Israeli War, at the end of October 1956.

Israel initiated hostilities on October 29 by invading Gaza and the Sinai and then moved into the Suez Canal zone on October 30. The United States, furious with Israel, Britain, and France and motivated even more by the understandable fear that the Soviet Union would be drawn into the fray, sponsored a U.N. resolution condemning the attack, which passed on November 2. Meanwhile, British and French troops, an ultimatum to Israel and Egypt having been ignored as expected, were busy trying to take control of the Canal Zone. Hostilities ended on November 6 after a ceasefire took effect. In December, a U.N. emergency force was stationed in the area. The Suez Canal was then returned to Egypt. This was one of the pivotal moments in world history where the child (the U.S.) became father to the man (England and France). From then on, there was no question that the Americans were wearing the pants in this relationship. And while Nasser was the loser militarily, he was the big winner politically. His stature in the Arab world rose sharply, quickly dwarfing other leaders like Jordan's King Hussein and Iraq's Nuri al-Said who were perceived to be too beholden to Western interests.

In 1957, Yasir Arafat, a civil engineer living in Kuwait, together with Khalil Wazir and Salah Khalaf, formed the Palestinian movement al-Fatah ("conquest" in Arabic; also, in reverse, an acronym for Harakat at-Tahrir al-Filistini, "Movement for the Liberation of Palestine").

In 1963 and 1964, Israeli and Syrian forces battled twice over water and cultivation rights on their common border. 1964 also saw the founding of the Palestine Liberation Organization.

In April of 1967, another border clash between Israel and Syria broke out over cultivation rights. In May, Nasser mobilized his Egyptian army and moved into the Sinai Peninsula in support of his Arab brethren in Syria. When he then blockaded the Gulf of Aqaba and signed a five-year mutual defense pact with Jordan's King Hussein, Israel mobilized for war.

The third Arab-Israeli War lasted six days between June 5th and June 10th, 1967. It was a huge victory for the Israelis, and by the time an armistice was declared, Israel controlled the Gaza Strip, the Sinai Desert, the Golan Heights in Syria, and the West Bank, including the ancient regions of Judea and Samarra. Perhaps most importantly, for the first time in 1,800 years, the whole city of Jerusalem was under Jewish sovereignty. This was a humiliating defeat for the Arab nations.

The United Nations on November 22, 1967 issued Resolution 242 calling upon Israel to withdraw from "territories occupied in the recent conflict." The resolution underscored "the inadmissibility of the acquisition of territory by war," and "the sovereignty, territorial integrity, and political independence of every State in the area and their right to live in peace within secure and recognized boundaries free from acts of force." Resolution 242 also called for a "just settlement of the refugee problem." A fundamental problem with U.N. Resolution 242 was that there were two versions, one French the other English. The French version stipulated that Israel was obligated to withdraw "from *the* territories" occupied during the war, while the English version read only "from territories." Israel was to argue fifteen years later in 1982 that it had complied with the latter sense of the resolution when it returned the Sinai to Egypt. In a problem with such complexity and almost intractable obstacles to peace, even a word as small and insignificant as "the" assumed immense importance.

In February 1969, Israeli Prime Minister Levi Eshkol died and was succeeded by Golda Meir. On June 15, 1969, Golda Meir was quoted in the Sunday Times of London as saying, "It was not as though there was a Palestinian people in Palestine considering itself as a Palestinian people and we came and threw them out and took their country away from them. They did not exist...."

At the Olympics in 1972, Palestinian commandos assassinated members of the Israeli Olympic team at Munich. Eleven Israelis and five Palestinians died. Israel avenged this attack the following year, with an attack by Israeli commandos led by Ehud Barak, the future Prime Minister, on PLO headquarters in Beirut, Lebanon. In this attack, three high-ranking PLO officials the Israelis claimed were responsible for the Olympic killings were assassinated.

In October of 1973, the Arab states, led by Egypt and Syria, launched a surprise attack against Israel on the holiest day of the Jewish Calendar, Yom Kippur, or Day of Atonement. The Arabs were motivated this time by the desire to redeem their honor after their major defeat in the 1967 Six-Day War. The Israelis were initially caught off guard, and suffered heavy casualties. Before long, the United States was airlifting supplies to the Israelis, and the Soviets were doing the same to their Arab counterparts, threatening for a time to evolve into a full-scale war between the two major powers. The Israelis recovered, and once again their forces proved too much for the combined Arab armies. Stung by yet another defeat at the hands of their Jewish enemies, and angered at the U.S. support of Israel, the Arabs, including Saudi Arabia, employed a full-scale oil embargo on the United States, with the result that the price of a barrel of oil rose from $4 a barrel to $30. The Americans, stung by rising gas prices and long lines at the pump, embarked on a new strategy to control the flow of oil from the Middle East by whatever means necessary—a policy that continues to this day.

13 / israel 1974–2006;
david becomes goliath

MUCH HAS BEEN WRITTEN ABOUT THE LESSONS that our government has learned from 9/11, and not much has been written about whom the government is learning them from. Since 1973, the United States has supplied Israel with enough fighter planes, attack helicopters, tanks, missile systems, and assorted other military equipment to enable it to become the fourth largest army in the world. If you add in the estimated 200 nukes, the battle-tested troops and the veteran leadership that a never-ending state of war brings to the table, then you could rank them higher. Little David's Army is all grown up. Having said that, the Israelis are teaching the Americans precisely the wrong lessons in how to bring an asymmetric insurgency to an end.

Proving decisively that it could defeat all Arab comers in the wars of 1948, 1956, 1967, and 1973, the Israelis now became *the* dominant power in the region. This came at a price, of course, for not even victory tastes sweet in the Middle East. The Israeli leadership became increasingly intransigent and more hard-line. In 1973, the conservative Likud Party came to fruition and the first Likud Prime Minister was Menachim Begin, elected in 1977. A former leader of the hard-line paramilitary (some say terrorist) Irgun, he helped initiate the bilateral peace process with Egypt, which resulted in the Camp David Accords and the 1979 Israel-Egypt Peace Treaty. It was in 1977 that Egyptian President Anwar Sadat visited Jerusalem and addressed the Israeli Knesset, an act that probably cost him his life, in 1981, at the hands of Islamist extremists in his own Army.

In the absence of a final peace settlement with all of the Arab combatant nations, the continued Israeli administration of areas captured in 1967 is subject to constant international concern and criticism. However, it is the establishment of Israeli homes and communities in those areas that has often generated condemnation. Over 500,000 Jewish settlers now live in areas captured during the 1967 war. These settlements have been declared illegal in no less than four United Nations Security Council resolutions and by the International Court of Justice. The settlements have also been a source of tension between Israel and the U.S., who have always tried to balance their "special relationship" with Israel and their "special relationships" with Saudi Arabia and Egypt. Despite these tensions, the United States during this period has increasingly looked at Israel as the bulwark of democracy and capitalism in the Middle East and the first line of defense of the oil fields in the region. To that end, the U.S. has given Israel billions upon billions of dollars in aid, the biggest increases coming after 1973. While our successive governments have talked publicly about fairness and balance and a "two-state solution" to the Israeli-Palestinian problem, it is obvious to anyone with a calculator whose side we favor.

One of the misconceptions that Westerners, especially Americans, have of the Arab Middle East is that it is some sort of monolithic entity. We had the same misconception about communists. The truth is, many of the loyalties in that region are still tribal, or clannish. It makes sense that since Jordan has only been "Jordan" for about 60 years (before that being part of Greater Palestine), this country would be the natural refuge for displaced Palestinians, and sure enough, it was. Along with the refugees came the PLO, though, and the PLO wanted virtual autonomy in the refugee areas. This led to a bloody clash with the Jordanian government and their army in 1970, called "Black September" by the Palestinians, and the PLO was expelled. Seeking a new place to call home, the PLO took up residence in Lebanon.

In 1982, fed up with cross-border attacks on civilians by PLO fighters from bases in Southern Lebanon, the Israeli Army launched a massive invasion of Lebanon to root out and destroy the PLO fighters and their sanctuaries. The Israeli government had authorized the army to only go forty kilometers inside of Lebanon, but, led by General Ariel Sharon, the Israelis chased the PLO fighters all the way into Beirut. Two months later, the Palestine Liberation Organization, including Yassir Arafat and 14,000 fighters and members, were evacuated from Beirut and relocated to Tunis, Tunisia, not to return to Palestine for twelve years. The removal of the PLO did not stop the violence however, especially in Lebanon. In one of the biggest massacres in the modern history of the Middle East, Lebanese Christian Phalange units, allowed by Israeli forces to enter the Palestinian refugee camps of Sabra and Shatilla just outside of Beirut, murdered between 400 and 800 Palestinian civilians. No action was taken by Israel to stop the massacre.

In Lebanon, where there were 400,000 Palestinian refugees, the situation was complicated by a Civil War. Into this mess the Americans came in 1983, trying to bring some order to a very complicated situation. There were the Christian Phalange fighters, the Muslim Druze militia, the Syrian Army, the PLO, the Israelis, and now the Americans and the French. The Americans under Ronald Reagan were trying to rebuild their post-Vietnam image, and trying to reassert their influence in an area of strategic (read: oil) interest. Some of these factions did not see the Americans as neutral peacekeepers, but saw them instead as allies of the Christian dominated Lebanese Army, which, in fact, they became. On October 23, just after dawn, 241 Marines died when a truck packed with explosives blew up a Marine barracks at Beirut International Airport. At that same moment a similar explosion blew up a French military barracks a few kilometers away, killing 56 French troops. The October 23 suicide bombers used the identical technique that had been used six months earlier to blow up the American embassy. The same technique would be used again on December 12 in Kuwait against the American and French embassies. It would be used again in September 1984, in East Beirut at the American embassy, with 13 deaths. We did not learn very fast.

In 1987, the *Intifada*, or "Awakening," was spontaneously started by young Palestinian men and youths as a reaction to several incidents of Israeli brutality. At first, this involved the throwing of rocks and stones at Israeli soldiers, but later, under the auspices of the PLO, Hamas, and Islamic Jihad, the demonstrators graduated to Molotov cocktails and even hand grenades. By the time the Oslo Accords were signed in 1993, 1,124 Palestinians and 90 Israelis had died. It was during this time that the Palestinians could have used a real leader; one who could have led the people in non-violent resistance and stated the case of the Palestinian people eloquently to the world. The Intifada was on the right track, it just didn't have that person to lead it. As it was, the Intifada brought the plight of the Palestinian people to the forefront of world opinion, and was not a good thing for Israeli public relations. David was turning into Goliath.

In 1993, Yitzhak Rabin, the Prime Minister of Israel, and Yassir Arafat, the Chairman of the Palestinian Liberation Organization signed an agreement known as the Oslo Accords. In this agreement, among other things, the PLO acknowledged Israel's right to exist, and Israel accepted the PLO, under its newly appointed governing body, the Palestinian Authority, as the sole representative and government of the Palestinian people.

In the past, the Israelis had refused to negotiate with the PLO, whom they deemed as a terrorist organization. Yet when they negotiated with anyone else, that Palestinian representative would have to consult the PLO before responding. When Rabin became Prime Minister in 1992, the Israelis opened secret talks with the

PLO through the auspices of Norwegian diplomats, and thus the Oslo Accords were born. The Oslo Accords took the United States and just about everyone else by surprise.

While these agreements were a start, and better than nothing, they were carefully constructed as a "Declaration of Principals," and an "Interim Agreement." The Oslo Accords left the major negotiating for later: an independent Palestinian state, the status of Jerusalem, and the status of refugees and their right-of-return to their former homeland. The Israelis handed over limited sovereignty in some parts of the West Bank and Gaza in stages to the Palestinian Authority, while retaining control of all borders, much of the security, and all of the foreign policy.

Viewed in over twelve years of cold daylight, the Oslo Accords have to be seen as a failure. The Israelis came to the meetings with a huge advantage in organization, technical engineering, detailed maps, and skilled negotiators. Once again, the lack of a viable alternative to the autocratic improvising of Yassir Arafat was obvious to all who were present. The upshot of this is that the Israelis have turned the West Bank into an incredible series of small, noncontiguous cantons in the valleys for the Palestinians, surrounded by large, modern Israeli settlements occupying the hills. This impossible situation is made worse by the fact that wherever you are in the Palestinian areas, you can't get *there* from *here*. Access to *anywhere* is restricted for Palestinians, with time-consuming waits at innumerable checkpoints and humiliating searches. As one writer put it, Israel owns this house; in it they've allowed the Palestinians the use of a few bedrooms, but they're not allowed to use the halls or the bathrooms. The Israelis claim, with justification, that this situation is made necessary by the numerous Palestinian suicide bombings that have plagued Israel for the past twenty years.

This violent Palestinian response to their plight deserves to be scrutinized. Many Palestinians claim that given the overwhelming military superiority of the Israeli Defense Force (and overwhelming is really an *under*statement), all the Palestinian people have to fight with is a few guns, some mortars, and their own bodies, to which explosives are attached and detonated at strategic locations. This is viewed by many as the ultimate heroic sacrifice, and these young men (and, increasingly, young women) are seen as martyrs and heroes.

Imagine, though, how different our history would be if young Negro boys and girls had strapped on explosives and blew themselves up at department store counters, entrances to colleges, on buses, and on crowded urban streets in Birmingham, Atlanta, and Nashville in the early 1960s. The response to their plight would have been completely different. While the conditions of Southern blacks would have still been intolerable, sympathy from the outside community would have certainly shifted to the slain white civilians. Federal troops, far from being used as a buffer *against* the continued violence of whites aimed at Negroes, would have probably been positioned against the blacks themselves. The blacks were in a similar, hostile, repressive situation against a much larger and better-equipped foe. They had what might be viewed by some as a legitimate right to strike back at their oppressors; instead they chose a path of non-violent resistance and because of this, they delineated clearly for all to see their position as victims, and their oppressors as the brutal racist thugs they truly were.

Of course, black Americans had the incomparable Martin Luther King, Jr. to state their case; but they also had James Bevel, and Diane Nash, and John Lewis, who led a movement of young African-Americans committed to non-violence and civil disobedience. These people studied how to do this—it didn't just happen. They trained their cadres and prepared them as fully as possible for what was going to happen to them—including what to do when they were beaten. The immense courage that it took to know you were going to probably get your head smashed in, or a bone broken, or worse, and not strike back—this was the essence of the movement. The thing people forget about using non-violence against repression is that it's only non-violent in one direction.[15]

The Palestinians have always lacked their version of Martin Luther King Jr., or Nelson Mandela, or even Gandhi. Instead, they got stuck with Yassir Arafat, with a sidearm on his hip, and not much eloquence coming out of his mouth. How the course of history can change when one brave, prophetic person can put his own well being aside and lead a people to freedom in the face of impossible odds.

If only...if only the Palestinians could take this vital lesson to heart, things would necessarily be much different. Every time a suicide bomber blows him or herself up in a crowded market, or in a club full of young Israelis, or at a wedding, the Israelis have all of the justification they need to lock down villages, throw up roadblocks, build Berlin-style walls, cause endless humiliations to harmless women and children, and worse, to blow up houses and kill civilians in retaliation. The court of world opinion, already inclined towards the Palestinians, would be so much louder if it weren't for the suicide bombers. Above all, America would be placed in a much more difficult situation, morally, if the Palestinians were using only non-violent techniques; as it is, every time a suicide bomb kills Israeli civilians, the American government is quick to condemn the terrorism and it tips the scale back on the moral side of Israel.

Imagine, though, a Palestine of non-violent resistance, with a Nelson Mandela-type, or a Martin Luther King, or a Gandhi, or even a Vaclev Havel leading the way. Imagine these young Palestinian men and women, steeped in non-violent training, sitting down on roads, obstructing traffic, marching peacefully, singing songs, and filling the jails faster than they can be arrested. For starters, you'd have every Bono-style celebrity activist marching with them within days. There's Harry Belafonte! There's Martin Sheen! Here comes the legendary Mandela! The situation would be completely different—American religious leaders and peace-movement activists would be going to jail in solidarity with the Palestinians. This would all be way too much for the Israelis, who would suddenly look like the purveyors of apartheid that they really are.

At least one man is really trying. Dr. Mubarak Awad is a Palestinian who is internationally recognized as an expert in nonviolent strategic action. As the director of Nonviolence International, he and his group are working tirelessly from village to village in the West Bank and Gaza, teaching nonviolent techniques to all who will listen. The work is hard and slow, and old ideas diehard. But Dr. Awad is convinced that his work will eventually be successful, and he has the support and respect of like-minded Israelis just over the border.

What happened in the meantime was the second, or al-Aqsa Intifada, spurred on by the collapse of yet more peace talks, and Ariel Sharon's ill advised visit in September of 2000 to the Al Aqsa Mosque, the Muslim holy site in Jerusalem that is also the site of the Temple Mount. Israeli and Palestinian violence associated with the Intifada had claimed 1,782 Palestinian lives, 649 Israeli lives, and the lives of 41 foreign nationals by the end of March 2003. Israel took full advantage of the 9/11 tragedies by equating al-Qaeda with the Palestinian suicide bombers, knowing that America in its vengeful mood would look the other way. Sharon's tanks, Apache helicopters, huge bulldozers, and F-16 fighters turned the West Bank city of Jenin into rubble, killing hundreds of civilians.

In the summer of 2005, Ariel Sharon convinced his reluctant Cabinet to allow him to unilaterally withdraw all 8,000 settlers from the Gaza Strip. On the surface, this seemed to be a grand gesture towards peace, allowing the Palestinians true autonomy over one of the Occupied Territories. A closer look reveals that, unlike the West Bank with its 500,000 Jewish settlers, the Gaza Strip had never become the destination of choice for any but the most hearty or militant Israelis. The few settlements in place were isolated and lightly populated. Sharon sacrificed the Gaza Strip settlements and their 8,000 inhabitants for the "facts on the ground" in the West Bank. It seems as though for now they've given back all the land they are going to give.

On January 4th, 2006, Ariel Sharon suffered a massive stroke that permanently incapacitated him. Power was transferred to his 2nd in command, Ehud Olmert, whose Kadima Party (a party founded by Sharon) won the majority of seats in the March elections and made Olmert the new Prime Minister.

Another election in January was more troubling to Israel and its supporters. Hamas, the Islamic militant organization, won 74 out of 132 seats in the Palestinian legislative election and became the majority party in Palestine. Among other things, this posed an uneasy dilemma for the United States, which has been pushing hard for democracy in the Middle East. Hamas, which is committed to the destruction of Israel, was elected by the people of Palestine in a relatively free and fair election.

As for the nation of Israel, a few things are fairly clear to me. For starters, they have to start acting their age. They have to realize that they are the elephant in the living room. Playing the victim isn't cutting it anymore. As the last living people who were victims of the Holocaust pass into eternity, today's generation of Israeli Jews must come to terms with the fact that it has now been sixty years since the death camps were liberated, and as truly horrible as it was, and understanding that it should never be forgotten, it is time to stop thinking of themselves as victims. Victims don't possess the 4th or 5th most powerful army in world; victims don't own 200 nukes; victims don't win four wars in a row; and victims don't oppress other minorities.

You must admit, much of the Arab world has made it its life's mission to destroy Israel. Under this constant looming threat, what would you expect?

In 1948, Israel was like a baby lion surrounded by a pack of hungry hyenas. With the memory of the Holocaust fresh in the world's consciousness, most nations outside of the Arab world, even the Soviet Union, were partial to a Jewish state. And like the United States after 9/11, Israel has squandered away its considerable bank of sympathy through its over-zealous militarism and uncompromising and repressive position against the Palestinian people. The last fifty years have seen David indeed turn into Goliath, except that David doesn't seem to know it. For nowhere, not even in the United States, are the myths of a country and a people so powerfully and fatally ingrained as in Israel. They have constructed and learned a version of their young history as a nation in which they have been the victims in every act of their play. As a result, most Israelis can't conceive of being oppressors; their script has always called for them to be the oppressed. The few eloquent and lucid voices of sanity in Israel remind me of the Whos in Whoville shouting loudly but vainly from their dust-speck amidst a jungle of self-righteous violence.

The Israelis fought four wars (some would say five, if you include the 1967–1970 War of Attrition) from 1948 to 1973, or in their first twenty-five years of existence, to deal with the fact that the neighboring Arab world was bent on their destruction. They won every one of them, and haven't had another one in the last thirty-two years. Egypt, Jordan, and the PLO have all renounced their earlier policies and have declared Israel's right to exist. Israel no longer needs to act as though it is fighting every day for its own existence. It is now the Palestinians who are fighting every day for *their* own existence.

The Palestinian people are fighting a battle against time, which may be a reason, but not an excuse, for the flailing, violent actions of some. The Israelis are using a strategy that embraces "the facts on the ground," which is to say that every day, month, and year that goes by adds permanence to the settlements that have sprouted up all over the Occupied Territories. They kept building and building, ignoring the spirit, if not the letter of any and all interim agreements negotiated with the Palestinians. Now, thirty-plus years later, they can say, "You can't possibly expect us to tear *all* of this down!" They have not only built all of these settlements, but have carefully constructed a network of roads in and out of them that are only to be used by Israeli Jews. This, along with the Security Fence, or Apartheid Wall, whichever you choose to call it, has effectively trapped the Palestinian people into a matrix or spider web that is virtually impossible to traverse. This situation has no resemblance to justice. It is apartheid.

If the Palestinian people have any hope of getting anything close to their former lives back, they *must* renounce all acts of violence so that they can gain the upper moral ground and expose the Israeli position for the apartheid that it is. Until then, the "facts on the ground" will continue to speak louder than any single cry in the West Bank.

Where should the government of the United States be in this miserable state of affairs? I think that the United States needs to quit treating Israel like the 51st state. Did you know that we give Israel one quarter of *all* of our foreign aid each year? This may have been okay when Israel was a baby lion, but baby's all grown up now, and is starting to eat the neighbors. Alas, being kind to Israel is one thing all sides of the ideological divide seem to agree on. Being "soft" on Israel is kind of like being "soft" on Defense—no one wants to be accused of it. If this is the case, and everybody knows it, we should stop pretending that we're being even-handed about it, and recuse ourselves from the peace process. After all, we can only really be of any help as a parent showing some tough love to Israel—and it appears as if we don't have the political will to do that. So, administration after administration play their role of power broker, with occasional successes, such as the Israeli-Egyptian Peace Agreement (although it didn't work out too well for Mr. Sadat), but mainly overseeing agreements like the Wye River Accords that end up with a Palestinian entity that looks amazingly like a piece of Swiss cheese. To his credit, George W. Bush was the first U.S. president to officially call for a Palestinian state. While this is an improvement on his predecessors, it is a long way from coercing the Israelis to change "the facts on the ground." I just don't see this happening any time soon, not with George W., not with Hillary Clinton, or Barack Obama, or John McCain—not with anybody on the immediate horizon.

As for us, the Christians, how should we feel about all of this? Who's side should we be on? Should we even take sides?

Conservative evangelical Christendom comes down hard on the side of Israel. Strike me down with a bolt of lightning right now, but I've never *really* understood this great love/brotherhood from the Christians to the Israelis—I mean, an over-the-top, favor-one-side-over-the-other kind of love. There is a whole sect of conservative Christians who call themselves pre-millennial dispensationalists who believe that everything that is going on in Israel, and happening to Israel, both good and bad, has to happen in just this way for Jesus to return. They seem to rather perversely pray for as much violence as possible to accelerate the completion of this prophecy. On the other hand, this is the religion that rejected and *still rejects* the basic premise of our faith in the person of Jesus Christ. This is a *pretty major* divide. I don't mean that we shouldn't love them, or that we should side *against* them, I just don't understand why we should come down so strongly *for* them over the Palestinians. (I'm gonna be killed crossing the street tomorrow.)

My position is, I'm on the side of peace. I'm on the side of whoever is on the side of non-violence. If there is an Israeli peace movement, I'm with them. If the Palestinians start marching for peace, I'm with them, too. I'm especially for those brave souls on both sides who, against overwhelming odds, come together for a better understanding of the other's position and try to arrive at non-violent solutions. This is whom I believe the Christian church should support. This idea that we should support Israel because we have a Biblical...*obligation*, is contrary to Jesus' teaching. He said, "Blessed are the peacemakers." He didn't say anything about bulldozing houses, or suicide bombers, for that matter. But he wouldn't have liked either one.

14 / a parable about the war on terror

THERE'S A MAN WHO LIVES IN MY NEIGHBORHOOD who has a wife and four children. His name is Charles. Charles is a pretty good guy; he works hard, seems to love his kids, and takes his family to church on Sundays. Charles hired some Mexican guys to take care of his lawn once a week. One day, while Charles was at work, one of the gardeners came to the door and asked Charles' wife, Sarah, for a glass of water. Sarah, unwisely, let the man into her house, where he proceeded to brutally beat and rape her, leaving the poor woman near death. This man escaped out a back door, and melted into the large immigrant community.

The police learned through their investigation both the last place this man had lived, and many of the people that he associated with. Charles, beside himself with rage, and certain that the police were never going to give this horrible man the justice that he deserved, took it upon himself to administer what he felt was proper justice. Many of Charles' friends, while concerned that Charles would only get himself in trouble and make a bad situation worse, quietly applauded his grim determination, and had to admit that they, too, would at least consider doing the same thing if a loved one of their own was attacked in this way. This is what Charles did:

First, he found out where the house was that the Mexican gardener had been staying. In the middle of the night, he poured gasoline in a ring completely around the house and on the roof, and proceeded to burn the house down, killing a man, the man's mother, his wife, her brother, and three children who were living and sleeping there. The Mexican gardener was not there. He had been staying there at one time, but he didn't stay there any more.

The next morning, Charles found the main office of the gardening company that this guy worked at. He drove up to the front door, went inside, and shot every person who happened to be there. The Mexican gardener that he was looking for wasn't there. He had been there, but he wasn't there when Charles shot the people in the office. On the way out of the office, Charles shot a guy getting out of his car who looked somewhat like the Mexican gardener who had raped his wife.

Although some of Charles' friends were concerned that Charles had gone a little overboard, especially considering that he hadn't found the rapist/gardener, others took a more balanced view. "Although I'm sorry to see women and children die, those people should've known what they were in for when they let that beast sleep in their house," said one friend. As for the people in the gardening office, another remarked, "I've wanted to pick a few of those guys off myself when they start cranking up those noisy blowers!"

What Charles did next, though, was more puzzling, especially to those who didn't know what a Good Man Charles was. There was a Japanese gardening company that had serviced many of the houses in Charles' neighborhood in the past, including his for a time. Charles had fallen out with this particular gardener, named Ryuchi, over a dispute concerning rhododendrons. It seemed that many people in the neighborhood considered Ryuchi's company overpriced and his gardeners rude and haughty, which is why the Mexican gardeners were there in the first place. Charles had it on good authority that not only did Ryuchi and his men know the Mexican gardener, but in fact, in a bit of revenge over being fired, had put the Mexican up to the crime. This information came to Charles from a rival Japanese gardener named Hideki, who was looking to get work in Charles' neighborhood. Charles had little trouble finding Ryuchi's house, as Hideki drove him to it. Before Charles settled the score with Ryuchi, though, he burned down the Hokkaido House, a restaurant that many Japanese people, including some gardeners, liked to frequent. He then went to Ryuchi's office and killed everyone that even remotely looked like a Japanese gardener. Charles proceeded to Ryuchi's house, where he killed all of Ryuchi's family, and took Ryuchi hostage.

People who didn't know Charles as well as his friends did were really beginning to question Charles' motives, if not his tactics. "I was right there with him when he went after the Mexicans, but I really don't see the Japanese connection," said one. Charles' friends, however, continued to stand solidly behind him. "You people don't understand," said one. "Charles is a Good Man, a church-going man, a prayer warrior. If Charles says there was a Japanese connection then, by God, there must be a Japanese connection. The Japanese have to learn that their gardeners can't go around doing these kinds of things without consequences."

Meanwhile, after many long hours of torture, Ryuchi gave up the names of several Home Depot employees working in the gardening department, and a man who sells seeds at Lowe's, who he says were co-conspirators in the crime against Charles' wife. As I write this, we are awaiting Charles' next move.

15 / iraq

The statesman who yields to war fever must realize that once the signal is given, he is no longer the master of policy but the slave of unforeseeable and uncontrollable events. —Sir Winston Churchill

ANY ATTEMPT TO COME UP WITH A RATIONAL response to the attacks on 9/11 did not immediately land one at the door of Saddam Hussein. In his response to the attacks, President Bush articulated these main themes: that the United States would make no distinction between the terrorists and the regimes that harbored them; that the War on Terror was likely to be longer and more involved than other wars, and, as we weren't necessarily attacking nations *per se*, we would be looking for terrorists groups in up to sixty different countries; and, we would particularly focus on keeping weapons of mass destruction out of the hands of terrorists.

In attacking the Taliban in Afghanistan for their refusal to turn over Osama bin-Laden, the United States was making good on it's threat. If the administration then wanted to follow through with the idea of making no distinction between terrorists and the regimes that harbored them, there were over a half-dozen countries other than Iraq that were more legitimate targets: Iran, Syria,

Pakistan, Saudi Arabia, Egypt, Libya, Sudan, and Indonesia. Even Germany had known Islamic militants within their grasp (the main 9/11 al-Qaeda cell was originally based in Hamburg) but their own post WWII constitution forbade any intrusion into the religious practices of minorities. Many of the countries listed here are our "strategic allies," which is a nice way of saying that we look the other way when it's they who are harboring terrorists, or when it's they who are repressing their own people, because they have something we need. Between the Saudis, the Pakistanis, and the Egyptians, you have 95% of all the ingredients that went into the birth of Islamic radicalism.

When I'm weeding in my garden, it doesn't do me any good to chop off the heads of the weeds, because they'll just be back next week. You have to get down in the dirt and pull up the roots...pulling up the roots means identifying where they are. What we did was go into Afghanistan and chop off some heads, and then instead of attacking the roots, we used whatever capital we might have had left in the court of world opinion to settle an old score with Saddam Hussein and attempt to secure the free flow of oil to the West for the foreseeable future.

In the run-up to the second Gulf War, the majority of American people meekly accepted the obvious procession of Monty Python-esque fabrications foisted upon them by the administration, aided and abetted by their mouthpieces in the press.

Here is Monty Python's "Dead Parrot Sketch." What is a Monty Python comedy sketch doing in a book like this? I believe the "Shop Owner" is an almost perfect representation of the Bush administration in the run-up to Gulf War II. The skit begins when a customer walks into a pet shop:

Mr. Praline: I wish to complain about this parrot what I purchased not half an hour ago from this very boutique.

Owner: Oh yes, the Norwegian Blue.... What's wrong with it?

Mr. Praline: I'll tell you what's wrong with it. 'E's dead, that's what's wrong with it!

Owner: No, 'e's uh...he's resting.

Mr. Praline: Look, matey, I know a dead parrot when I see one, and I'm looking at one right now.

Owner: He's not dead, he's, he's restin'! Remarkable bird, the Norwegian Blue idn'it? Beautiful plumage!

Mr. Praline: The plumage don't enter into it. It's stone dead.

Owner: Nononono! 'E's resting!

Mr. Praline: All right then, if he's restin', I'll wake him up! 'Ello, Mister Parrot! I've got a lovely fresh fish for you....

(Owner hits the cage)

Owner: There, he moved!

Mr. Praline: No, he didn't, that was you hitting the cage!

Owner: I never, never did anything....

Mr. Praline: *(yelling and hitting the cage repeatedly)* 'ELLO POLLY!!!!! Testing! Testing! This is your wakeup call!

(Takes parrot out of the cage and thumps its head on the counter. Throws it up in the air and watches it plummet to the floor.)

Mr. Praline: Now that's what I call a dead parrot.

Owner: No, no.... No, 'e's stunned!

Mr. Praline: STUNNED?!?

Owner: Yeah! You stunned him, just as he was wakin' up! Norwegian Blues stun easily, major.

Mr. Praline: Um...now look...now look, mate, that parrot is definitely deceased, and when I purchased it not 'alf an hour ago, you assured me that its total lack of movement was due to it bein' tired and shagged out following a prolonged squawk.

Owner: Well, he's...he's, ah...probably pining for the fjords.

Mr. Praline: PININ' for the FJORDS?!?!?!? What kind of talk is that? Look, why did he fall flat on his back the moment I got 'im home?

Owner: The Norwegian Blue prefers keepin' on it's back! Remarkable bird, id'nit, squire?

Mr. Praline: Look, I took the liberty of examining that parrot when I got it home, and I discovered the only reason that it had been sitting on its perch in the first place was that it had been NAILED there.

Owner: Well, o'course it was nailed there! If I hadn't nailed that bird down, it would have nuzzled up to those bars, bent 'em apart with its beak, and VOOM!

Mr. Praline: "VOOM"?!? Mate, this bird wouldn't "voom" if you put four million volts through it! 'E's bleedin' demised!

Owner: No no! 'E's pining!

Mr. Praline: 'E's not pinin'! 'E's passed on! This parrot is no more! He has ceased to be! 'E's expired and gone to meet 'is maker! 'E's a stiff! Bereft of life, 'e rests in peace! If you hadn't nailed 'im to the perch 'e'd be pushing up the daisies! 'Is metabolic processes are now 'istory! 'E's off the twig! 'E's kicked the bucket, 'e's shuffled off 'is mortal coil, run down the curtain and joined the bleedin' choir invisible!! THIS IS AN EX-PARROT!!

For those of us who grew up on this kind of humor, the parallels were sadly striking. I believe that the Bush administration counted on the majority of Americans to still be so bent on revenge, so gung-ho, so jingoistic, that they could say almost anything that they wanted to, and then change that, and then do a 180 degree turn on *that*, and most people would fall in lockstep behind the flag and "National Security." In sounding the moral imperative to rid the world of the evil Saddam, the Bush administration undermined their case by blatantly lying about their evidence. Some are quick to point out that President Bush had the almost full support of Congress and "they saw the same intelligence that he did." That is a false statement. The handful of senior Senators and Congressmen to whom the White House was obligated to show intelligence were shown edited and incomplete versions of the whole picture. The evidence was carefully sifted through, and only the things that supported the administration's view were presented. Dissenting views were not allowed, or were sent back to be "corrected." There have been numerous credible reports from several former administration members testifying to these facts. It has been corroborated, through the minutes of a British Cabinet meeting, the infamous "Downing Street Memos," what many people have known all along—that the American and British governments had decided to go to war with Iraq a long time ago and needed the intelligence to fit their case so that they could at least present the cover of legality. Poor Colin Powell's performance at the UN in February of 2003 was one of the most dishonorable moments in diplomatic history—full of lies, speculations, half-truths, obfuscations, and misinformation. He knew it, too, but being the loyal soldier, he took the bullet for the team.

- The report of Iraq buying uranium from Niger that President Bush used in his State of the Union address? It was a hoax, a forgery. A pretty clumsy one at that. There were names of Niger leaders that weren't even in power on this "contract." (*'E's uh,.. he's resting*)

- The "proof" that Iraq was linked to al-Qaeda? This would be through Ansar al-Islam, a small, 600-man Islamist group in the Kurdish region of northern Iraq. This charge was immediately dismissed by Ansar's leader, Mullah Krekar, a longtime, bitter foe of Saddam—and his "factory of chemicals and poisons" turned out to be a bakery. The area in question was not even under Saddam's control, and this organization sought the overthrow of Saddam.

- The claim that Mohammed Atta, leader of the 9/11 hijackers, met with Iraqi intelligence agent in Prague? This claim was supposed to be more evidence that linked Saddam with al-Qaeda, but it was denied by both Czech, and eventually, U.S. intelligence.

- In an interview with the New York Times on January 9, 2004, Colin Powell said this about the linkage of Saddam and al-Qaeda: "I have not seen smoking-gun, concrete evidence about the connection." (*'E's pinin' for the fjords*)

- The "mobile biological weapons laboratories" central to the evidence? They turned out to be food-testing trucks and hydrogen gas generators used to inflate weather balloons. Powell himself admitted on April 2, 2004 that that information "appears not to have been that solid." (*'E's not dead-'e's stunned*)

- In a September 7, 2002 press conference with Prime Minister Tony Blair, President Bush referred to a report from the International Atomic Energy Commission, based on Hussein's nixing of inspections in 1998. "I would remind you that when the inspectors first went into Iraq and were denied—finally denied—access, a report came out...that they were six months away from developing a weapon," the president said. "I don't know what more evidence we need." But the next day the commission claimed that no such document existed. "There's never been a report like that issued from this agency," Mark Gwozdecky, head of the group, told Reuters. Asked why Bush referred to an apparently imaginary document, the White House claimed he was really talking about a report from 1991. But Gwozdecky told Reuters no paper to that effect was issued by his agency in 1991, either.

- The British "secret spy dossier" entitled, "Iraq: It's Infrastructure of Concealment, Deception, and Intimidation," depicted by the British government to be an up-to-date and unsettling assessment by British intelligence, and praised by General Powell as "a fine paper," was found to be lifted from magazines and academic journals, grammatical mistakes and all.

- Scott Ritter, the former UN chief weapons inspector in Iraq, and self-described "card-carrying member of the Republican Party who voted for George W. Bush," believes that between 90% and 95% of Iraq's weapons of mass destruction were destroyed by the UN and the remainder were probably used or destroyed during "the ravages of Gulf War I."

- The steel tubing that "proved" Saddam was reconstituting his nuclear program? The Defense department "expert" analysts that made that claim didn't even bother to check with anyone in our Energy department or anyone at the Oak Ridge Nuclear Facility in Tennessee to see if these tubes were legit. If they had, the scientists could have easily told them that they weren't the right size for nuclear reactors. They were casings for 122-mm artillery.[16] By the way, President Bush gave job performance awards to these same analysts for the third year in a row for their excellent service to our country. George Tenet, the Director of the CIA, on whose watch 9/11 happened and whose famous "slam dunk" line George Bush used as confirmation that Saddam had WMDs, was given the rare and highly prestigious Medal of Freedom, our nation's highest civilian honor. Condoleezza Rice, the president's National Security Advisor, and the person most responsible for disseminating all of the various intelligence information and presenting it to the president, was rewarded with a promotion to Secretary of State. As for Colin Powell, the only voice in the administration of moderation, he was "resigned" at the end of Dubya's first term. It seemed to me that he had been sucking on a sour lemon for three years.

Some of the statements that in the end proved to be most laughably false were unverified claims from Iraqi defectors provided by the Iraqi National Congress headed by Ahmad Chalabi. In a poll taken by Oxford Research International in Iraq in June 2004, Chalabi outpolled Saddam Hussein by a measure of three-to-one as the least trusted politician in Iraq. A report by the Defense Intelligence Agency after the war had started concluded that most of the information given by the Iraqi defectors "was of little or no value, with much of it invented or exaggerated." One of the most infamous was an Iraqi who defected to Germany code-named "Curveball." Mr. Curveball proved to be a serial liar, but despite German Intelligence informing the Americans of their serious reservations about the veracity of this defector's information, the Bush Administration used Curveball's material in speech after speech.

Where did the Iraqi National Congress and Ahmed Chalabi come from? When I first heard about the INC, I assumed that it was much like the Polish government-in-exile in World War II. The Poles were based in London and were awaiting an Allied victory so they could establish a new government in Free Poland. That never happened because of a guy named Stalin, but that's another story.

In this case, the Iraqi National Congress was virtually the creation of one man, John Rendon, head of a propaganda firm named the Rendon Group. The Rendon Group was hired by the Pentagon to engage in what Rendon terms "perception management," or manipulating information. Initially, though, Rendon was hired by the CIA to put together a credible opposition group to Saddam Hussein and find a suitable replacement as leader. He organized a conference of Iraqi dissidents in Vienna, Austria, gave it a name, the Iraqi National Congress, and chose Ahmed Chalabi to head it. Rendon was given over $300,000 a month to pass along to the INC to create a worldwide propaganda campaign against Saddam.

After 9/11, the Rendon Group was given a contract by the Pentagon to plant false stories in the media and hide their origins. It becomes easier to see how even a veteran reporter like Judith Miller of the New York Times could file a front-page article on December 20th, 2001, titled, "An Iraqi Defector Tells of Work On At Least 20 Hidden Weapons Sites," which was based on an interview that Ms. Miller did with a known liar who had failed a CIA polygraph test only days before. The man was a 43-year-old Iraqi defector named Adnan Saeed al-Haideri, and he had been coached and prepped for the polygraph test and the subsequent

interview by an INC member and former Rendon Group employee named Zaab Sethna. Everything the man said in the article by
Miller was false, but the damage had been done.[17]

*"The truth is that for reasons that have a lot to do with the U.S. gov-
ernment bureaucracy, we settled on the one issue that everyone could
agree on which was weapons of mass destruction."*
> —Deputy Secretary of Defense Paul Wolfowitz,
> in an interview with the magazine *Vanity Fair* in May 2005.

None of this information provides a moral reason why we
shouldn't have gone to war with Iraq. From a moral point of view,
the facts remain that Saddam Hussein was a horrible man and his
regime had tortured and murdered countless numbers of people.
He did, in fact, defy numerous U.N. resolutions, even if he was
playing a deadly game of bluff. So it would not be a stretch to
make the case that at some point, being the largest and most powerful nation on earth, we might have a moral obligation to intervene on the Iraqi people's behalf. There have been many credible
arguments made from reasonable people that on a purely humanitarian level, this is the moral imperative of the world's largest liberal democracy. Not that there haven't been numerous other circumstances around the world that, if you take that position, we
should have also intervened in, most notably the genocide that
happened in Rwanda, and more recently the genocide in the
Darfur region of Sudan. The Bush administration only took the
"saving the poor people of Iraq from the evil tyrant" position after
all of this other hogwash was proven to be irrefutably false. In the
process, and maybe this was the grand master scheme, they've
turned Iraq into a giant piece of flypaper for terrorists.

*No matter what you thought of the reasons for going to war, didn't
seeing the Iraqi people voting make it worth it? Didn't that make an
impression on you?*
The same George W. Bush who declared during the 2000 campaign that his administration was not going to be into nation-

building settled on nation-building as the final resting place for his rationale for invading and conquering Iraq. Of course, you'd have to be pretty cold-blooded if you didn't feel anything but admiration for the courage of the Iraqi people in braving intense violence just to go to the polls. It was a great moment. Unfortunately, it was a huge right turn that the United States made on its way to the War on Terror. This is not what was advertised. Would you want your son or daughter to be killed for this? What part of America exactly were we protecting? No, this has nothing to do with the War on Terror. General Brent Scowcroft, former National Security Advisor to George Bush Sr., and no dove himself, said this, "This (war in Iraq) was said to be part of the war on terror, but Iraq feeds terrorism." We now have over 150,000 troops in Iraq and only 17,000 in Afghanistan. Are there—were there—al-Qaeda members in Iraq? There certainly are now. And if it is to be believed that al-Qaeda has cells in over 60 countries, than the law of averages says that yes, there probably were at least some. Keep in mind, though, that it is estimated that there are, or were, allegedly over 100 al-Qaeda members in the United States.

The War on Terror should be about rooting out the terrorist infrastructures in Pakistan and stopping the seething hatred and unlimited billions of dollars spewing from Saudi Arabia. Instead, we've spent over $700 BILLION dollars and counting in Iraq, much of it to fix what we broke. Instead, we brought Iraq to an open civil war. Instead, we have traded the poor Iraqi people one hell for another. What, or who, gave us the moral right to do this? This Saddam Hussein, bad as he was, was *not* Adolph Hitler, and any attempt to play the Hitler card in this circumstance is an insult to anyone who knows the slightest bit about it. We were not intervening, as we did in WWII, to save an entire hemisphere from being overrun. He was not threatening to take over the world. He couldn't even take over the no-fly zone in his own country! From a completely different point of view, the Iraq of Saddam Hussein was a secular, yet Sunni-led country, providing a strategic counterweight to Shiite Iran. Now that we've intervened,

Iraq is a Shiite-led (hopefully moderate) Islamist country, with much closer ties to Iran. This is good?

This "insurgency" is as much about the Shia-Sunni divide as it is about anything else. The fact that the U.S. was initially there fighting on the Shia's side is what made this mess an "insurgency." The vast majority of Arab Muslims are Sunnis, with the rather large exception of Iran. Although Iraq is a Shia-majority country, as stated earlier, Sunnis governed it. Before we intervened, though, Iran was surrounded by Sunni countries—Afghanistan (and Pakistan, for all practical purposes), Iraq, Saudi Arabia, Turkey, and Turkmenistan. Keep in mind that the Sunni Wahhabists think of the Shi'ites as *kafir*, or infidels. Now there is a Shi'ite block that extends from one end of Iraq to the other end of Iran, which is upsetting the religious balance in the region, to say the least.

Keep in mind, as well, that the Bush administration had no plausible exit strategy because in their hubris, they thought they wouldn't need one. In an almost unbelievable misreading of the tea leaves, and swallowing the information that the Iraqi exiles in London were feeding them (they were savvy enough to tell the administration what they wanted to hear, unlike some intelligence officers), the Americans thought they would be greeted as liberators, with flowers and cheers from a grateful Iraqi public. Instead, the Iraqis saw them as the invaders who had starved them for over ten years, and now were further destroying their infrastructure. Just because the Iraqi people may have loathed Saddam Hussein and would like to have seen him gone, it does not necessarily follow that they wanted the United States to do the job. This is something that I think a lot of people don't understand. "When we want your help, we'll ask for it." The latest reputable poll from Iraq states that 80% of Iraqis want the U.S. to leave, and 45% think it's justified to kill Americans.

What about the Surge? You're not going to tear that down, too, are you?
In January 2007, over three-and-a-half years after President

Bush's "Mission Accomplished" speech aboard the U.S.S. Abraham Lincoln, the President finally gave in to the reality on the ground and ordered 20,000 more troops to Iraq. Prodded on by his more realistic Secretary of Defense, Robert Gates, and his visionary new commander of U.S. troops in Iraq, General David Patraeus, the President's new strategy, dubbed "the Surge," was born. Gates realized what many American generals had been saying all along: there weren't enough troops in the field to provide even a minimum amount of security to the Iraqi people given the terrible sectarian violence. General Patraeus wrote the Army's manual on counter-insurgency, and was finally given a chance to put his strategy to use. In reducing the level of violence in Iraq from catastrophic to merely bad, the Surge has to be seen as a tactical and strategic success.

But any assessment of the Surge must also take into account several factors. One is that the most dangerous areas of Baghdad were already in the process of being ethnically cleansed and walled off from each other, creating mini West Bank-like cantons. Another factor is exhaustion and/or attrition. The young males on both sides of the Sunni/Shia divide have mostly been killed, wounded, driven into exile, or bribed into submission. The Sunnis in Anbar province, many of whom are the same Baathists that we were there to overthrow, have been convinced both by the indiscriminate violence of al-Qaeda in Iraq and by tens of millions of American dollars to switch sides and fight against the foreign terrorists. Finally, Muqtada al Sadr's large and well-armed militia has gone into a cocoon, and the Shia leader appears to be willing to keep his powder dry and wait the Americans out.

Conservatives who renounced those against the war from the beginning as being unpatriotic traitors now point to the Surge as confirmation that they were right all along. When faced with overwhelming evidence that the war, the idea of the war, and almost everything connected to the war has been a catastrophic failure for the United States, its people, and its reputation around the world, these same right-wingers resort to Mark McGwire-like tactics during the steroid hearings on Capitol Hill and "don't want to talk about the past," as if it is so far back in the mists of time that it is now irrelevant. They then make the leap that because the Surge has met with tactical success, it somehow absolves them of the terrible judgment of supporting the war in the first place. Who didn't think that if we poured enough American troops into Iraq that we would eventually pacify the insurgency? Raise your hand if that is what you thought we sent our young men and women into Harm's Way to die for. In my opinion, spouting off now about the effectiveness of the Surge is like wildly celebrating the scoring of a touchdown when your team is losing the football game 42-7.

The reason it absolutely *is* important to keep remembering the origins of this war (and right-wingers would love us all to forget it and just keep thinking about the Surge) is that we as a nation were lied to in the most despicable way by the leaders of our government, with the generous help of a sycophantic and compliant mainstream media. This is the same media that gets constantly mislabeled as *liberal*. The truly liberal media, including such publications as *The Nation*, or the website *Common Dreams*, were against the war from the beginning and saw the lies and manipulation of the American people for the crime that it was.

After the Vietnam War and the Watergate scandal, many Americans optimistically thought that it would not be possible for our government to lie to the American people so blatantly and get away with it, not with mainstream investigative journalism at the height of its power. With the consolidation of the mainstream media into the hands of just a few large conglomerates who all crave a seat next to those in power, the field of critical investigative journalism has been left to the so-called "fringe" media. These reports are then dismissed and marginalized because they are seen as coming from the fringe.

Among the many ways that the war in Iraq must be considered a failure is that President Bush completely lost his ability and power to influence events, here in the United States, but especially on the world stage. He was rendered irrelevant. No one believed a word he or his Cabinet said about anything. No one took anything he said about freedom and democracy at face value anymore. In the face of the greatest financial crisis since the Great Depression, the President of the United States was a pitiful bystander, unable to lead the American people through it because his approval ratings were at historic, all-time lows.

Because we took our eye off the ball in Afghanistan and committed so much blood and treasure to the tragic folly in Iraq, the Taliban and al Qaeda have been able to reconstitute themselves into a force more dangerous and deadly than at any time since 2001.

"Saddam Hussein is a terrible person, he is a threat to his own people. I think his people would be better off with a different leader, but there is this sort of romantic notion that if Saddam Hussein got hit by a bus tomorrow, some Jeffersonian democrat is waiting in the wings to hold popular elections. (Laughter.) You're going to get—guess what—probably another Saddam Hussein. It will take a little while for them to paint the pictures all over the walls again—(laughter)—but there should be no illusions about the nature of that country or its society. And the American people and all of the people who second-guess us now would have been outraged if we had gone on to Baghdad and we found ourselves in Baghdad with American soldiers patrolling the streets two years later still looking for Jefferson. (Laughter.)"

—Colin Powell, during a press briefing, in 1992.

Four Truths

Here are four true statements:

• Hummers aren't gas-guzzlers when compared to F-16 fighter jets.

• The Washington Nationals are a great baseball team when they are playing against The Holy Sisters of the Poor.

• I shot a 69 one time over nine holes of golf.

- Saddam Hussein's brother-in-law, who was definitely in a position to know, told interrogators that Iraq did indeed have WMD's, but that they were either destroyed during the 1st Gulf War, or they were subsequently destroyed by UN weapons inspectors.

Here are the four statements again applying our government's "selective use" of information:

- Hummers aren't gas-guzzlers.

- The Washington Nationals are a great baseball team.

- I shot a 69 one time.

- Saddam Hussein's brother-in-law, who was definitely in a position to know, told interrogators that Iraq did indeed have WMD's.

Whither Israel?

"If Iraq does acquire WMD's, their weapons will be unusable, because any attempt to use them will bring national obliteration"

—Professor Condoleezza Rice,
writing in *Foreign Affairs Magazine* in 1999

If I were captain of one of the sides in a War to End All Wars, the Mother of All Wars, the Israeli Armed Forces would be my 1st pick. They have, pound for pound, the best military in the world. It is a badly kept secret that Israel's arsenal contains at least two hundred nuclear weapons. They have been in a state of perpetual high alert for fifty-eight years. Israel's intelligence agency, the Mossad, is also viewed as one of, if not *the* world's best spying organizations. Israel has already demonstrated the will, and the ability to unilaterally meet threats that compromise its sovereignty or threaten its people. In July of 1976, Israeli Special Forces slipped into Uganda and stormed a hijacked Air France airliner, rescuing virtually all of the Jewish and Israeli hostages taken by Palestinian terrorists. In 1981, Israeli warplanes bombed the Iraqi nuclear facility at Osiraq, completely destroying the reactor, which was one month away from being fueled.

If any nation should have felt threatened by Iraq from the mid-nineties to the weeks and months after 9/11, it would have been Israel. Israel stood by during the first Gulf War like a Doberman chained to a fence while the kitten Hussein mockingly lobbed Scud missiles overhead. If Iraq had any weapons of mass destruction left, the country most likely to feel the sting of them would have been Israel. If Israel, with arguably the world's best intelligence agency, didn't feel threatened enough to take action or at least threaten to take action, doesn't that tell us something?

Maybe Israel was afraid of igniting a wider conflict.

Everything in Israel's past and its character tells us that Israel would take preemptive action if they felt directly threatened. Saddam Hussein was a classic bully/coward who didn't want his neighbors to think he didn't have WMDs, lest he be thought of as weak. But the UN weapons inspectors knew better, and so did the Israelis.

Why didn't they share that information with the U.S., their strongest ally in the world?

If the U.S. wanted to take down Saddam, the Israelis weren't going to spoil it with something silly like the truth. Besides, the UN inspectors did tell the U.S. government and the world that Iraq did not possess WMDs, and the Bush administration didn't want to believe them.

The fact of the matter is, Israel had the most to lose, being so geographically close to Iraq; it has an excellent intelligence agency in the Mossad, and it has never been afraid to take care of business unilaterally when it feels that its sovereignty (or in the case of WMDs, its very existence) is threatened. I think in this case, Israel's silence speaks volumes.

16 / abu ghraib and guantanamo

The arrogant cannot stand in Your presence; You hate all who do wrong. You destroy those who tell lies; bloodthirsty and deceitful men the LORD abhors. —Psalm 5:5-6

Only the winners get to decide what were war crimes. —Garry Wills

THE ABUSES OF PRISONERS AT Abu Gharib and Guantanamo are where many of the issues that I have raised in this book come together: issues of morals, patriotism, supporting the troops, the arrogance of the Bush administration, where you get your news and history from, who you believe and why, and, especially, how we as Christians should react to this news. Rehashing the many ignominious details of the abuse won't get us anywhere. Somewhere in the narrative of these events lay lessons that are too important to let drift into the ether of yesterday's news. We have also arrived at the three-way intersection of the secular deeds of our government, the supporting of this Republican president and his administration, and our fundamental obligation to be—first and foremost—Christians, which means being followers of Jesus Christ.

137

In our thirst for vengeance and retribution after 9/11, we stormed into Afghanistan and swiftly and overwhelmingly crushed the Taliban, in search of Osama bin-Laden and members of al Qaeda. In fact, our troops swept through so easily, that one might almost think the Taliban had disappeared right before the Americans got there. The Pakistani Army, second only to the Saudis in playing both-ends-against-the-middle, just may have tipped off the Taliban (who were essentially their creation), as to the imminent arrival of the Americans. The Taliban headed for the proverbial hills.

One of the principal shortcomings of American foreign policy in this region had been the lack of human intelligence assets. The CIA had very few, if any agents able to blend in with the natives in the area or fluent in the various languages of the region. (Anyone out there looking for adventure that speaks Pashto?) All of the bombs in our massive arsenal weren't going to be as helpful to us as a timely piece of information on the whereabouts of the elusive bin-Laden. It was like trying to find a needle in a very large haystack, in which the hay is actively working against you.

The CIA and the Special Forces units in Afghanistan enlisted the help of the Northern Alliance, a motley collection of various militias united only in their dislike of the Taliban, to provide them with badly needed sources of information concerning bin-Laden and the missing Taliban leaders. Also providing assistance were some of the other notorious warlords that ran parts of the country, along with the double-dealing Pakistani Intelligence Service. The deal was info for cash. Since the Americans had no real solid intelligence of their own on the ground in Afghanistan to discern between the "good" Afghans and the "bad" Afghans, they had to rely on these "assets" of questionable integrity and easily change-able loyalties to tell them who was who. They would pay a price-per-man (about $5000) delivered to them.[18] Talk about giving the fox the keys to the henhouse! Along with actual POW's from what battlefields there were, the Americans were provided with all kinds of Afghan men, from taxi drivers, to shop owners, old men and young men, and men from tribes that needed old scores settled. As has been the case for over twenty years in this remote cauldron of turmoil, the Americans were fed just enough real information to keep on paying. It's like a card shark letting a mark win just enough games to keep him from quitting.

There is the well-documented case of two men, *Weegers*, or Chinese Muslims from Xianxian Province near the border of Afghanistan, who were rounded up by Pakistani Intelligence agents and "bought" by the U.S. forces in February of 2002. They had languished in prison for over three years, first at a base near Kandahar, and then at Guantanamo, largely because their U.S. captors couldn't find a translator that spoke the *Weeger* language. Their case was brought to the attention of a high-powered corporate Boston law firm, where an attorney named P. Sabin Willett, hardly a left-wing radical, agreed to take the case. The pair were finally cleared of any wrongdoing in March of 2006, but remained incarcerated at Guantanamo because of extra-judicial powers that the president has assumed since 9/11.[19]

Back in Washington, the Bush administration was developing legal language to circumvent the Geneva Convention of 1949 concerning the rights of prisoners of war. In yet another flouting of recognized international law, the U.S. government declared these prisoners "unlawful combatants" and claimed that as such, they were not subject to the protections afforded under the Geneva Convention. The thinking initially was that if these prisoners were given fair trials in the USA, they might be found not guilty because most of the evidence against them would have to come from very hard-to-collect places such as the mountains of Afghanistan. They would then have to be set free and would be able to commit further heinous crimes against the American people. (Gee, I would have thought that this is exactly the kind of thing the International Criminal Court was to be used for, but what do I know?)

As a result, the system of international provision for prisoners taken during the course of conflict between combatants that was strict enough for Nazi Waffen SS, Japanese fighters, the Vietcong, and North Koreans, was rendered incapable of being sufficient to handle Afghan and Arab mujahedin. This meant that in the course of trying to extract information from these people, the U.S. could basically use whatever means they chose to get it, keeping these detainees in a "legal black hole," without charges and without legal representation. Keep in mind, that for every legitimate enemy fighter in custody, there were probably two that were rounded up for being in the wrong place at the wrong time.

The ramifications of this profound change in American standards of behavior are immense. In seeking to defeat the evil in the world it is of the utmost importance that we don't become the evil we are trying to defeat. The neo-cons in the Bush administration apparently came to the opposite conclusion. The reason one is proud to be an American is not the name on our jersey or the number of nukes we possess, but our system of laws and jurisprudence, and the fact that we *don't* resort to extralegal means of treating prisoners of war, and we *don't* invade countries whenever we feel like it, the rest of the world be damned. This issue of fairness is one of the seminal characteristics that has made our country great. The *true* American patriot should be appalled at what has been done to two hundred-plus years of carefully crafted laws. (The same neo-cons are the ones most liable to cry for "strict constructionist" judges who don't "legislate from the bench" and alter one hair on the body of our precious Constitution!)

These heinous taxi drivers and shop owners were then either stuffed in huge metal containers at Bagram Airbase outside of Kabul, or sent to the prison constructed at the U.S. Naval Air Station at Guantanamo on the tip of Cuba, where they were subject to, if not outright torture, then large-scale abuse. As much as administration apologists would like to tell us that the prisoners are being treated "just fine," the evidence to the contrary is mounting. (One well-respected man at my church, while almost popping a vein in his neck over the comparison of Guantanamo with other infamous detention facilities of the 20th century, said he didn't see what all the fuss was over "turning the temperature up and down on these people a little bit.") Reports from freed prisoners may be easy to dismiss, but internal reports from the FBI, the CIA, members of the staff at Guantanamo, including chaplains, the Red Cross assessments, and reports from Pentagon insiders themselves are not so easy to brush off. Quoted reports from FBI and CIA officials alone include "prisoners lying in their own feces, military guards slapping prisoners, stripping them, pouring cold water over them and making them stand in stress positions until they got hypothermia." Prisoners were left in strait-jackets in intense sunlight with hoods over their heads for hours, according to a Pentagon adviser. This was, for many of them, the "recreation periods" that the Bush administration assured critics that it was granting.

Since it is easy to question the veracity of these claims—if you doubt them—I would urge you to do your own research. There is way too much information from credible sources to even begin to put in this chapter. The key is to simply look just beyond the mouthpieces of our government. If you have Rush Limbaugh on in the car, and Fox News on in the house, then you are merely getting an amplification (to put it mildly) of exactly what the Bush administration has wanted you to hear. This doesn't mean resort-ing to Air America in the car; then you are getting loud ranting from the other side implying that everything the administration is doing is always wrong. (What I have found enlightening is to do a "Google" search on a word like "Guantanamo." Literally thou-sands of pieces of information come up, with many points of view, but the end result is a profoundly more rounded view of a subject than the bits and pieces you get on these one-sided "rant" shows.)

One of the less altruistic and more practical reasons for treating enemy prisoners-of-war decently is that it is a well-known fact that Jesus' commandant to "Do unto other as you would have them do unto you" is a universal principal in wars of all kinds. U.S. soldiers in enemy custody have, for the most part, been historically treated well by their captors because the other side has known that, by and large, the Americans will treat their combatants humanely. It's common knowledge that the German soldiers at the end of both World Wars were quick to surrender to the Americans in lieu of having to do the same to the dreaded Soviets, or anyone else for that matter. The treatment of these "detainees" at Guantanamo and Abu Ghraib changed all of that. Now, there is no more reason for radical Islamists or any other enemy of the U.S. to treat our soldiers any differently than any other hostage they may take.

In our family, we often talk to the older children about role modeling for the younger ones. Well, we now have the situation around the world where authoritarian, repressive regimes can call their political opponents "terrorists" and treat their political prisoners with reckless impunity and claim that, "if the Americans can do it, so can we!" (Can anyone say Putin in Chechnya?) So in conclusion, I would say to anyone who says that "to support the troops you must support the mission," this part of the mission has assuredly put American troops in greater danger for the foreseeable future, and so to support the troops would mean to strongly disagree with the methods being used at Guantanamo.

Abu Ghraib presents another set of problems to consider. No one could argue, at least at the outset, that the Iraqis being rounded up and herded into Abu Ghraib were "unlawful enemy combatants." (I mean, they *did* argue that, but it's absurd.) Another bad thing about making up new rules as you please is that once you've done it, it just gets easier and easier to keep doing it. Having created a whole new class of incarceration in Guantanamo, the Bush administration decided to transfer the methodology to Iraq. For their shining new City on a Hill, they unfortunately chose one of the worst symbols of the *ancién regime*: Saddam's old torture chamber at Abu Ghraib. The Americans could not have picked a worse place than Abu Ghraib to act like the bullies and barbarians many people around the world think we have become. The War on Terror is as much a war about ideas as it is anything else, and *any* possible credibility our government had left in the world of ideas went down the tubes at Abu Ghraib. Again, President Bush preached to the world that it would be a safer place after we, unprovoked, stormed into Iraq and toppled the brutal dictator, causing billions upon billions of dollars worth of damage and untold numbers of civilian casualties (they're untold because our government won't tell you how many). He made grand, sweeping pronouncements about Freedom and Democracy, and how happy the Free Iraqi people were going to be. What the world saw were some of the worst images of the last century, (Rush Limbaugh called it "frat hazing") happening at a place that was the very symbol of what was so awful about the regime we just toppled. In our attention deficit culture, this already seems like so much "last year's news," but in the places that spawn the hate that continues to threaten us, this has had lasting consequences. (Secretary Rumsfeld actually had the gall to protest the parading of five American POWs, captured early in the war by the Iraqis, in front of Iraqi TV cameras as being "against the Geneva Convention!")

If you are one of those that bought into the "few bad apples" defense put out there by our government, please, *please*, consider that proposition carefully and soberly. After 9/11, President Bush conjured up memories of John Wayne, Clint Eastwood, Charles Bronson, Sylvester Stallone, and many other heroes of the American Cinema with his "smoke 'em outta their holes" lingo and confident swagger. Some of that was probably soothing to many Americans unused to the idea of being attacked on our own soil. We are used to our celluloid Good Guys turning the tables on the Bad Guys and always prevailing in the end. This swagger passed from President Bush to Vice President Dick Cheney, and then to Secretary of Defense Donald Rumsfeld, and on down the chain to his deputy, Paul Wolfowitz. Most of these guys didn't need the cue.

Rumsfeld's press conferences during the early, militarily successful stages of the war were seminars on glibness and confidence bordering on the arrogance and hubris that would come to define the Bush administration. Parrying and jibing with reporters, answering questions with witty questions and cutting remarks of his own, "Rummy" was the very epitome of a man supremely confident of his own infallibility and the absolute righteousness of the American cause. There was absolutely *no way* that this "Wyatt Earp come to clean up this town" attitude was not going to trickle—or should I say gush—its way down the chain of command. The coach sets the attitude of his players. Each subordinate below Rumsfeld wanted to show the coach that they could be as tough as their boss. We heard over and over again that this was a new kind of war, and it was going to have to be fought in a new kind of way. We had to show these terrorists that they couldn't f*ck with the U.S. of A. without feeling it the next morning. Damn straight.

Whether Donald Rumsfeld or any of the people directly under him *actually* knew the details about what was going on inside of Abu Ghraib is irrelevant. That's why they call it a "chain of command."[20] It also recalls a phrase made popular by the Nixon administration: plausible deniability. The Bush administration transmitted the attitude of swaggering arrogance, of "we're the frickin' U.S.A. and we can do anything we damn well please," and "if we don't like the rules, we'll make up our own," that came directly from the *very* top on down. It was the spoiled, rich brat with the biggest car and the lawyer/bigwig daddy that was portrayed so well in the remake of the movie "Shaft"; the never apologize, never admit that we have ever, *ever*, done *anything* wrong or that we didn't absolutely intend to do (which is going on to this day, as I write this). This is the unmistakable message that these untrained and ill-equipped soldiers at Abu Ghraib learned from their leaders. And this message is one that is being sadly and most unfortunately being preached from pulpit to pulpit across the United States in a tragic and misguided attempt to "support our leaders, and support the troops." This misreading of Scripture, and *especially* the words of Jesus Christ, has influenced millions of

Christians everywhere who look to their spiritual leaders for answers and guidance to these huge issues of the day.

Throughout His life, Jesus modeled the use of power, through healing, instilling life, and feeding others. Jesus also understood that poverty was a weapon of mass destruction and cared for the poor, the outcasts, and the powerless. Jesus taught His followers that they were not to return violence when violence was directed at them (Matt. 5:38-48; Lk 6:27-36). That did *not* mean that he meant them to be passive victims, but rather through endurance and their willingness to sacrifice that they could outlast and overcome evil (Matt. 24:9-14; Lk 21:9-19). His command to "turn the other cheek" was *not the sign of acceptance of defeat but rather one of defiance, demonstrating to the attacker that their spirit had not been broken* and that there were ample internal resources of a resistance that couldn't be broken by conventional ways.

What's In A Phrase II

Think of the phrase "freedom fighters." It's a very slippery phrase. My freedom fighters might be your terrorists. In the American government's lexicon, freedom fighters are any indigenous resistance group fighting a guerilla war against a government or country not of our liking. Otherwise, anybody doing exactly the same thing in countries that we like is called an "insurgent" or a "terrorist."

The original insurgent/terrorists were the American Indians. To many outside observers (of the non-European, colonial types), they might have been seen as freedom fighters, as they were fighting a desperate, and ultimately losing battle for their homeland. They certainly weren't portrayed as freedom fighters by the American government or press when we were wiping them out and rounding them up in the name of "progress."

You could actually make the case that the American colonists were the original insurgent/terrorists. After all, the Revolutionary War started as more of an insurgency on the colonists' part, and the Boston Tea Party was an act of economic terrorism. In our glorious past, they are viewed as the ultimate freedom fighters, toss-ing off the yoke of British colonialism. In Britain at the time, they were surely viewed as insurgents.

During the Civil War, the southern Confederates were viewed as either insurgents trying to undermine the Union, or freedom fighters defending the principles of their home states.

The next insurgent/terrorists on the American horizon came in the Philippines, after we "bought" the islands from the Spanish after defeating them in the Spanish-American War. The Filipino people were initially happy to be free from the Spanish yoke, and thought the freedom-loving Americans were coming to grant them their independence. They were in for a rude awakening as they came to the realization that they had only traded one colo-nial master for another. So let's pose a question: Were the native Filipinos who resisted the colonial occupation with violent acts against the American soldiers freedom fighters or insurgents/ter-rorists? Four thousand American soldiers died before the Filipino resistance was finally subdued.

In World War II, as the Germans occupied country after coun-try with seeming ease, resistance groups started to undertake guerilla actions in the German rear, blowing up train tracks, sev-ering supply and communication lines, and picking off German soldiers and officers. Let's pose another question, courtesy of Tariq Ali: If, during the Second World War, Jewish groups in France, Germany, Poland or Hungary had carried out suicide bombing raids against their (German) oppressors, would posterity have condemned their methods or lauded their courage? Freedom fighters or terrorists?

Jewish fighters in Palestine, including a couple of future Prime Ministers, carried out brutal and deadly attacks against colonial British soldiers and officers in the run-up to gaining their inde-pendence in 1948. Freedom fighters or terrorists?

In Vietnam, the Vietnamese resistance threw out the Japanese, then the French, and then the Americans in what they consider a continuous 30+-year struggle against foreign occupation. Freedom fighters or insurgents?

In Hungary and Czechoslovakia, rebellions against Soviet domination of their countries were brutally crushed by Soviet tanks in 1956 and 1968, respectively. Insurgents or freedom fighters?

Latin America has seen so many coups and counter-coups and insurgencies and counter-insurgencies that it is literally impossible to begin to list them all. One thing seems constant—today's insurgents are tomorrow's freedom fighters, depending on who's in power on any given day and whether we like them or not.

In Afghanistan, the very *mujahedin* that we backed to the tune of hundreds of millions of dollars—and labeled "freedom fighters" for throwing the Soviets out of that country—are now most definitely labeled terrorists for trying to throw *us* out of the Middle East.

In the Occupied Territories of Israel, Palestinian people strap on bombs and blow themselves up because they have no other weapons to fight the enormous might of the Israeli Army. Are they freedom fighters or terrorists? That's a tricky one, isn't it?

This brings us to Iraq again. In light of all of the above examples, have the Iraqi resistors to the U.S. occupation been freedom fighters or insurgent/terrorists? And if there have been Arabs from other countries assisting the resistance would they automatically be considered terrorists? Why, if there were soldiers from Poland, the UK, Italy, and Ukraine helping the Americans, shouldn't there have been Arab/Muslim soldiers helping their Arab/Muslim brethren? This was a well-planned resistance. It is believed that they have enough weapons to hold out for at least five years. They are fighting to remove the occupiers from their country. In the eyes of many people around the world, if not ours, they are freedom fighters.

Let me pose a "what if?" historical question. The French were very helpful to the American colonists in their quest for independence from the British. What if the French monarchy decided to land 50,000 troops in America to 1) root out the remaining

Tory resistance, and 2) to make sure that we chose a government of their liking? Remember, until 1789, France was most definitely a monarchy, and there is little doubt that the French Revolution was inspired by events in America. Having seen this American Revolution up close and personal, the French wanted to quell this outbreak of democracy before it spread. What would the Americans have done? If the Americans resisted, what would they have been called by the French?

17 / supporting the troops

THERE ARE THOSE WHO BELIEVE THAT in order to support the troops, we must support the mission. I happen to think that's incorrect. I'm sure the good German people in the early 1940s supported their boys as they fought their way across Europe, but you probably wouldn't have blamed the more enlightened of them if they didn't support the mission.

How dare you compare what we are doing in liberating Iraq to Nazi Germany!

I'm not. What I'm saying is, throughout history, boys have marched off to battle on missions of all kinds—some righteous, some not. Some are battles of conquest. Some are battles of liberty. Some are in response to a back-room deal that their government made with another government. Some are the prideful choice of their leader. One thing they all have in common, though, is that once in the armed services, one has little or no choice but to fight, and sometimes, to die. No one asked the privates in World War I if they agreed or approved of the decisions to send them over the top, row after row, division after division, to be mown down like blades of grass, fighting over mere yards of territory that changed hands on a daily basis. Meanwhile the

Generals would use words like "attrition" to describe the condition; "attrition" meaning "we'll accede to the butchery of as many of our boys as necessary, as long as at the end of the day we've butchered more of our enemies' boys."

I believe that under most conditions, despite one's feelings about the mission, it is absolutely the right thing to support the troops. I thought it was unconscionable that the American Left treated returning troops from Vietnam so badly. Many of those who disrespected soldiers were able to get deferments from the draft because their parents could afford to send them to college. Those who were not so fortunate, a disproportionate number of whom were poor and minorities were sent to fight and die in the jungles of Southeast Asia. It wasn't their fault that the mission was, to put it mildly, questionable. Governments, no matter how much folly goes into their decisions, will always try to convince their citizens that the mission is just, the mission is noble, and the world will be a better place for the sending of their soldiers into Harm's Way. This hasn't changed since war itself began.

Something that *has* changed since the Vietnam War is the way war is covered (or not) by the media. Vietnam was the high-water mark in bringing the horror of war home in all of its bloody gruesome details to the American living room. The film reporting also played a huge part in the public awakening to a conflict in which an abstract theory was presented (The Domino Theory) that made sense on paper, but remained a remote idea until dead American boys started appearing on the nightly news. It was only then that people who might have previously supported their government's abstract theories started saying, "Wait a minute—our boys are 6,000 miles away from the United States dying for *what?* It sure doesn't *seem* like our country's in danger."

The military and our government learned a valuable lesson from Vietnam, although it's not the one that's going to bring us peace any time soon. They learned that if they don't want the American people to get all upset about war, by all means *don't* show them pictures of dying American soldiers. Have you noticed that we haven't seen *any* film, or still pictures for that matter, of dead American soldiers in Iraq or Afghanistan? They won't even show us the *coffins* for gosh sakes! Yeah, I know that seeing American soldiers dead on the side of an Iraqi highway is a horrible and sickening sight, but isn't the danger obvious in *not* allowing these images to ever be shown? As long as dead American soldiers are just a number, with no untidy images to make them real, then Americans are one giant step removed from what this is really costing. Unless we *personally know* one of these kids who have lost their lives, the whole business stays in the realm of the abstract. The government doesn't even want us to see the coffins, because they want to keep us as detached from the actual cost as possible for as long as possible. As long as it's just a number, and it isn't our kid, or our brother or sister, or our husband or wife, we can stay in the abstract, and hear about the "brave soldiers who are making the ultimate sacrifice for freedom," and we don't have to dirty up our minds with unsightly images of the pain and the suffering and the blood and the shattered limbs that these men and women are actually living and dying through. The government knows it's only a matter of time between the showings of these images and when the real protesting begins.

I realize that these soldiers are volunteers; nobody *made* them go into the military, but many of these young men and women are National Guardsmen who had no idea what they were getting themselves into when they signed up. Furthermore, their tours of duty have been extended far beyond what they signed up for.

I want to support the troops by working as hard as I can to bring them home. If the idea of supporting the troops includes supporting this mission in Iraq, I hope and pray that before it's one of *our* sons or daughters, or one of *our* husbands or wives who get blown to bits by a roadside bomb, we will realize that instead of supporting the War on Terror, we are supporting the overthrow of the right-wing dictator of a *secular* Arab regime. This pre-emptive action unleashed a civil war that our young men and women in the armed forces were caught in the middle of. The War on Terror is for all practical purposes on hold until we can find a way to slither out of Iraq with as much dignity as we can muster, while over 4200 of our brave soldiers will only be coming home in pine boxes that Americans are not even allowed to see.

By Their Deeds

Whenever someone brings these issues up, they are immediately accused by many on the right of not supporting the troops, or being unpatriotic, or being "blame America firsters." Sorry, but it's simply not true. Support of the troops would mean, in my view, sending them on the mission that was advertised in the first place—which was supposed to be the War on Terror—instead of having them fight and die for an Imperialist administration bent on remaking the world in their image of free-market capitalism.

Being patriotic means supporting and upholding what is best about our country, not perpetuating what is worst. As far as "blaming America first," I'd like to think that I'm in the "blame America also" camp. There's nothing evil about that. I certainly don't believe that you can lay all of the world's problems at America's doorstep. Being critical of the government is an obligation that too many journalists seem to have forgotten. When a nation's citizens stop being critical of their government's actions or policies, no matter what they are, or how many people suffer because of them, then the government has the people right where they want them. This is what has been happening in Israel for quite some time, and it is happening in our country today.

My point here is if you didn't vote for these guys, you should be angry; but if you did vote for them, you should be outraged, especially as a Christian. If you are a Republican, for whatever reasons, that's fine. Just remember, you're a Christian first. Just as you were outraged by Bill Clinton's immoral behavior, so you should be even more upset by this war which is costing us human lives—lives that can never be returned to their loved ones. What we the people did instead was give this administration a ringing vote of confidence that we in fact endorsed this tragedy by re-electing them. I've heard it said over and over again by my "favorite" talk-show hosts: Americans *did* vote on the war in Iraq by re-electing George Bush. As Christians, we need to let our leaders know that we will not be repeatedly lied to by anyone—and we won't be placid sheep meekly accepting whatever they tell us.

At a little Christian college located outside of Grand Rapids, Michigan, the students, faculty, and alumni did just that in the spring of 2006. Calvin College is a Christian liberal arts college affiliated with the Christian Reformed Church, and is home to the largest collection of John Calvin's works in North America. Michigan was a tightly contested battleground state in the 2004 election, and, in a practice common with all political leaders over the years, President Bush's handlers chose Calvin College as a suitable place for the president to give a commencement address. Nothing unusual here—just a safe way to spend a little political capital. Or so they thought. For the first time, the very people the Bush administration counted on to be good little Christian soldiers took out an ad in the Grand Rapids Press that said this:

"By their deeds ye shall know them," read the paid advertisement, quoting the Bible. "Your deeds, Mr. President—neglecting the needy to coddle the rich, desecrating the environment, and misleading the country into war—do not exemplify the faith we live by. Moreover, many of your supporters are using religion as a weapon to divide our nation and advance a narrow partisan agenda.... We urge you not to use Calvin College as a platform to advance policies that violate the school's religious principles." More than 750 alumni, students, and staff signed the ad. Sean Hannity, on Fox News' Hannity & Colmes, while interviewing two of the signers, called them "friends of the terrorists."

What a shock—you found a liberal Christian college....
Over 85% of the Calvin College students and faculty surveyed voted for George W. Bush.

18 / patriotism & dissent

"When a whole nation is roaring Patriotism at the top of its voice, I am fain to explore the cleanness of its hands and purity of its heart."
—Ralph Waldo Emerson, *Journals*, 1824

"Patriotism is your conviction that this country is superior to all others because you were born in it."
—George Bernard Shaw (1856-1950)

I'M SICK AND TIRED OF THE WAY the words "patriotism" and "patriotic" get misused, especially by conservative pundits and talk show hosts. The fact that they speak louder and faster than anyone else doesn't make them any more patriotic, or correct, for that matter, than anybody else. Just because someone dissents from current administration policy doesn't make him or her unpatriotic—that's idiotic. These folks are confusing the word "patriotic" with a new word: "partyotic." Partyotic is where you support everything your particular political party does, no matter whether it's legal or moral, or no matter how it actually effects the country as a whole or the rest of the world. This is not actually "patriotic," because it puts party ahead of country. It assumes that, if your party is in control, then what the leaders of your country are doing must be right. No less than Teddy Roosevelt said, "To announce that there be no criticism of the president, or that we are to stand by the president, right or wrong, is not only unpatriotic and servile, but it is morally treasonable to the American public." This particular behavior is not the exclusive property of either party, although I must say that conservative Republicans are by far the largest offenders. Democrats, by their nature, tend to argue more with each other, and are less inclined to fall in lockstep with their party. This, perversely, is one of the Republican Party's strengths.

Patriotism is a love of one's country, and the principals that one's country stands for. These principals aren't fluid, depending upon who happens to occupy the White House. I've listened to Rush Limbaugh for many, many years, since he was a local guy on Sacramento radio. In the eight years that Bill Clinton was president, I never heard him, even *one time,* say that Bill Clinton was right about *anything.* These talk show hosts are also confusing "patriotism" with another word: jingoism. Jingoism is defined by the Merriam-Webster dictionary as "extreme chauvinism or nationalism marked especially by a belligerent foreign policy." This word was first used just before the turn of the 20th century to describe the young and virile United States flexing its muscles against the tottering Spanish regime. In another piece of flexible history, the United States claimed that the Spanish, or an agent of theirs, blew up the battleship *Maine* as she docked in Havana, Cuba, in 1898. A more recent examination of the facts has revealed beyond the shadow of a doubt that the explosion was caused by an accident in the ammunition magazine. This didn't stop our excitable press from whipping up the nation in a jingoistic fury against the now-hated Spaniards, and, led by Mr. Jingo himself, Assistant Secretary of the Navy and soon-to-be President Teddy Roosevelt, we taught those nasty Spaniards a lesson and got ourselves a trio of fine colonies in the bargain, Cuba, Puerto Rico, and the Philippines.

Jingoism is what went on in our country in the run-up to the

Iraq War and its first two years. Jingoism was fabricating a hero named Jessica Lynch and filming a dramatic staged rescue presented in "night-vision" neo-realism. Jingoism was making a sham out of a real hero's funeral.

Pat Tillman was a professional football player who forsook guaranteed millions of dollars from the NFL to voluntarily enlist in the army. He didn't take a desk job, either. He went right into the heart of battle, doing a tour first in Iraq, and then moving on to Afghanistan in the spring of 2004. He was tragically killed in Afghanistan in a friendly fire accident. The administration, mired at the time in the Abu Ghraib scandal, saw a chance to divert attention away from that mess and onto a real hero in the person of Pat Tillman. They held a huge, televised memorial service, which would have been fine, except for one thing. The army neglected to tell Pat's parents—or anyone, for that matter—that Pat was killed by friendly fire until after the memorial service. They made the troops that were with him swear to secrecy and they made up a story about how he was killed by enemy fire leading his men up a hill. I guess they figured that the truth would've made Pat look like less of a hero, and they needed one badly at that moment. "Pat had high ideals about the country; that's why he did what he did," said Mary Tillman, Pat's mother in her first lengthy interview since her son's death. "The military let him down. The administration let him down. It was a sign of disrespect. The fact that he was the ultimate team player and he watched his own men kill him is absolutely heartbreaking and tragic. The fact that they lied about it afterward is disgusting."[21]

It has also come to light that Pat Tillman was no fan of the Bush Administration, or the war in Iraq. The well-read athlete thought he had signed up to go after bin-Laden in Afghanistan and was quoted by several of his closest army buddies as believing that the Iraq war was illegal. His mother confirmed that Tillman had also made arrangements to meet one of his favorite authors, the left-wing MIT professor Noam Chomsky, when he came home. Noam Chomsky is viewed by many on the right as the antichrist; when

Ann Coulter heard this about her "masculine manly hero" Pat Tillman, she simply refused to believe it.

If a person wasn't jingoistic about this administration's foreign policy in the wake of 9/11, then they were deemed to be unpatriotic. This was hogwash then and it remains hogwash today. The people of this country, left and right, truly were patriotic in the days and weeks following the 9/11 tragedies. President Bush had the broad support of all but the very outer fringe of the American people, and much of the world. When it was determined that Osama bin-Laden was behind the attacks, and the Taliban regime in Afghanistan wouldn't turn him over to the Americans, a forceful and determined George Bush made the decision to go after bin-Laden in Afghanistan, toppling the Taliban in the process. The overwhelming majority of people in this country, whether they differed on exactly how or to what extent it was done—myself included—were in agreement with this move. Our country was attacked, and we had a legitimate right to go after the people who did it. It was also *legitimate* to at least *bring up the point* that *maybe* we should at least *look at* what we *might* have done that would cause these fanatics to do something as horrible as this. Anyone who had the nerve to do so was roundly shouted down, their patriotism severely questioned, and their political affiliation determined to be to the left of Stalin.

Nonetheless, at this point, there was the real possibility that out of the ashes of the Twin Towers and the Pentagon would come a true coalition of concerned nations with the common goal of working together to solve the problem of international terrorism. This was a new kind of enemy, slippery and elusive, and massive military force would not be as effective as shared intelligence, coordinated international police efforts, covert operations, and a global shutdown of the terrorist funding pipeline.

Unfortunately, previous to 9/11, the United States had embarked on a unilateralist agenda marked by the repudiation or opting-out of several important, widely supported multilateral treaty frameworks, including the Kyoto Protocol, the ABM treaty, the Comprehensive Test Ban Treaty, the Ottawa convention banning the production, trade, and use of antipersonnel land mines, the Biological Weapons Convention, the refusal to attend the World Conference on Racism, and my personal favorite, nonparticipation in the International Criminal Court, a court that we were signatory to creating, in 1998. And now the Bush administration needed the very international cooperation that it hitherto had worked so hard to throw in the trashcan.

The real chasm between patriotic and partyotic, between patriotism and jingoism, came in the run-up to the 2nd Gulf War. President Bush's War on Terror now took him to Iraq. To anyone who bothered to delve any further than the colored boxes on the front of USA Today, this was a curious choice. Iraq's economy was in ruins, thanks to the decade-long sanctions insisted on and imposed by the United States and Great Britain. The pounding that it took in Gulf War I had reduced its army to a mere shell of its former self. It's dictator, Saddam Hussein, was a classic bully—mean and cruel to his own people, but by his very cruelty had managed to keep the three distinct ethnic religious groups stuck together, not unlike Tito in Yugoslavia. Hussein had become like one of the Banana Republic dictators of Latin America—a repressive killer of his own people, but nothing more than a nuisance to the countries around him. The truth is, the Iraq of 2003 might have been able to beat Lebanon in a war, but that's about the only country in the area that couldn't have handled them one-on-one.

Being patriotic doesn't mean you have to fly a 15-foot flag off of your front porch, or stand at attention and dab a tear from your eye every time you hear Lee Greenwood sing, "I'm Proud To Be An American," or wear a flag lapel pin, or agree with your country's decision to go to war. It doesn't even mean you have to support your country's policies once they are at war. G.K. Chesterton said it best: "'My country right or wrong' is like saying 'my mother drunk or sober.'"

Dissent

"The spirit of resistance to government is so valuable on certain occasions, that I wish it always to be kept alive."   —Thomas Jefferson

One of the great things about our country is that we are endowed with the right of dissent. We are a nation founded upon dissent. If our citizens hadn't rebelled against the authority of the British Crown, our history would obviously be very different. When a government starts to make its citizens believe that to oppose its decisions is somehow unpatriotic then we've started down the road to repression. We've been down that road in this country before, in times of war.

In 1798, Congress passed the infamous Alien and Sedition Acts, which among other things gave the President (John Adams) the right to expel any foreigner he considered "dangerous." Also, in clear violation of the First Amendment, it made any "False, scandalous, and malicious" writing against the government, Congress, or the President a crime punishable by fine and imprisonment. Most of those punished were Jeffersonian editors.

During the Civil War, President Abraham Lincoln suspended the writ of *habeas corpus* and allowed military tribunals to try civilians outside war zones. While there was damage to civil liberties, Lincoln took great pains to mitigate the excessive actions of his subordinates.

The most infamous example of the repression of free speech came during the administration of Woodrow Wilson during World War I. People were arrested and given long jail sentences for even uttering any discouraging words about the war. Citizens were encouraged to spy on their neighbors, and turn them in to the authorities if they heard anything unpatriotic, all in the name of morale.[22]

President Franklin Roosevelt made Freedom of Speech one of the Four Freedoms he promised the world after World War II, but the internment of over 100,000 Japanese-Americans during the war is one of the darker episodes pertaining to civil liberties in the history of our nation.

Free speech and the right to dissent was probably the determining factor in the ending of the Vietnam War and the decision of Lyndon Johnson not to seek a second term as President. The release of classified government documents called the Pentagon Papers and the Supreme Court's upholding of the legality of publishing them even though it was certain to affect the war effort was a major victory in the history of American dissent.

I have a bumper sticker on my car that reads "Peace Is Patriotic." A small statement, not too radical, harmless enough. I can't tell you how many Christians have snickered at that bumper sticker, mainly in good fun, but with the attitude of "That's just Brent—the village lefty!" I take that for the compliment that it wasn't intended to be.

Part of my motive for writing this book is to try and find out why, for many Christians, "Peace Is Patriotic" is a funny, silly thing to put on a car. We believe in the Prince of Peace, we try to emulate His ways in everything we do. Jesus said, "Blessed are the peacemakers, for they will be called the sons of God." I've had Christians say to me, "Well, yeah, but *that's* not what He meant." What, then, exactly, did He mean? It seems that many Christians have a New Testament-style view of their personal lives, but take an Old Testament view of our nation's place in the world. I'm not sure that we're supposed to hop back and forth as it's convenient, depending on the circumstances. Similarly, it seems to me that many Christians use Jesus when they want to talk about concepts of love, peace, forgiveness, tolerance, loving one's enemies, and inclusiveness; on the other hand, they invoke God when it comes to vengeance, war, violence, wrath, and, sadly, patriotism. It just surprises me that so many Christians line up so solidly behind war. Let me be clear, I'm not talking about supporting soldiers. I'm talking about war itself. I hear so many Christians, as they're shaking their heads, say, "I don't like war. It's terrible, but it's the price we must pay for our freedom," or words to that effect.

The Bush Administration has done a good job of embedding the concept in many Americans' heads that the War in Iraq is actually a war being fought for our freedom, or on alternate days, for the Iraqi people's freedom. I might be more persuaded if they said that this was a war being fought to protect our freedom *of movement*, being addicted to gasoline like we are, or our freedom of *trade*, as we continually seek to remake the world in our economic image. The last war we actually fought for *our* freedom was World War II. And I hate to tell you this, but we are already more than paying our share. The United States spent $466 billion dollars on military expenditures in 2004. The rest of the world, combined, spent $500 billion. We outspent the next closest nation, China, by over *seven-to-one*! In 2009, the White House is requesting $711 billion for Defense expenditures! This is 98.6 times more than our current bugaboo, Iran, is spending.[23] To be fair, as a percentage of our GDP (around 4%), the number becomes more digestible. On the other hand, to put this figure into perspective, the budget request for education in the fiscal year 2009 is just over $60 billion.

The U.S. has over 700 military bases in over 90 countries. On the high seas, the United States possesses nine "supercarrier" battle groups. The rest of the world has none. In the air, we have three *different kinds* of stealth aircraft. The rest of the world has none. What, or who are we afraid of again? *We're* afraid of appearing weak to other nations? Even as we, on the one hand, are strongly discouraging any nation that doesn't already possess nuclear weapons not to even *try* and develop them, to the point of threatening economic sanctions or even military action, we, on the other hand, continue to develop and test ever more modern and powerful weapons of mass destruction. Why are we doing this? Is this our God-given right? Are we getting ready to take on the whole world? It puzzles me as a Christian what my reaction to this should be. It makes me sad, but it doesn't make me proud.

This whole spiel is typical, liberal, America-bashing. Do you really hate your country that much?

I don't hate my country. I truly love the United States of America. It is our government, especially the last one, that I take strong issue with. One of the many great things about this country is our right to find fault with our leaders, and say so if we choose. This is a right that many of the peoples across the world still don't have. Sure, I don't like what this administration has done in foreign policy, but what has been revealed to me through investigation and study is that this foreign policy is really just a continuum of eleven administrations since WWII, five Democratic and six Republican. I want this policy to be known, because with knowledge comes the power to make intelligent, informed decisions, based on what is morally right. We can't just blindly accept what our government tells us. Our government should reflect the will of its people, but the problem with this is "the people" only get about half of the story at any given moment.

It says in the Bible that we should support our leaders, you know, "Render unto Caesar what is Caesar's," and "Submit to the governing authorities...etc." in Romans.

I believe that we should follow the laws that our government has made, pay taxes when they are owed, and pray for the people who have the grave responsibility of making decisions that put lives at risk. But I don't think this means blindly following our leaders like lemmings over a cliff. I'm sure that the leaders of Nazi Germany would have liked the priests and pastors of the German churches to quote this scripture to their faithful, and I wonder what the church leadership's position should have been? After all, many good people were not in a position to have access to the information that we know now or even that some of the people knew then. Propaganda being what it was in Germany at the time, there was definitely only one side of the story being told. So, many people either didn't want to believe the rumors, or buried their collective heads in the sand, not wanting, or more likely, too afraid to get involved. The German people were, by and large, intelligent and industrious; their composers, philosophers, and scientists rivaled any in the world. The German people certainly thought of themselves as a Good People; this they transferred to the Nation as a whole. I honestly don't know what Scripture has to say about following leaders like these, except that we should follow Jesus before we follow any man.

There was dissent in Philadelphia during the writing of the Declaration of Independence and at the Constitutional Convention. There was a great deal of dissent in the early years of our nation between the Federalists and the anti-Federalists, who favored States Rights. Dissent has been part and parcel of the health of this country since before its inception; it is one of the things that keep us from becoming an authoritarian dictatorship. Dissent is not slander; dissent is not partisan attacks based on nothing more than party politics. Dissent is intelligent disagreement with the current policy or policies of your government.

On February 15th, 2003, just before the United States of America attacked the nation of Iraq, tens of millions of demonstrators in six hundred cities across the globe marched in opposition to this coming war. George W. Bush's response to the largest demonstration of any kind in the history of the known world? "I don't listen to focus groups."

19 / a just war or just a(nother) war?

EVERY WEEK OR SO, ONE OF MY conservative friends, with the best of intentions, used to send me an article or something from the web to "help" me with the research for this book. One such missive was an essay titled, "Is War With Iraq Justified?" and was written by Dr. Woodrow Kroll, of *Back To The Bible* fame. This piece was written just before we started in with "Shock and Awe." In it, he framed his discussion around the Just War Principles, which were mainly attributed in his article to St. Thomas Aquinas:

• *A just war can only be waged as a last resort, after reasonable attempts to bring justice have been exhausted.*

A last resort or what? Saddam was going to invade us? He was going to invade whom? With what? Israel alone could have rolled his army up in about three days. They also possess enough WMDs to turn Iraq into a parking lot. While it is true that Saddam defied many UN resolutions, the Israelis have defied their fair share as well. The vast majority of nations around the world did not see the situation in its "last resort." The UN inspectors were begging for more time.

- *A just war can only be waged by a legitimate authority. People, vigilantes, terrorists do not wage just wars; only a legitimate government is permitted to wage a war that can be considered justified.*

The United States is a legitimate government. But preemptive war violates all known international law on the subject. When the U.S. unilaterally decided to go to war in Iraq, they proceeded to throw away almost 60 years of international law. It has been argued by some that international law is outdated and doesn't have enough teeth to deal with tyrants like Saddam Hussein. This is a slippery slope; now that this law has been breached, it opens the door to abuse by nations copying the United States' precedent.

- *A just war can only be fought to address wrongs that have been committed. A first strike attack on a nation that has committed no atrocities cannot be considered justice; that's aggression.*

This is where you can make any argument you want. If this is the case, then almost any nation on earth is fair game, including us. Atrocities are in the eye of the beholder—would it have been justified for the Chinese or the Russians to bomb us for the My Lai atrocity in Vietnam? There are so many examples of atrocities. I guess it needs to be pointed out that Saddam Hussein committed the worst atrocities of his heinous regime when he was our buddy fighting the Iranians. Every atrocity is horrible—ask the Tutsis in Rwanda or the Muslims in Darfur. Our government took this and twisted it around to justify an attack on a nation that, as bad as their leader was, wasn't anywhere near to committing an atrocity against us. It was aggression.

- *A just war can only be fought with "right" intentions. War is not justified to gain control of another nation, its assets, or its people. If the right intention for going to war is not present, justice is not present.*

First of all, how could our intentions be "right" when we kept changing what it was we were attacking Iraq for? First it was for

WMDs, then it was the link to 9/11, then it was to remove the evil dictator and spread democracy to the Middle East at the point of a gun (and isn't the world a better place without Saddam?). Secondly, if the hawks in the government have their way, we're going to be in Iraq for the next fifty years to make sure that no one else gets their paws on Iraqi oil. Call it what you like, but we're taking control of their greatest asset. Oh, nominally it will be under their control, but if it walks like a duck, and quacks like a duck....

- *A just war can only be fought if there is a reasonable chance of success. Deaths and injury incurred in a hopeless cause are not morally justifiable.*

No one doubted that we would easily prevail over the Iraqi army. That comes part and parcel with the fact that Saddam was not much of a threat to his neighbors anymore. Then again, no one doubted that the Germans would roll over the Poles, either. That doesn't make this a just war. Success is a slippery word. As of this writing, in spite of the Surge, the success of the overall mission is still very much in question. We are now four-plus years from Dubya's famous *Top Gun* moment on the U.S.S. Lincoln where he declared "mission accomplished." I'd hate to have to define this war as a success in a court of law.

- *A just war can only be fought if the ultimate goal is to re-establish peace. More specifically, war is not justified if the situation in a country cannot reasonably be expected to be better after the war than before.*

I think any reasonable person would agree that the ultimate goal of this war was to re-establish peace, although Iraq was not at war with any other nation before we got there. I can't think of any war where the ultimate goal was to keep fighting. On the other hand, the Bush administration has prepped the American people for perpetual war. They even had a name for it for a while: The Long War. As to the second part, I think this is a point where reasonable people could disagree. I don't think that there's any question that the Iraqi people and the rest of the world are better off without Saddam Hussein in power, but I think it is debatable whether Iraq and the Middle East in general is better off because of our preemptive invasion. There certainly has been more overt violence going on in Iraq in the last five years than before the invasion.

- *A just war must never allow the force used to be disproportional to the need. Nations must be prohibited from using force not necessary to attain the limited objective of addressing the wrongs that have been committed.*

From 40,000 feet, it doesn't feel disproportional. "Shock and Awe?" No, that wasn't disproportional. Again, our government kept changing the "limited" objective. First, it was to eliminate the spread of WMDs, and then it was to remove Saddam Hussein, now it is to allow time for the Iraqi military to defend itself. (How can we miss you if you never go away?) I'm also wondering what the fourteen permanent bases that we are building in Iraq have to do with the "limited objectives of addressing the wrongs that have been committed?"

- *A just war must employ weapons and tactics that discriminate between combatants and non-combatants. Innocent civilians are never permissible targets of war, and war can only be just if every effort is made to avoid civilian casualties.*

This comes down to the crux of the issue; I'm sure that George W. Bush, Dick Cheney, Donald Rumsfeld, *et al*, didn't want to intentionally kill civilians. I'm pretty sure it still bothers them deeply. But the only way to avoid civilian casualties is to avoid war. I don't care how "smart" the bombs are, some of them are going to veer off course or malfunction, and inevitably, civilians are going to be killed. Mothers. Babies. Children. Old people. People in hospitals. Wedding parties. The reason that war should be a last resort is because innocent people are always going to get

killed. When George W. Bush decided to attack Iraq, he con-
sciously decided to kill innocent people as well. He didn't *have* to
attack Iraq. He better have his answers straight on Judgment Day.

Dr. Kroll comes to the conclusion in this article that, based on
these principles, the United States "has a pretty strong case." I
would argue that, by the very principles that he has set out on
these pages, the opposite is true. But that's not the real problem
here. Dr. Kroll is a very influential man, and when he trots out the
Principals of Just War and then gives his "thumbs up" to the U.S.
government, this has immense repercussions on his large audience, many who are confused about how or what to think. He
also skews his audience's opinion with this: "If you feel that war
as the last resort may be justified in certain cases, and you believe
the atrocities committed by Saddam Hussein is one of those cases,
be supportive of your President. Write your Senator or
Congressman. Express your beliefs, whatever they may be. That's
a privilege of a democratic society, but rarely are unpopular decisions like this one supported by letters or e-mails." He's basically
telling his faithful, "if you support the war, tell your politicians. If
you don't, don't bother."

I don't know Dr. Kroll, and he's probably a nice and godly man,
but this is *not* good theology. This is about as far away from the
Jesus that I know as it gets. And the really sad thing is, this type
of coercion has been played out from pulpits all across America
week after week, month after month, year after year. This "I'm not
gonna tell you how to vote, but...." or "I'm not gonna tell you how
to think or feel, but...." or "I'm not trying to justify the war,
but...." is turning Christians all over the country into apologists of
aggression. We're supposed to be *against all* war, except in the
most drastic or dire cases. This war, in no way, could ever be justified as a drastic or dire case.

20 / christian love = weakness?

"Nonviolence is the answer to the crucial political and moral questions of our time; the need for mankind to overcome oppression and violence without resorting to oppression and violence. Mankind must evolve for all human conflict a method which rejects revenge, aggression, and retaliation. The foundation of such a method is love."
—Martin Luther King, Jr.

A COMMON AND, SOME WOULD SAY, fair reaction to the main points I have presented would be to regard me as an appeaser of terrorism or of our enemies; that I would do nothing in a situation that demands action; that it is essential to meet this enemy where they live so we don't have to deal with them where we live. In a word, I am weak. This situation calls for strength, for courage. To the latter two points, to use a friend of mine's favorite phrase, I don't disagree. We do have to take this fight to the enemy, and to do so requires a great deal of strength, courage, and patience.

I believe that the solutions to these great problems that we face are political, economic, and moral, not military. We are not facing a Great Power like the Soviet Union, nor are we trying to slow down the Nazi blitzkrieg. We are probably at least a decade away from a possible conflict with China. We have been born and raised with the idea that, when in doubt, send in the heavy bombers. The United States of America reached its apex of bombing "success" when we dropped the atomic bomb on Hiroshima, Japan, effectively ending World War II. From three days later, when we unnecessarily dropped a second bomb on Nagasaki, to "Shock and Awe" in Iraq, it has been all downhill. Oh, we've had successes; we've killed plenty of bad guys along the way, but it is my opinion that since the end of WWII our chosen method of resolving conflict has done the world and ourselves more harm than good.

In Vietnam, we bombed and strafed, and bombed with napalm; we spread Agent Orange (and its harmful byproduct, dioxin) from the air; we bombed the North to a staggering degree...and the North Vietnamese peasants died and hid, and lived in tunnels and caves, and came out occasionally to try to harvest what remained of their crops. They hunkered down in holes, and rode out the fury of the most powerful nation on earth. For what? What did they do? All the poor peasants wanted to do was farm their crops, sell some of them at market, and live a simple, rural life. They couldn't have cared less if they were communists or capitalists. The original partition of Vietnam was completely artificial. The true leader of the Vietnamese people, all of them, was Ho Chi Minh. The "Ahmed Chalabis" that we brought in to run the South could never compete with Ho for the people's loyalty and affection. So it didn't matter how much we bombed them, we weren't going to win that war. It was their country, and they were fighting to defend it. We were the invaders, not the liberators. They weren't insurgents—they were freedom fighters. The fact that we didn't happen to agree with their economic system doesn't make them any less.

Look what happened in the aftermath; Vietnam is a communist country, at peace with its neighbors. We have treated the country honorably in defeat. They have been gracious in victory. The sky didn't fall, nor did the dominos. 58,000 American soldiers and somewhere in the neighborhood of four million Vietnamese soldiers and civilians died in the liberation of Vietnam. There are untold numbers of people in both countries suffering from the effects of Agent Orange to this day. My brother-in-law and his family took a bicycle trip across Vietnam a few years ago and said the people were as friendly as the country was beautiful.

One of the forgotten elements in the aftermath of the Vietnam War was the fact that the United States, its desire to defeat communism trumping all other factors, supported one of the most murderous regimes in history in Pol Pot and the Khmer Rouge when the newly reunited Vietnam tried to intervene in the "Killing Fields" massacres in Cambodia.

We couldn't expect the politicians of that era—Lyndon Johnson and Robert McNamara, Richard Nixon (Quaker that he was) and Henry Kissinger—to consider the moral implications of what we were doing over the *realpolitiks* of the Cold War. They felt that even if they *lost* Vietnam, they showed the Soviets and the Chinese that we would fight to stop communism. The moral fight fell to people like Daniel and Philip Berrigan, brothers and priests, who staged some of the most significant protests against the Vietnam War during the 1960s and '70s. Their civil disobedience landed them in jail for their beliefs, and at one time on the FBI's most wanted list. Another surprisingly moral stance was taken by heavyweight boxing champion Muhammad Ali, who refused to serve in the Army during Vietnam, saying: "I got nothin' against no Viet Cong. No Vietnamese ever called me a nigger." For this, he was stripped of his title, and given a suspended sentence of three and a half years. Martin Luther King, Jr., bravely spoke out against the Vietnam War even though members of his own inner circle thought he was going to damage the cause of civil rights by doing so. His speech at Riverside Church in New York City on April 4th, 1967 declaring his unambiguous opposition to the war still ranks as one of the greatest speeches of all time.

If I am weak, then I hope that I am weak like Jesus was, or weak like Gandhi was, or weak like Martin Luther King was. No less a man than Dwight D. Eisenhower once said, "Though force can protect in emergency, only justice, fairness, consideration, and cooperation can finally lead men to the dawn of eternal peace." If we are truly to act in the way Jesus wants us to act, then we as Christians cannot support the violent, hypocritical, militaristic, and definitively unchristian ways of our recent government. Because here's the thing: your tax dollars and your votes are doing just that. Instead of forgiving African debt so that the people of Africa have half a chance at life, we are dropping bombs laced with radioactive residue in Iraq. The money usually goes to one at the expense of the other.

Both Gandhi and Dr. King proved time and time again that the use of non-violence was definitely *not* for the weak. It takes a tremendous amount of courage to be a member of something like the Nonviolent Peaceforce, or Christian Peacemaker Teams, two of the organizations that stand between warring parties. The Reverend John Dear was incarcerated for eight months for protesting at a nuclear weapons factory, and the Franciscan priest Fr. Louis Vitale has been imprisoned numerous times for acts of civil disobedience in the name of non-violence and peace.

Appeasement

"I believe it is peace for our time."

—British Prime Minister Neville Chamberlain, upon returning from his fateful meeting in Munich in 1938 with Adolph Hitler

With that sentence, Neville Chamberlain sealed his fate to be ever associated with the word appeasement. In fact, no modern discussion of accommodation, dialogue, alternative solutions, understanding of the other side's position, trying to find the root causes of conflict, or anything short of bombing the holy hell out of our enemies can even be started without the right-wing spluttering on about appeasement, and in short order, reminding everyone of the infamous arch-appeaser Neville Chamberlain. This is one of the ways that rational discussion is quickly ended.

Once the Right gets someone on the defensive about appeasement, the discussion is over. This is the tactic of using a word or
a phrase inappropriately but saying it loudly enough and with
enough blather that the average person who is only catching bits
and pieces of the monologue will hear the headlines,
"Appeasement = Anything but Bombing the Crap out of Our
Enemies." It is then assumed by a whole lot of SAS (short attention span) citizens that any solution to conflict in the world other
than massive military force constitutes the act of appeasement.
This is dangerous and unchristian-like thinking. There are a
whole range of ideas that fall between appeasement and the use of
disproportionate force that inflicts collateral damage. First,
though, it is necessary to debunk the comparisons of being
against the War in Iraq to the famous Chamberlain-Hitler
appeasement, the Mother of All Appeasements.

Appeasement is the act of granting concessions to potential enemies to maintain peace. Neville Chamberlain thought he could
reason with a completely unreasonable human being in Adolph
Hitler. The idea of granting concessions to a man with the largest
army in Europe, and with a record of the most apocalyptic utter-
ances (both on paper and in speeches), was a dangerously ludi-
crous fantasy. No one that I know of wants to reason with radical
jihadist nutcases. They need to be tracked down and put in a jail
cell for the rest of their lives, and if they put up resistance, then
send them on to their 72 vestal virgins, or wherever they're going.

Some people talk in absolutes; there are the pacifists, who consider any violence against anyone, no matter how justified, is
wrong. There are others who think the solution to every problem
is to put in a call to the U.S. Air Force. My opinion is that there
are times when violence simply cannot be avoided. I certainly
think that it's pretty ridiculous to expect a nation to be pacifist. I
have a great deal of respect for the intelligent arguments of pacifism, but I'm not a pacifist. It's funny—if you tell people you're
against the war in Iraq some of them jump straight to, "Ohhhh,
so you're a *pacifist*." A real pacifist wouldn't hit a man who was

raping his wife. I would have no problem with committing violence in that case. A real pacifist would not use violence on anyone at any time, and this includes nation against nation. There are
instances in our nation's history where I think military force was
justified, although it's interesting that when you read about wars
in general, so many of them were not *necessary.* It's hard to tell the
family of a soldier that died in an unnecessary war that his death
was... unnecessary.

One thing that has to be made completely clear is that pacifism
and the discipline of non-violence is *not* the same thing.

Hitler had the ambition, the military force, the scientists, the
manpower, the industrial capacity, and the will to seriously threat-
en the whole world. He had to be stopped. Saddam Hussein may
have had the ambition, but he lacked everything else. He could
have been *contained.* He *was* contained. This is important, because
it will help explain my position on using violence. Each and every
life that has been lost on both sides of this conflict is precious—
precious to God, and precious to their loved ones. If my son *ever*
had to give up his *life,* all of his potential, the loss of his seed to
the next generation, the songs he would never write, the father
and husband he would never be...*it better be absolutely undeniably
necessary.* The people who send our soldiers into Harm's Way
know this, which is why they will never, ever admit that they were
wrong to do so. Once they have made that commitment, they
must defend it forever, or risk having innocent blood on their
hands.

In Baghdad, a suicide bomber slammed into a group of people
on a street in Baghdad, and blew up twenty-seven people. When
it happens in London, it's huge news for a month. When it's
Baghdad, it's just another day. The difference in this day, though,
was that the dead in this instance were mostly children. They
were all gathered around a U.S. Army Humvee, and the American
soldiers were passing out candy. This is an absolutely heartbreaking story. Here we are, a nation of *good people,* as exemplified by
our brave, yet kind soldiers, who are doing everything they are

asked to do *and* handing out treats for the little kids, and some brainwashed lunatic comes along a blows up these kids. How could *anyone* think they're going to heaven for that?

Now certainly these soldiers, some of whom were injured, bear little or no responsibility for this horrific crime against humanity, although some of them probably had pangs of guilt. Our government, on the other hand, once again has the blood of the innocent on their hands. I know this is a harsh indictment. There is a harsher judgment awaiting them. If some of our brave soldiers were killed in the mountains of Afghanistan or Pakistan fighting Al-Qaeda or Taliban jihadists, or if some of our Special Forces were killed in a covert operation in Saudi Arabia while apprehending the authors of this vile slime that is being passed off as Islamism, and even if, *even if* innocent civilians were tragically killed in crossfire, this could unfortunately be seen as the price our nation and the world must pay for freedom from this scourge. This is what our military is for. Civilians do die in wars. These twenty-seven children in Baghdad didn't have to die. This war in Iraq in no way passes the *absolutely undeniably necessary* test. Some of the 4,200-and-counting men and women in our armed forces who have died in Iraq might have died in some other theater of war fighting some other battle at some other time, but the mothers and fathers and wives and husbands and children of these soldiers will never know. We can dispute this all we want, until the soldier that dies is from our family.

What about the Ukraine? And Georgia? Democracy is breaking out all over. How can you say that what we are doing in Iraq is wrong when we are helping them become a democracy?

I don't recall our armed forces having anything to do with democracy triumphing in either Ukraine or Georgia. The people of those countries did it themselves. To the extent that we helped, it was covert, through either financial help or CIA involvement. It's actually two examples of how we *can* help spread democracy without blowing a place to smithereens. Those two countries are also considerably more ethnically homogeneous than Iraq. We're trying to shove a three-sided peg down a round hole. It *just might be possible* that due to the artificial way that Iraq was cobbled together after World War I, and the tribal nature of its people, combined with three distinctly different groups that either ethnically or theologically don't see eye to eye, this conglomeration of humans are not ready to be thrown together in a democracy. What is *much more likely* to happen, sooner or later, is that by being forced to be a democracy before they are ready, unlike the Ukraine or Georgia, these three groups of people are going to tear each other apart until a military or civilian leader of strong will and character assumes control of one of the armies, and crushes the opposition one by one and creates yet another repressive authoritarian dictatorship in the name of finally giving these people some peace. Either that, or they finally separate into three countries, like Croatia, Slovenia, and Serbia did in Yugoslavia. Or first one, then the other.

The United States has a dismal record of spreading freedom and democracy by force. Just look at the record during the Cold War. In most cases, one of two things happened: 1) The guy who we supported was elected, but the opposition doesn't accept the result, so in order for the new leader to keep the peace, repressive, authoritarian measures have to be taken to pacify the opposition. These measures become permanent, and we have a dictatorship. 2) A left-leaning guy is elected, and *we* don't like the result, so we engineer a *coup*, and replace him with the guy in scenario #1. This represents much of the modern history of Latin America.

Most democracies that succeed are homegrown. When the people are ready, they take matters into their own hands.

I believe that to the extent appeasement has gone on in this country, it has been that we, as citizens, hand in hand with the mainstream media, have granted our government the concession to act in almost any way they see fit in order to maintain our extravagant standard of living at the expense of the many around the world who are too weak to object. I consider myself fully convicted of this indictment, as I have never lifted a finger in protest in all of my years on this planet until the day I started writing this book.

21 / a new marshall plan[24]

"From everyone to whom much is given, from him much will be required."   —Luke 12:48

I LOVE THE IDEA OF A NEW MARSHALL PLAN to help alleviate poverty in the world. I believe that the War on Terror is, to a large degree, a war of ideologies, not unlike the Cold War.

Immediately following World War II, American and Soviet forces basically froze in place along the lines they held when Germany surrendered in May of 1945. Obviously, at the time, most of Europe was a complete disaster area, a recipe for radical governments. Many European nations had tried various forms of socialism between the wars, with varying degrees of success, and there was a considerable flirtation with communism. During WWII, communists in France, Italy, Greece, and Yugoslavia were among the front-line members of the Resistance to the Nazis in each of those countries, and their efforts did not go unnoticed by the local populations. When the war ended, there was a very real possibility in all of these countries that communists would at the very least become part of coalition governments. In Yugoslavia, this quickly became the reality, as communist Josef Tito was a national hero for his leading role in the Resistance. In all of the countries overrun by the Soviet Union, the Soviets had given lip service to the idea of free and fair elections, but in reality, after suffering over twenty million dead in the war, they were determined to have a buffer of friendly states between them and Germany. One by one, in Rumania, Bulgaria, Hungary, Czechoslovakia, Poland, and in the part of Germany they controlled, communist governments were either "elected" or installed. There was nothing that the Americans could do about it, short of going right back to war, an idea that appealed to no one, with the possible exception of General George Patton.

In Greece, a civil war erupted between the communists and the royalists. In Italy and France, communism was a very real alternative to their war-ravaged people. By 1947, the United States—which had emerged from the war largely unscathed and the richest nation on earth—had decided to invest many billions of dollars in the rebuilding of Western Europe, through what was known as the Marshall Plan. This action committed money where it was needed most, and is largely credited with defeating communist inroads in every Western European country in which they were gaining strength.

Now I know that it is a common response to say that throwing money at poverty is a typical liberal solution, and it has been proven that in most cases, it doesn't work. The United States government, both Democratic and Republican administrations, throws massive amounts of money to some pretty strange bedfellows overseas when it thinks it is in our national security interests to do so. We gave literally billions upon billions of dollars to the same guys we're trying to kill right now because they were doing to the Soviets in Afghanistan what they are doing to us now in Iraq.

The War on Terror is more closely aligned to global poverty than it is to the folly in Iraq. This will only be true however, if we as a nation act in a morally just way to the poor on this earth, following the teachings of Jesus Christ and the prophets that came before Him. The poorest nations have always been ripe for radical ideas and upheavals, just as they were ripe for communism's appeal to level the social structure. When you are desperately poor, leveling the field sounds pretty good. Our solution to the temptation of communism in the Third World, which is still gloated over by many in this country, was in many cases to install repressive authoritarian dictatorships, some civilian, some military, and give them massive amounts of money to keep control over their subjects. These dictators bought billions of dollars worth of American military hardware, and squirreled much of the rest of the loot away in Swiss bank accounts, leaving their countries destitute, but not communist.

Now that communism has been discredited and defeated as a political and economic system, the new peril is radical Islamism. The poor people on this earth are still vulnerable to radical ideologies, and in this case the rival ideology has a spiritual element to it, whether it is flawed or not. We defeated the political system of communism not on the battlefield of war, but on the battlefield of economics, because ultimately capitalism proved to work better than communism. We will never defeat radical Islamism on the battlefield, despite our ridiculously overwhelming military advantage. You can't bomb an idea. You can't "Shock and Awe" people who consider it an honor to be blown up by one of your bombs. Sure, you can take out a dozen or so of these guys here and there, but the "collateral damage" caused, both physical and psychic, creates a new set of jihadists for every set that you kill. You most certainly can't "wipe the Middle East off the map," as has been suggested by some of the more irrational callers to right-wing talk shows—even the hosts of those shows agree that you can't. There is no army to fight. There are no battlefields. There are no tanks, or navies, or planes (except ours). It is a desperate ideology/theology, and it must be defeated by a better theology. I'm not talking about a Christian military solution, i.e., another Crusade. I'm talking about the teachings and principals of Jesus Christ. The only killing we need to do is with kindness. This is where the New Marshall Plan comes in.

The seeds of this plan are already in the planting stage. The first step in any recovery program is the admission that one has a problem. The Western world is finally awakening to the enormous problem of the have-nots, and more importantly, to the direct effect that this problem is having on them.

The War on Terror has obviously siphoned off not only funds available for alleviating poverty, but attention and energy as well. There are those who would say that you couldn't fight a War on Terror and a War on Poverty at the same time. Former British Prime Minister Tony Blair and his Chancellor of the Exchequer (the equivalent of our Treasury Secretary) and new Prime Minister Gordon Brown have understood very well that they are intimately related. They have both been at the forefront of the initiative to relieve the crushing debt burden of the world's poorest countries, while being simultaneously at George W. Bush's side in fighting terrorism.

It has been pointed out that many of these jihadists and a majority of the 9/11 hijackers were not poor, were by and large educated, and were from middle class families, and this proves that the problem of Radical Islamism is not related to poverty issues. The answer to that is that they were also by and large Saudis, and could afford to go to universities instead of straight into the work force or worse. It is the men who are well off enough to go to these universities that get educated by the most fundamentalist Wahhabi *imams*, and come out radicalized. It is also the middle class from Muslim communities in both the Middle East and in Europe who can afford to send their sons to *madrassahs* in Pakistan for intensive training in the Koran. The "good" *madrassahs* are the equivalent of sending your kid to Bible College. The "bad" *madrassahs* are the equivalent of sending your son to a right-wing militia training camp with classes taught by David Duke and Timothy McVeigh. There isn't really a functional equivalent in the United States, with the possible exception of the Ku Klux Klan of a bygone era. The point is the poorest people in the Developing World are mainly stuck where they are, and to the extent that they can be made into exportable jihadists depends on the largess of the terrorist financiers.

History has taught us that poverty is not a condition that government or politics is going to "fix." In this country the Left and the Right have taken swings at the issue of poverty and all have struck out. The Left would like to attack poverty through governmental social programs like Welfare, Head Start, free school lunches, subsidized childcare for working mothers, more subsidized healthcare for the poor, and subsidized affordable public housing. The Right hates that word "subsidized," and considers it a synonym for "dependency." History has borne this out to a reasonable extent. The Workfare programs conceived of and started by largely Republican governors have been viewed by most people on both sides of the aisle as an improvement over the Welfare system. There is truth to the claim that too much governmental help in the lives of the poor creates a cycle of dependency. But there is also a tendency on the Right to believe in simple mantras and catch-all phrases like "everyone in America is allowed the chance to succeed," and "the poor just need to pull themselves up by their bootstraps," when the problem is much more difficult and complicated than that. There is a tendency to paint all poor people with the same brush—as if it's mainly their fault that they are in the position they are in. Some, yes; many more, no. Drug abuse, alcoholism, parental abandonment of children, spousal abuse, and gang violence all do exist among the poor; these things can be a cause of poverty, or the very same things can be a result of poverty. The children of poverty don't deserve to be punished for the sins of their fathers (and mothers).

George W. Bush made a big deal about faith-based initiatives, which was good, but then did very little to support them. His mind was apparently preoccupied with other things. There are over three thousand references to poverty and the poor in the Bible. Jesus' teachings on our responsibilities to the poor are numerous and very clear. The Global Marshall Plan proposed by Rabbi Michael Lerner would ask every Western nation to devote

5% of their Gross Domestic Product for the next twenty years to alleviate world hunger and poverty. This idea will almost certainly never get off the ground in this country because our government, both the administration and the Congress, is convinced that we the people would rather they spend the money on missiles, new plutonium research, new research in chemical and biological weaponry, bigger, faster, and more lethal airplanes, and new bases for our troops overseas. As Christians, we represent one of (if not *the*) largest voting bloc in America. If we spoke as one on this most Christian of issues, it would definitely be heard in Washington. As simplistic as it may sound, what would Jesus prefer us to spend the money on?

Therefore let us pursue the things which make peace and the things by which one may edify another. —Romans 14:19

Getting At the Root

We hear the phrase "the root causes of terror" so much—as in, "If we could just address the root causes of terror," or, "Maybe we should pay more attention to finding the root causes of terror." This has produced much hand wringing on the Left, and a similar amount of scorn on the Right. While alleviating poverty is part of the holistic solution to terrorism, it is by no means the only solution. I believe that one of the root causes of dissatisfaction in fundamentalist Islam (that ultimately leads the extremists in their community to acts of terror) is economic and cultural globalization. Now, globalization is a Big Word, and lots of Important Books have been written about it, and the word inspires Passion and Protest and Pronouncements by Rock Stars and Politicians, and much hand-wringing on the Left, and a similar amount of scorn on the Right.

There are many facets to globalization, and many other books to read on the subject. What I want to concentrate on here is cultural globalization. In the Muslim world, there are many fundamentalists who are not jihadists, and who do not preach or advocate violence, but are very religious conservatives trying to pre-

184 | Brent Bourgeois

serve a way of life that they feel is being corrupted by outside, secular forces. Does this sound familiar to anyone? It sounds to me
like a certain group of people in this country.

Take Mel and Norma Gabler of Longview, Texas.[25] Actually, the
Lord has taken Mel, in 2004, at the age of 90. Understanding the
Gablers of Longview is important because if you get where they
were coming from, then it becomes much easier to understand
the average fundamentalist Muslim. The Gablers, staunch fundamentalists themselves of the Christian persuasion, were, up until
Mel's passing, the two most powerful people in American education. The Gablers had, for over forty years, the final say on what
textbooks public schools in Texas use or don't use. Books used in
Texas public schools had to be on a list approved by the Gablers
and their organization if the schools were to receive state money
for their purchase. Because Texas is the nation's largest purchaser
of textbooks, the Gablers' approval could either make or break a
textbook nationally.

The Gablers emphasized a traditional curriculum of reading,
math, and grammar, as well as patriotism, high moral standards,
dress codes, and strict discipline. They believed that inferior,
improper, and blatantly destructive textbooks have been responsible for destroying confidence and pride in America, for under-
mining Judeo-Christian values, and for creating a society in which
crime, violence, drugs, pornography, venereal disease, abortion,
homosexuality, and broken families have become the norm. That's
quite a textbook.

They criticized material that in their view encouraged change,
rebellion, or protest, although they spent most of their time
protesting...change. They took a hard line on any book that spoke
unkindly of free enterprise or didn't strongly condemn socialism
and communism. They objected to writers like Edgar Allan Poe
for being "morbid" and "negative." They also objected to any
material that drew parallels between Christianity and other religions, or material that contained any hint of moral relativity. Sex
Education was strictly *verboten*. They didn't like any book written

in slang, or with "improper use of the English language," which threw out a whole host of authors from Mark Twain to Alice Walker. They wouldn't accept any history textbook that was more than faintly critical of any American policy ever. This is where many, many of us learned our history, because as the Gablers spoketh, so did most other states listen.

The Gablers represent a large slice of America that feels like the evils of secular America are closing in all around them, and to have any chance of survival, moral walls have to be constructed around their schools and communities. It is what is sometimes referred to as living inside the Christian bubble. They wish to return to a simpler, slower, more homogenous time when men were men, women stayed in the home, and sex stayed in the bedroom of married couples. In this scenario, the United States is the one and only virtuous country in the world, and anyone who thinks otherwise is probably an outside agitator, a communist spy, or a pervert. The outlying radicals of this way of thinking would be the John Birch Society, right-wing survivalist militia groups, and the Ku Klux Klan.

If you understand the Gablers, you now have an open window into Islamist fundamentalism. Most of these people don't want to harm us; they just want us to leave them alone. They are very Gabler-esque in their thinking; they long for a simpler time, before Coca-Cola, and Levi's, and Britney Spears, and hip-hop, and Nikes, and *Dallas*, and *Charlie's Angels*, and bikinis, and the Internet, and Girrrl Power, and Tinky Winky, and McDonalds, and pornography, and Wal-Mart, and Raider jerseys, and Marlboros, and sex, and sex, and sex. It is all overwhelming the fabric of their lives. If you can imagine the shock and horror that the Gablers have felt in Longview, Texas, then you can start to appreciate the upheaval that is going on in Lahore, Pakistan, or Riyadh, Saudi Arabia, or Tehran, Iran, or Khartoum, Sudan, or Leeds, England for that matter.[26]

The cultural war that is raging in these places begins to explain why the *imams* and the *ulamas* are fighting a desperate battle for the souls of the youths in these countries. Think Jerry Falwell and Pat Robertson on steroids and you have that picture. This is also why parents choose to send their sons to *madrassahs*, the Islamic equivalent of "get thee to a nunnery." The same cultural backwash that Christians object to in this country is being exported to Muslim countries in the name of capitalism and free enterprise. Add to this scenario a standard of living that is far below the West, and a feeling that the West, and the United States in particular, has exploited the mineral wealth of this region while installing repressive regimes friendly to its own purposes and goals. On top of *that*, there is America's unrelenting support for Israel over the Palestinians, and finally, the invasion and war in Iraq, and there begins to emerge the "root causes of terror." The outlying radicals of Islamist fundamentalism are the jihadists and the terrorists. When the fundamentalists in the American South felt threatened by the rising of black people to equality, spurred on by the "outside agitators" of the North, who rose to defend the fundamentalists' former way of life? The outlying radicals like the Ku Klux Klan. What methods did they use to defend the status quo? Terror.

The average conservative fundamentalist Muslim family is probably not all that different in their worldview from the average conservative fundamentalist Christian family. Both families have a strong faith at the center of their lives. Both see the family in a more traditional structure than their secular counterparts: the husband/father is the head of the household, and the wife is discouraged from working outside of the home, and is in charge of the care of the children. Both would like to keep outside, secular influences from their children as much and as long as possible. Both demand modesty in the appearance of their females, the difference here is in degree. Both are generally more patriarchal societies than their more modern counterparts. Both, in fact, would like to slow down modernity and return to the good old days of their grandparents and beyond.

All religious cultures, whether Christian, Jewish, Muslim, or Hindu, have internal battles between orthodox isolationists, and secular assimilationists. If we as Christians understand our own battles to a greater or lesser degree as being concerned with keeping the worst of Hollywood and Madison Avenue out of every facet of our own lives, maybe this can allow us to have some empathy for our Muslim counterparts' lack of enthusiasm over the cultural globalization that has permeated their society. And maybe, just maybe, this might be a warning sign that what might be good for the bottom lines of our large multinational corporations may not be in our own best interests in the War on Terror.

I am not advocating the closed off lifestyle described above. We are called as Christians to be salt and light in the world, and as a follower of Jesus, nothing could be clearer than His constant determination to mingle with the lowest characters around. I believe it is a mistake to wall ourselves off from the culture at large, but instead many of us are called to be the "Roaring Lambs" that the late Bob Briner so eloquently described in his book of the same name.

I also think that there are many wonderful products and cultural gifts that we have given to the world, like soft-tissue toilet paper, and Louis Armstrong, and Fed-Ex, and baseball, and Martin Luther King Jr., and Thomas Edison, and the Blues, and Billy Graham, and Katherine Hepburn, and funny animation, and Jerry Lewis...well, only in France.

I don't pretend to know what is best for a culture that I have never been a part of; these are age-old problems of advance versus retreat, playing themselves out in a place that is thousands of miles away both literally and figuratively. Progress is good—how one defines it is key. I just think it might be a good idea for the culture capitalists to lay off this market for a while in the interests of the common good.

22 / the capitalist paradox

I'VE NEVER BEEN ABLE TO COME TO TERMS with the teachings of Jesus as I understand them, and the unfettered free-market capitalism that most people in our country, Christians included, bow down to. Page after page, quote after quote, Jesus seems to refute this economic system completely. I wonder how much of this brand of capitalism, in the current form that is now foisted upon the world, would Jesus have approved? Or, what kind of an economic system most closely resembles Jesus' life, all of the things that He said, and all of the things that He did? The issue that I'm raising in this chapter is big enough for another book altogether. I have been afraid to even raise the subject of capitalism due to a) my lack of qualifications to talk economic theory, and b) even *I* know there are some things that are *so* deeply embedded in our nation's psyche that to even broach the subject in a negative way is tantamount to heresy or treason. I think it is simply too important not to include at least a preliminary discussion of it here in this book. Mel Gabler is rolling over in his grave right about now.

Many people get our form of government—which is a representative democracy, or a republic—confused with our economic system, which is capitalism. A nation can be capitalist without being a democracy, as in the example of current-day China. A nation can be a democracy without being capitalist, as many of the European countries were socialist democracies in the 20th century.

Modern capitalism has its origins in 18th-century Britain. The earliest form of capitalism was called mercantilism, which is simply defined as the distribution of goods in order to realize a profit. Practiced from the time of the Roman Empire on through the golden age of Islam and into the Middle Ages, mercantilism gradually evolved into the economic practices that would eventually be called capitalism. Since Britain led the way into the Industrial Revolution, and since they had both the largest navy in the world and the largest empire, the British government of the late 18th and early 19th centuries became, by far, the foremost advocates and purveyors of free-trade capitalism.

What this free trade meant then, and what it's still supposed to mean today, is "you let us sell anything of ours in your country, and we'll let you do the same in our country." The problem with this idea, as nice as it sounds, is that each and every country on this planet is at a different stage in their development, whether that means industrial, economic, political, educational, or anything else. This has the potential to create an extremely unlevel playing field. The "developed" nations have all sorts of advantages over the "underdeveloped" ones.

The rule of thumb throughout the history of mercantilism, and later capitalism, is that lesser developed nations would protect their "infant industries" by levying tariffs, or import taxes, on the products from other countries that matched those from these "infant industries." This would make these foreign products considerably more expensive and thereby less attractive to buy than the domestic ones. The advocates of protectionism, as it was called, argued that this was the only way to grow an industrial economy of one's own instead of being relegated to providing nothing more than raw materials and cheap labor to the more developed countries.

Obviously, the more developed countries didn't look kindly on protectionism. At the same time, they would hypocritically protect certain elements of their own economy, most often agriculture. Britain, for example, during her climb to the top of the capitalist ladder, banned the export of woolen products from her colonies, thereby killing the superior wool industry in Ireland. A few years later, it did virtually the same thing to the excellent cotton products coming from India, debilitating that industry as well. This action by more developed nations in defense of their own industries has been called "kicking away the ladder."

Any guesses as to which country in the world acquired the well-deserved reputation of "the mother country and bastion of modern protectionism" of its infant industries? Why, it was the fledgling United States of America. It was our own Alexander Hamilton, in his role as Secretary of the Treasury, who is credited with being the father of the infant industry argument. He argued that the only way new industries in America would become internationally competitive was with the generous help of the federal government in the form of import duties (tariffs), or, in rare cases, prohibition of imports. Interestingly enough, the foremost economists of the time, especially Adam Smith, thought the United States should focus on agriculture and warned sternly against infant-industry protection. Smith wrote the five-volume series entitled *The Wealth of Nations,* universally acclaimed as the Bible of capitalism, and is a man whom we're supposed to revere but not actually read. Thankfully, for the future prosperity of our nation, the U.S. government at the time dismissed this patronizing suggestion and throughout the 19th and well into the 20th century, the United States was the most protectionist country in the world.

After World War II, with the British Empire on the outs, the now-mighty United States acquired the religion of Free Trade, while at the same time quietly protecting its own steel industry and its farmers with protective tariffs and massive subsidies. It, too, began the process of "kicking away the ladder."

By the time Ronald Reagan and Margaret Thatcher joined ideological hands in the 1980s, they had agreed to do away with the
ladder altogether. In cahoots with the International Monetary
Fund, the World Trade Organization, and the World Bank, the
United States and its now junior partner, Britain, threatened, bul-
lied, coerced, and cajoled the poorer Developing Nations to aban-
don all protectionist tariffs like the ones that had so helped both
Britain and the United States in their periods of industrial growth.
They forced these nations to liberalize the flow of money in and
out of their countries, thereby allowing Western multinational
corporations to not only buy up the very infant industries that
might allow these poor nations a chance to break the cycle of
poverty and dependence, but also allowing blatant speculation
and manipulation of their currencies, much to the benefit of Wall
Street hedge funds, but likewise much to the detriment of these
developing nations. Finally, they removed all government regula-
tions that might have given these nations a small chance at someday becoming real, functioning capitalist countries instead of the
weak, dependent, vassal states that we see so many of these days.
To add insult to these grievous injuries, the United States still
hypocritically protects, through subsidies and tariffs, the only two
industries that the poorest of nations have any chance of reaping
export capital from, textiles and agriculture.

The United States, led by the Clinton administration, pushed
hard for NAFTA, or the North American Free Trade Agreement,
which created an open zone of supposedly free trade from Mexico
to Canada. The problem is, the U.S. still protects whatever it feels
like protecting, and even when the courts that are supposed to
oversee violations find them guilty, they ignore these courts with
the impunity of a big brother playing his little brother in a game
of backyard football. The Canadians were incensed over the U.S.
tariff on imported timber, and while the United States timber
industry was happy about this, the price of a 2-by-4 is now considerably more expensive to American homebuilders (and by
extension, American home buyers) than it would be otherwise.

This is especially important in light of the Hurricane Katrina disaster.

With the collapse of the Soviet Union and the end of the Cold War, capitalism reigned alone and supreme throughout the world. There was no longer any need for the United States to even pretend that what they were doing was fair to the Developing World, for we possessed the military and economic weapons to force recalcitrant nations to either play the game by our rules, or face becoming isolated, outcast nations.

This form of economic hegemony is one area in which Democratic and Republican administrations seem to be in almost perfect harmony. The only difference is in tone, or style. Bill Clinton used a velvet hammer to get what he wanted–George W.'s was more like a mailed fist. Bill Clinton preferred more partners in crime, the Bush administration preferred working alone.

Today, multinational corporations roam the earth like giant predators. Many of the largest corporations have operating budgets much larger than some developing nations. (This is an interesting list. According to the Institute of Policy Studies, of the world's 100 largest economic entities, 51 are now corporations, and 49 are countries.) With the help of the American government, the IMF, the WTO and the World Bank, whose leaders play musical chairs in and out of the CEO positions in these corporations and then back into the government, the center of world economic power is increasingly incestuous, the checks and balances more and more minimal.[27]

This form of hyper-capitalism, the privatization of everything, is creating an ever-larger gap in the world between the haves and the have-nots. You can call this bleeding-heart liberalism, or you could call it a refutation of everything that Jesus Christ ever lived and died for. Wasn't it Jesus who said in Luke 6:46, "Why do you call me Lord, Lord, and do not do the things I say?" The problem isn't that the cheerleaders of this form of capitalism are wrong about the efficiency of markets or the creativity of enterprise. It's that they have made false idols of both, usually without ever acknowledging that markets work best when well regulated, that private enterprise simply can't meet every human need, that government has always played a crucial role in our economy, and that the profit motive can be socially and environmentally destructive as well as dynamic.

The main opponents of government intervention and government regulation have always sung the same tune. "Government is incompetent, government is corrupt; there is too much government already in our lives; private citizens in open competition with each other can do a much better job and provide much better services than some faceless bureaucrats in Washington." And on and on. I would simply insert the word "bad" every time in front of the word "government"—then I might agree. But it seems pretty obvious to me that the deregulation of everything has brought on a flood of corporate malfeasance the likes of which the world has never before seen. Human nature is such that greed is too much of a temptation without the strong checks and balances that good governance can provide.

The politicians are in the pockets of the corporations! They can't be objective arbiters when they owe their seats to the same people they are supposed to regulate.

I couldn't agree more if I said it myself. Our current system of government is corrupt. We've replaced political government with corporate government. Politicians and corporations are so hopelessly tangled up with one another that it is simply ridiculous to think that the government in its current state could fairly and impartially regulate corporate America.

In the meantime, is it truly fair and just that basic needs such as water and electricity and *health care* are in the hands of private corporations whose sole *raison d'être* is to make a profit, and who, by their very nature, do not have the welfare of the people as its primary goal? This contrasted with government, whose primary goal *is* the welfare of *all* of the people, not just the ones who can afford their services, and is not by its nature supposed to be concerned with profit. Whether government works as it is supposed to (it usually doesn't) is another issue.

It should be our goal as Christians as well, for it says in 1 John 3:17, "Whoever has this world's goods, and sees his brother in need, and shuts up his heart to them, how does the love of God abide in him?" If government has not properly fulfilled this role, the answer is to fix what is wrong with government. The answer is to disentangle the government from the corporations, get them out of bed with each other. The government cannot possibly fulfill its role as the guardian of the people when its influence has been bought by entities whose purpose has nothing to do with the welfare of the people with the exception of its own shareholders and executives.

The odious corruption scandals on Capitol Hill featuring Jack Abramoff centered mainly on Republicans because Republicans were the party in power at the time. Now that the tables are turned and Democrats are Kings of the Hill, unless something drastic is done, I have little doubt that they, too, will seep to the depths of their ideological counterparts.

The only way for politicians to truly disengage from the influence of corporate America is to not allow corporate money in any elections. The government should pay for elections. Each viable candidate should receive the same amount of funds, and the campaign season should be shortened, as it is in Britain and throughout much of Europe. There have been a few brave politicians fighting for campaign finance reform, but they seem to be pushing a large rock uphill.

Hannah Arendt, probably the most referenced political philosopher of the twentieth century, said this: "All our experiences—as distinguished from ideologies and theories—tell us that the process of expropriation (the transfer of another's property to oneself) which started with the rise of capitalism does not stop with the expropriation of production; only legal and political institutions that are independent of economic forces and their automatism can control and check the inherently monstrous possibilities of this process. What protects freedom is the division between governmental and economic power."

Ok, smart guy; you sure are long on problems and short on solutions. Assuming anyone buys into any of this, what does one do? What can anyone do?

You're right about that—I probably am short on solutions. My goal here is simply to raise awareness of these issues, and that goes for the rest of the book as well. People who ask, "What can I do?" need to remember that it's a marathon, not a sprint. My first task is to make people aware of the questions, or that even these sorts of questions exist before we can ever begin to tackle the solutions. Knowledge is the key, but curiosity is the spark. Once people start to accept that some of these deeply held concepts that are buried in their psyches might be built on rickety foundations, then, and only then, will their minds be free enough to challenge some of these concepts, and from there, discuss possible solutions.

I truly believe that as Christians, or I should say, as *true* followers of Jesus, we have in His life, in His works, in what He said, and in His death, a moral and ethical blueprint for how to treat our fellow humans. It's all there. Sometimes I get the feeling that Jesus is also someone who we are taught to revere but not to actually read. Many of the actions taken by our government *on our behalf* that we condone seem so antithetical to what Jesus actually *says* that it defies all logic. The only explanation for this is that for all we think we know about Jesus and the concepts that He taught, we are actually bombarded from a very young age with a very different set of concepts about patriotism, loyalty, and the unquestioned righteousness of our economic system. There's this idea that as *Americans* we can do no wrong, even if this means doing to others what you most certainly would not want done to you. Jesus said, "You cannot serve God and mammon," and, "For what is highly esteemed among men is an abomination in the sight of God" (Luke 16:13&15), and yet from the time we are

barely conscious as toddlers we are spoon-fed the joys of consumerism, the righteous pursuit of material wealth, and the step-
on-your-neighbor-on-the-way-to-the-top mentality that pervades
our society in the name of unbridled capitalism. These two sets of
paradigms manifest a dichotomy that Christians learn to accept
and live with, because they simply believe that there is no other
way. Alternatives are quickly branded with a host of pejoratives
designed to frighten away the curious. We are supposed to remain
loyal, meek, and unquestioning. Governments are well aware of
the awesome power of public opinion—that is why they work so
very hard to control it. That is why it makes the government so
happy when the mighty strength of Christian opinion is largely
consumed with two issues, abortion and gay rights. Abortion *is*
important. It is an important issue *precisely* because it goes to the
very heart of how we treat our fellow man, the innocent who has-
n't been given a fair chance at life. I believe it is *no more or less*
important than how we treat our fellow man in every other life
and death situation. Paul says in Romans, "Let no one seek his
own, but each the other's well-being." "For out of the abundance
of the heart (a man's) mouth speaks," says Jesus.

The gay rights issue, on the other hand, is a big, fat, red herring.
And I'm afraid that the evangelical Christian community has fall-
en for it hook, line, and sinker. The fact that Mike and Mike, or
Jill and Jill want to be married by a Justice of the Peace and maybe
even adopt a child is *nowhere near, NOWHERE NEAR* as important
as the way that our government systematically treats the poor in
our own country, or allows huge corporations to gobble up basic
industries in poor nations, thereby perpetuating the cycle of
dependency. It is nowhere near as important as the arrogant
impunity it takes to bomb anyone anytime our government feels
like, with such disdain for international law that it won't even join
the International Court of Justice. Nowhere near as important as
a government that continually lies to its own citizens in an absurd
tragicomedy called The War on Terror, where up is down, in is
out, and we are all supposed to shut up and believe it all in the

name of their beloved *patriotism*, no matter how immoral or obscene or *unchristian* the situation becomes. This is a government that comes up with a catchy slogan called "The Clear Skies Initiative," which is immediately seen for the farce that it is by the fact that this administration has done everything in its power to block environmental protection, and until very recently, officially denied the concept of global warming.

Greed and hypocrisy, hypocrisy and greed. These are the sins Jesus spoke of over and over again. Our current form of unfettered, unregulated capitalism is brimming with greed and hypocrisy, hypocrisy and greed. It is our duty as Christians, and our right as American citizens, to express our opinions on *all of these* large issues.

One must remember that large shifts in public opinion take time. Abolition, Women's Suffrage, and the Civil Rights movement all took quite a bit of time to change the deeply embedded concepts in the public's collective brains. In each case, there stood a few lonely, brave souls willing to challenge the status quo against insuperable odds, and in many cases, real danger to their lives.

We, in our busy lives, find little room in them for such lofty projects. That's okay, at least for now. Our charge is to equip ourselves with knowledge, information, and awareness. We can't even begin to contemplate change unless we understand what it is that we have to change.

Globalization

Globalization is one of those $10 words that is both easy to define and hard to explain. Quite simply, globalization is the integration of the world into one marketplace of ideas and products, one labor-force, and one economic system. That's the easy part. What is not so easy to explain is why some aspects of globalization are a good thing, while many of the economic aspects of it are positively tragic for the Developing world.

With the introduction of the Internet, high-speed communications, powerful computers, and the constantly improving conditions of global travel, the advent of the Age of Globalization was a foregone conclusion. When I can both read the *Karachi Times* and then buy a guitar from a seller in London on my computer in California all before my second cup of coffee in the morning, I have engaged in the benefits of globalization. The marketplace of ideas has benefited greatly from globalization.

To the extent that a person wants to, he or she can find out almost anything about almost anywhere, armed with a decent computer and an Internet hookup. All that is needed is curiosity. The world is much less of a mystery to those who have accepted this largely free gift.

Have you noticed that the price of clothing has gone down over the past several years? Shirts that used to cost $80 can now be had for $35, pants, shoes, coats, virtually all clothing costs less than it used to. This is the work of globalization as well, but this is an aspect of it that is far less easy to put in the "positive" column. There is a heavy price being paid for cheaper prices, both here in America, and in the countries where these items of clothing are being manufactured.

When President Bush, or any American president in the modern era talks about spreading democracy and freedom around the world, they never mention by name the most important thing that they want to spread: free-market capitalism. This is the essence of economic globalization. The world is one giant open market. It sounds like a good idea, this global bazaar; the free flowing exchange of goods without governmental intervention or regulation, almost eliminating political borders. The market is king. The market is inviolable, inerrant. Whatever price a product can be sold at in open-market commerce is the right price; supply and demand will determine the correct price for that product.

To do real justice to the subject of economic globalization would require another book (and a more knowledgeable author). Suffice to say, globalization is the end game of free-market capitalism. In this global market free-for-all, the rich are definitely getting richer, while the poor are not only getting poorer, but there are constantly more and more desperately poor. The difference in this poverty, as opposed to the poverty of previous generations in modernity, is that it is not the result of scarcity, but of a set of priorities imposed upon the rest of the world by the rich. There is enough food in the world to provide every human being with 3,500 calories a day. Jeremy Seabrook, who has written an excellent book on globalization and poverty, says this: "The opposite of poverty is not wealth, but sufficiency." Through globalization, the poor are encouraged to bypass sufficiency and become consumers. Again, Jeremy Seabrook: "Poor people can expect consumerism instead of relief from poverty, economic growth instead of security, Coca-Cola instead of safe drinking water, junk food instead of adequate nutrition, and products from entertainment conglomerates as a substitute for ancient cultures."

The dirty little secret of economic globalization as practiced by the wealthy nations of the world is that it is just an updated form of colonialism. In the place of colonies are markets. It is a process of wealth extraction, from the poor to the rich. The poor are being driven off of their small plots of farmland and into large ghettos in ever-expanding megalopolises in the name of a "progress" that they see on billboards, but rarely if ever get to taste.

The genie is too far out of the bottle to reasonably expect a sea change anytime soon in many of the aspects of economic globalization. The have-nots of the Developing World are putting up what resistance they can, but the wealthy nations have all of the power. The United States and its economic allies hold almost all of the key seats at the IMF, the World Bank, and the WTO. It is a stranglehold that is going to be very difficult to break from the outside looking in.[28]

This is why I believe that the only way that this situation is going to change anytime soon is by changing the thinking of the people within the wealthy nations. For that to happen, citizens of these nations need to view this problem as a moral issue, not an economic one. For the moral issue of the effects of economic globalization to gain any traction in the United States, Christians need to stand together at the forefront and provide moral leadership.

23 / homophobics
& tree huggers

WE INTERRUPT THE SOLVING OF ALL of the world's problems
with a little aside on two subjects that have bothered me for quite
awhile. You can see by the title what the first one is. I'm not going
to try to defend homosexuality from a Christian perspective; it's
stated in some places in the Bible that it's a sin, and I don't want
to argue here about different interpretations. Whenever I've gone
down the rabbit-hole of, say, Leviticus 19–20, where there are all
kinds of things that were forbidden in those times, including
shaving the sides of your head, wearing wool and linen together,
and tattoos, that aren't forbidden now, I end up more confused
than when I started. What I don't understand is there are many
sins in the Bible, and many, many sinful acts. In Matthew, Jesus
mentions anger, mocking, adultery, lust, divorce, blasphemy,
boastfulness, hoarding, judging, false prophesying, faithlessness,
ungratefulness, stealing, lying, deceit, self-indulgence, hatred,
persecution, sloth, betrayal, and His two biggies, hypocrisy and
greed. It is obvious by His word that Jesus holds a "special" place
in His heart for hypocrites and the greedy. He never mentions
homosexuality. Some Christians seem to go out of their way to
make homosexuality a "greater" sin than almost any other, and to
demonize and/or satirize homosexuals. Making fun of gays seems

to be the current-day version of the derision and scorn that African-Americans put up with in generations past. There is a large and lingering disagreement among psychologists and people of faith about whether homosexuality is from "nature" or "nurture." I think it is wrong to assume that there is any definitive answer to this debate. I would just ask the common sense question whether it would be worth it to go through the harassment and bullying in high school, and the discrimination and further harassment later on if it were merely a choice.

I'm not trying to change anyone's mind about the actual act itself. I personally feel like *promiscuity* is the bigger problem, whether we're talking about hetero- or homosexuals. A father or mother who sleeps around and eventually breaks up a family would seem to be much bigger pox on society, in my opinion, than a couple of old gay guys who have been monogamous for thirty years. And yes, there are a whole bunch of angry, left-leaning, religion-bashing homosexuals out there. I must ask the question though: Who turned them into that?

The fact is that the vast majority of gay people just want to be left alone. Geez, those who want to get married are at least people who have made a commitment to each other, and who are vowing to be monogamous. The divorce rate among *Christians* is over 50%! You can't rank sins!! One of the most famous passages in the New Testament is: "And why do you look at the speck in your brother's eye, but do not perceive the plank in your own eye?"

There seems to have been a need over the last eighty years or so for fundamentalist evangelical Protestants to have a "them," or an "other" to demonize. There were always the blacks and the liberals, and early in the twentieth century there were the suffragettes, and then there were the labor unions, and the communists. After that there were the integrationists, and the communists again, followed by the anti-war protesters and the feminists. This in turn was followed by the communists again, who were then replaced by the Muslims and the homosexuals. The homosexuals seem to be winning out over the radical Islamists these days as the most demonized community in the evangelical Christian community. This is incredibly sad.

For all have sinned and fall short of the glory of God.

—Romans 3:23

This would be the place to bring up something that happened a few years ago that I thought said so much about what fundamentalist evangelical Christianity has come to mean for so many people.

Once a year Disneyworld in Orlando, Florida holds a Gay Appreciation Day. I'm not sure that's exactly what it's called, but whether it's Gay Pride Day, or whatever, you catch my drift. Disneyworld also annually holds "Night of Joy," which is actually several nights of Contemporary Christian entertainment set up all over the park marketed to church youth groups and is a rousing success. Well, even one day of Gay Anything was too much for the people at Focus on the Family, led by Dr. James Dobson. He organized a boycott of Disneyworld, in conjunction with the Southern Baptists, and they set up a picket line at the entrance to the facility. If you've ever been to Orlando in the summer, you know it could get mighty hot carrying a "God Hates Fags/Down With Disney" sign around for several hours in the middle of the day. So what did the morally contemptible people that run the Mouse House do in response to this righteous act of moral indignity? Why, they brought out a table to the entrance, and placed upon it cold drinks and cookies for the protesters. A more Christlike act, I can't imagine. It felt great to be a Christian that day.

Tree Huggers

"What is the use of a house if you haven't got a tolerable planet to put it on?" —Henry David Thoreau

While I'm on a roll, I thought I might wade into the environment debate for a moment. What, in God's name, are we doing to this planet? Individually, most people wouldn't toss a bag of garbage out of their car window when no one was looking, or pull up our neighbor's flowers and place them in a nice vase in our house, or empty a bucket of pesticides in the nearby stream, or even take a bottle of hairspray and spray it directly into a baby's crib, but collectively, as a nation, and as human beings on this planet, that's about what we're doing. How many scientists, experts on climate change, oceanographers, and geologists have to go on record to say that we're heading for a climate-induced catastrophe before certain radio talk-show hosts stop calling the whole bunch "tree-hugging environmentalist wackos?" Of course, there are always going to be the lunatic fringe out there on the edges of every righteous or reasonable cause, diverting attention away from the main issue. The reactionary types use these people to deny that there's anything wrong at all! In study after study after study, in computer models, and pictorial data, and in interviews with natives who have lived in the harsh nether regions of the world all their lives—the evidence is overwhelming that the ice caps are melting, the glaciers are receding, and the oceans are rising, all at an unnaturally accelerating pace. What possible motive other than selfishness or greed, could anyone have in denying this? It's the ultimate act of saying, "Look, it's probably not going to be a disaster in *my* lifetime, so why should I worry about it?" People can accuse others of being Chicken Littles all they want, but the fact is, this is the first time in history that both this amount of—and this potent—industrial and chemical pollutants have been loosed into the atmosphere. Under President Bush, the Environmental Protection Agency has gone from watchdog to lapdog. According to information gathered by the Sierra Club, the polar ice caps are melting at a rate five times faster than computer models showed *just five years ago*. It is true that the earth has been remarkably resilient, but it has never been assaulted from all sides like this before. Isn't this a Christian issue? Did God give us dominion over His creation to use and abuse it until it becomes unlivable for future generations?

On the other hand, we could always take the advice of Ann Coulter, who never fails to come up with just the right thing to say at the right time: *"God gave us the earth. We have dominion over the plants, the animals, the trees. God said, 'Earth is yours. Take it. Rape it! It's yours.'"*   —Hannity & Colmes, June 20, 2001

Thomas Friedman, the respected author and *New York Times* syndicated columnist whom conservatives would call a liberal and liberals would call a conservative (I happen to agree with both), lambasted the Bush administration on their environmental policies (or lack thereof) in a series of columns saying, "Enough of this Bush-Cheney nonsense that conservation, energy efficiency, and environmentalism is some hobby that we can't afford. I can't think of anything more cowardly or un-American."

I could cite fact after sad fact, from a multitude of sources, but one thing I read really stood out. It was an essay entitled "Warning To Humanity," written in 1992. Over 1,500 members of national, regional, and international science academies from sixty-nine nations, including each of the twelve most populous nations and the nineteen largest economic powers, signed this document. The list includes a majority of the Nobel laureates in the sciences. Now I don't profess to know the political leanings of these people. I would imagine you'd find representatives from both sides of the political aisle, some from places where there are no aisles, and some who could care less about aisles. The point is these are not wackos. Certainly not *all* of them. This is *not* a political document. It is a heartfelt plea from some pretty knowledgeable people. This Warning was written fifteen years ago, and very little has been done since then to remedy the situation. (This document can be read at http://www.worldtrans.org/whole/warning.html.)

In 1972 the U.N., for the first time, held a conference on the environment in Stockholm, Sweden, to consider global environment and development needs. On the 20th anniversary of that conference, the "Earth Summit" took place in Rio de Janeiro, Brazil. One of the outcomes of the summit was the Kyoto Protocol, which is an agreement to cut greenhouse gas emissions signed by 156 nations in Kyoto, Japan, in 1997. This agreement, while hardly perfect, was at least a positive step in the right direction after a hundred years of unrelenting industrial growth. One of the only countries in the world not to sign the agreement was the world's largest greenhouse gas emitter, the United States. This is the same country that makes up 5% of the world's population, and produces 72% of the world's hazardous waste. The U.S. claims that the changes, which call for a 5.2% reduction in greenhouse gases by 2012, would be too costly to introduce. As the world's wealthiest nation and its largest polluter, this stance is, to put it mildly, hard for much of the rest of the world to swallow. Our president has stated, on more than one occasion, that he has to make tough choices, not necessarily ones that are going to make him popular in other countries. He's right about that. He shouldn't make decisions that are vital to our nation's welfare based on popularity polls in other countries. But he should have signed the Kyoto Protocol, because, small step though it is, the United States, as the self-proclaimed "leader" of the world, should be setting a positive example for the rest of the industrialized nations that we take the matter of cutting greenhouse gas emissions seriously. The only reason he *shouldn't* have signed the Kyoto Protocol is if he *led* by introducing even more stringent cuts in greenhouse gas emissions. The whole world needs to act together if we want to slow down or even reverse the erosion of our environment. And it sure smacks of hypocrisy that we can't "afford" to do this, but we can afford a few more billion-dollar airplanes, and we can afford to spend a trillion dollars to rebuild a country that we busted up.

The Bush Administration treated the overwhelming evidence of global warming, the greenhouse effect, and overall environmental degradation remarkably like they treated the evidence leading up to the War in Iraq. If the evidence didn't square with their plans, then they simply changed the evidence. This was unbelievably arrogant, and took the citizens of this country for fools. The Bush administration counted on the smokescreens laid by their friends at right-wing talk radio and Fox News to once again diffuse, confuse, and bluster their way around this issue. This, though, was not about an opinion. There was a major scientific document called the National Assessment of the Potential Consequences of Climate Variability and Change. The National Assessment was the most substantial scientific document of its kind in the history of government-based climate change research. This 300-page report called on the services of hundreds of scientists who worked alongside the National Assessment Synthesis Team to create the most comprehensive and authoritative climate assessment yet to date. The National Assessment was an advisory committee report by a distinguished panel of experts—not a policy or regulatory document. It was all scientific information—cited for the purpose of developing priorities for scientific research. This document was the result of years of painstaking research and another sixteen months of careful and overlapping review.

Philip Cooney was the Chief of Staff of the White House Council on Environmental Quality at the time the report was ready to be presented. Mr. Cooney is a lawyer and has a bachelor's degree in Economics. He is also a former official with the American Petroleum Institute, the main lobbying arm of the oil industry. He is not a scientist. However, Philip Cooney took this 300-page document and made roughly 200 text changes to the review draft. Then, in the final review, he made about 450 comments throughout the document. Many of these changes were of the same, devious sort: changing the word "is" to a more uncertain "may be"; so, for example, when the scientists said that "the earth *is* experiencing significant climate and environmental change right now," he changed it to "the earth '*may be*' undergoing a period of unusual climate change." There were hundreds of little changes like this that added up to a result that was horrifying to scientists working for the government.

One scientist who was intimately involved in the entire process was Rick Piltz, who served as a Senior Associate in the Climate Change Science Program. When Mr. Piltz became aware of what

Philip Cooney had done to the National Assessment, he sent a 14-page letter to twelve principals across all of the various agencies involved. The letter detailed the inappropriate editing done by Mr. Cooney. He also contacted *New York Times* reporter Andrew Revkin, who wrote a front-page article about it the following day. Two days later, Mr. Cooney was suddenly "resigned," but miraculously, he landed a job the very next day...at ExxonMobil, the largest oil company in the world.

Of course, by the time the right-wing talk show hosts had finished putting this story through their House of Mirrors, enough confusion was created to make most listeners just scratch their heads and wonder what the big deal was all about, and why the Left keeps bringing up stories that have no basis in fact. Well, in fact, the facts are all there. These are government reports, and the paper trail is a mile long. In fact, the National Assessment was already a rather cautious document, stressing a gradual approach to solutions concerning climate change, before Philip Cooney got his unscientific hands on it. But even this was too much for the Bush Administration, who seemed hell-bent on leaving this planet much the worse for wear than when they became its foremost stewards. For shame.

The earth and its environment are neither conservative or liberal, Democratic or Republican. Although there are some short-term costs involved with cleaning up and preserving the environment, everyone loses if we don't. As Christians, this *is* a moral issue. Disregarding the degradation of the environment is a crime against future generations. If your favorite politicians aren't concerned with reversing the dangerous tide in climate change, deforestation, and ozone depletion, they should be. And we, as Christians, should be letting them know that this is an issue that we care deeply about.

24 / bias[29]

IMAGINE FOR A MOMENT THIS SCENARIO: Billionaire George Soros, who is very active in and supportive of left-leaning causes, purchases CNN. He immediately installs Al Franken as his lead newscaster. He gives Tim Robbins and his wife, Susan Sarandon, a nightly news/interview show. He gives Barbara Streisand a weekly opinion show. Regular contributors include Noam Chomsky, Alexander Cockburn, and Gore Vidal. Michael Moore is given the title of Director of News. The closest thing they have to a conservative on the network is a show featuring Mario Cuomo and Michael Medved, in which they debate the issues of the day. They come up with a catchy slogan, "The Truth and Only the Truth." How long would this network be on the air before it was being investigated for slander, unfair reporting, complete and utter bias, and misuse of the public trust? This, however, is the scenario one would have to concoct to be as outlandishly biased as the allegedly "Fair and Balanced" Fox News Channel. The fact is, liberal media bias is a myth and a hoax; an invention of the Far Right in the early 1970s that succeeded beyond their wildest dreams.

The first cry of "liberal media bias" came from segregationists who were upset at the press' depiction of the Civil Rights struggle in the South in the mid-'60s. The person who made the phrase "liberal media bias" popular was a *TV Guide* writer named Edith Efron, who wrote a book in 1971 called *The News Twisters.* Efron's book, which was described in reviews as "inaccurate," "dishonest," and "bizarre," based its entire claim on a flimsy pretext: she taped every broadcast of the three major television networks in the last seven weeks of the 1968 presidential campaign, and then marked the transcripts either "pro" or "anti" bias. Her claims were laughably subjective. For example, any reference to the Vietnam War that wasn't completely pro-government was labeled "liberal." Mere mention of the demonstrations outside of the Democratic National Convention in Chicago was branded "liberal." "The News Twisters" made it onto *The New York Times* best-seller list, a laudable achievement until it was revealed in 1994 by Charles Colson, special counsel to President Richard Nixon, that Nixon himself ordered Colson to take $8000 out of Nixon's reelection committee coffers to "get it on the best-seller list."

This phrase was picked up by the likes of Pat Buchanan and Spiro Agnew, who used it to fend off criticism of network coverage of the Vietnam War. So, when the administrations of both Lyndon Johnson and Richard Nixon were feeding the American public blatant lies about the success, or lack thereof, of our strategies in Vietnam, brave and persistent journalists went to Vietnam and came away with a completely different picture, which at the time was viewed by many, particularly the Right, as out-and-out unpatriotic left-wing bias. Time proved that the journalists, for the most part, were speaking the truth, as painful as it was for Americans to swallow. Likewise, Watergate was dismissed as a "left-wing" witch-hunt until the truth became too obvious for even the right to deny.

Exposés on the environment and public safety, from Rachel Carson's *Silent Spring* to Ralph Nader's unceasing lobbying for automobile safety, clean air and water, and worker's safety issues were all dismissed as left-wing drivel until subsequent investigations proved them prophetically correct.

The next milestone in the "liberal media bias" misinformation campaign came in 1981 in the form of a book by Robert and Linda Lichter, along with Stanley Rothman, entitled, *The Media Elite*. This study took a sampling of 238 journalists out of 210,000 editors and reporters and 47,000 TV journalists then working and compared their voting habits and personal beliefs to those of CEOs and other top executives at six Fortune 500 companies. Guess what? The journalists came out more on the Democratic side than did the CEOs! What a revelation! What is truly laughable about this is that the only issues that the journalists came out *possibly* more liberal than the general population was on the environment and women's rights. In terms of economics, the journalists were generally more *conservative* than the general public.

Now, just on the face of it, drawing any conclusions from a survey that only takes into account the opinions of 238 out 258,000 people is absurd on its own merits, but consider this: the reporters and journalists at any print publication do not set the tone or opinion of any individual newspaper or magazine. The publishers and editors do. Anyone with a job knows that one's first obligation as an employee is to one's employer, no matter what your own personal beliefs happen to be. Newspaper publishers (owners) are overwhelmingly conservative, and voted for George W. Bush by an over 2-to-1 margin nationally in the last two elections.

The Media Elite became the Bible for the liberal media bias campaign. The sloppy methodology notwithstanding, the right-wing has been regurgitating and repeating, and repeating and regurgitating this non-information over and over and over again for so many years that even liberals and others who should know better have come to swallow this canard. This has become a *deeply* embedded concept.

If you want a sober read about this entire subject, pick up *The Republican Noise Machine* by David Brock. Brock knows exactly what he is talking about—he was a writer at the conservative

Washington Times, was a research fellow at the Heritage Foundation, a right-wing think tank, and was an investigative writer at *The American Spectator*—impeccable credentials for telling this story. Brock lays out the whole sordid history of the conscious and deliberate effort of the far right wing, which included the spending of hundreds of millions of dollars, to convince the public that there was actually such a thing as liberal media bias. The fascinating thing about this is that the right-wingers themselves didn't think that they would ever be as successful at this deception as they ultimately were. Another excellent book covering this topic is *What Liberal Media?* by Eric Alterman. Alterman takes each of the various mediums, from television to radio to print, and provides ample evidence that far from there being a liberal media bias, there is considerable evidence of a conservative media bias.

When Hillary Clinton went on an early morning news program during President Clinton's impeachment hearings to decry a "vast right-wing conspiracy," I remember thinking at the time that this was just histrionics, or exaggeration at the least. The fact is there has been a multi-billion dollar effort to systematically change the public's perception about the media. There are right-wing media schools and dozens of think tanks spewing out the likes of Ann Coulter and Michelle Malkin, who do nothing but venomously bash anything from the right-center over in the most hateful ways, while claiming the whole time that liberals are mean-spirited and vacuous.

This was the right-wing's plan to create the illusion of liberal media bias:

In the first twenty-five or thirty years of television, the three major networks, ABC, NBC, and CBS dominated the airwaves and had a virtual triopoly on news coverage and current events. The news departments at these networks prided themselves on their journalism, and presented the news in a straightforward, dry way. Was there liberal bias? Only if you were a Southern segregationist or a Vietnam hawk would you think so. If you were looking at a standard 12-inch ruler, and the "6" was absolute objectivity, and "1" was the left wing, and "12" was the right wing, these networks were probably at 5 and-a-half on the ruler. The right-wing strategy was to call for "balance" on the networks by sending "12s" to the Sunday talk shows and news programs and demanding "equal time." This was the game, and it worked. We are seeing the results today.

There has been nothing close to liberal media bias. *The whole thing is a right-wing concoction.* In all the years of screaming liberal media bias, it is the most *radical* right-wingers who are all over the airwaves claiming it. Who has ever been the equivalent of Ann Coulter? Would it be Fidel Castro? Who is the equivalent of Bill O'Reilly or Michael Savage? Or Rush Limbaugh? There never has been any, until the left started pushing back in the last few years with the likes of Keith Olbermann and Bill Maher. These are now your mainstream commentators. To go that far to the left as you have on the right with Coulter, Savage and perky flamethrower Michelle Malkin you would have to be listening to Noam Chomsky all the time (only he presents an overwhelming accumulation of facts), or Abbie Hoffman—remember him? How about Angela Davis? I don't remember Gore Vidal ever being an evening newscaster. No one—*no one* from the far left gets one-tenth the face time on mainstream television that these far right-wingers get. These types used to show up late at night on Dick Cavett or Tom Snyder as a kind of novelty, but *never* giving opinions on mainstream news shows.

What about Air America?

Air America was a failure for a number of reasons. First of all, it was a poor imitation of the worst of right-wing rant radio. Just like the failed impersonation of Jon Stewart's *The Daily Show* on *FoxNews*, some things (like right-wing comedy) are better left alone. Secondly, the quotient of xenophobic, angry white males needed to sustain such a format was mercifully lacking on the left. And third, the advertisers needed to support Air America never materialized, as much of the bloviating was aimed squarely at the corporate hand that fed them.

Anyway, what the right did was to paint the networks as inherently left wing, which is false, and then put far right-wingers on to balance the "liberal media bias." What this has done, in effect, is move the center of the ruler from "6" to "9". Now, anything to the left of the "9" is seen as "liberal," so, for example, a report questioning the strategies or tactics of this administration, which in any other era would have been seen as responsible journalism, is now seen as "liberal bias."

If you believe that there somehow still exists a liberal bias in the media (and why wouldn't you, it's shouted from the rooftops by every right-winger from Maine to Hawaii), then you have probably accepted the notion that to watch *Fox News* is to somehow restore a "fair and balanced" view of the news. Actually, *Fox News* is *the* most biased news entity in the history of television. No one else has ever come close. You want to know what the liberal media bias version of Fox would be? You would literally have to be watching *The Nightly News with Castro and Chavez* to see the left-wing equivalent.

On the other hand, if you happen to wander into any local Christian bookstore, you will find books by convicted criminals Oliver North and Chuck Colson; you will find a book by Daryl Cole on the Christian case *for* war; and you will find up to eight different books on Ronald Reagan, three on George W. Bush's prayer life, and one each on former Republican Senator Bill Frist, Secretary of State Condi Rice, and American Idol runner-up Clay Aiken (well, you would before he came out of the closet). Don't misunderstand me—this is not a criticism of Ronald Reagan, or any of these other people. But what, pray tell, does Oliver North, or Condi Rice—as nice as her story may be—have to do with Christian living, other than the fact that they're Republicans?

The best example of this kind of bias in "Christian" bookstores would have to be a book by Christian talk-show host and author Hugh Hewitt titled *If It's Not Close, They Can't Cheat: Crushing the*

Democrats in Every Election and Why Your Life Depends On It. I was perusing the selections in a Nashville Christian bookstore recently when I came upon this book. Hugh Hewitt is obviously a well-respected author in this venue judging by the amount of copies of this selection that were displayed and the amount of copies of his newer book the store had on hand. The poor fellow at the register in this particular store was just going about his business when I marched up to the counter, book in hand, and said, "I know you just work here, but is this a Christian bookstore?" "Yes it is," he replied. "Then how can you sell this?" I asked as I tossed a copy of the Hewitt book down on the counter. "Wha..." was his attempt at a reply as he apparently looked at the book for the first time. "I'm a Christian and I can't believe you're selling a book called '*Crushing* the Democrats'—that's *not* okay," I said to the now attentive clerk. "It says that?" was all he could reply as I walked out the door. I've never been good at finishing this kind of conversation. I must admit that I couldn't bring myself to read Mr. Hewitt's book.

Isn't is a bit disingenuous not to mention going against much of what you've previously written to criticize a book you haven't even read?
I'm not criticizing the book, per se, although it is obvious from the title I probably wouldn't care for its contents. I have a much bigger problem with a Christian bookstore carrying this kind of book.

The other side writes these kinds of books, too—what's wrong with a little "balance" in the marketplace?
Once again, I have no problem with the fact that this type of book exists; I'm glad that our Freedom of the Press guarantees that all sides can be freely heard. The other side *does* write this kind of screed. This book should be sold where the rest of this type of books are sold—in a Border's, or a Barnes & Noble, or on Amazon.com. I have a real problem with a Christian bookstore selling such an obvious politically biased hatchet job, especially

considering the fact that the same type of store won't even touch many *Christian* authors with even a slightly progressive view.

What you won't find, with few exceptions, are any books about Christian pacifism or non-violence, or books by Christian authors critical of the policies of Republicans in general or this administration in particular. You won't find any books by qualified Christian authors and theologians that lay out the biblical case *against* the war in Iraq. You won't find any books by qualified Christian authors and theologians that lay Jesus' teachings side-by-side with the Bush administration's actions. You won't find any books by qualified Christian authors that show the disconnect between the rhetoric of compassionate conservatism and the poverty that exists in the United States today, with the possible exception of *God's Politics* by Jim Wallis. You have about a fifty percent chance of finding any books by Jimmy Carter, an avowed and very public Southern Baptist, who has dedicated his life after his presidency to peace and the reduction of poverty around the world. Where are Father John Dear's books? These books not only exist, they are for sale at places like Borders Books, Barnes and Noble Bookstores, Tower Books, Amazon.com, and many other secular places of business.

I have to ask, in all seriousness, why? Why must I go to secular bookstores to find these Christian authors? What sort of deeply ingrained bias is this? Believe me, I am not talking about fringe people here. These are leaders of churches, leading theologians with long résumés, authors with Jesus on their minds and in their hearts, with a strong desire for justice and peace, and a calling to end poverty in our country and around the world. It is a very telling statement on the condition of evangelical Christianity that you have to go to a Borders to find these types of books. This is beginning to remind me a little of the Dobson/Disney scenario; you have to go to the secular store to find books on Christian non-violence—that's just great.

Maybe the Christian Bookstore owners only stock the things they know they will sell—it's possible that they know their clientele better than you do.

This argument is brought to us by the same people who have told me that Christian radio's target demographic are the 35 year-old housewives in Peoria, so all of their focus groups are geared towards 35 year-old housewives from Peoria. It's a self-fulfilling prophecy. The 35 year-old housewives from Peoria in the focus groups confirm to the Program Directors at these stations that the music they like the best is music for 35 year-old housewives from Peoria. If Joe or Judy Christian is perusing the shelves of the local Christian bookstore and he/she sees *The Christian Case For War*, is it not unfair and presumptuous that Joe and Judy can't browse a copy of *The Christian Case Against War* and make up their own mind?

Can we at least agree that this is part of why we have received only one side of the story? The very most biased people there are have told us that there is a bias in the media. These same people have told us that "liberal" means the opposite of what it does. We have been told that to be a Christian, we must support this and this and this, without probably ever hearing the rational Christian case against the same. We have been told that it is our duty as Christians and our patriotic duty as Americans to support a lie masquerading as the War on Terror, and we have been told that to even listen to another *Christian* perspective on this is to be unpatriotic, a "friend of the terrorist," "an appeaser," or worse. We can't even find this perspective to make up our *own minds* in a Christian bookstore. The gatekeepers have made up our minds for us.

25 / rush

"Let no corrupt communication proceed out of your mouth, but what is good for necessary edification, that it may impart grace to the hearers." —Ephesians 4:29

"Let all bitterness, wrath, anger, clamor, and evil speaking be put away from you, with all malice." —Ephesians 4:31

"They are 12 percent of the population. Who the hell cares?"[30]
—Rush Limbaugh, to a caller
who said black people need to be heard

I TOLD MYSELF I WASN'T GONNA DO IT; I wasn't going to give him any more attention than he already gets. There have already been books about this fellow (Al Franken's, among others) that have done the yeoman's work in exposing the holes in his game and deconstructing the Limbaugh mystique—not that you should feel sorry for him. But Rush Limbaugh has too much influence to ignore. As I have already mentioned him several times, I might as well get it out there on the table—I think Rush Limbaugh is one of the most dangerous men in America. He would no doubt revel in that title, and in fact has used it to describe himself.

I have listened to Rush on and off for over twenty years. I lived in Sacramento when he had a slot on KFBK, before he went "big-time" with the EIB network and all of that. I used to listen to Rush all of the time, despite myself, because although I disagreed with about 90% of what he said, 1) he was always entertaining, 2) he was often funny, and 3) there was always the sense that he knew he was just entertainment, and he didn't take himself completely seriously. The song parodies that he had cooked up were hilarious, and his imitation of Bill Clinton was spot-on. I would often yell back at the radio at him, but at the end of the day, I was entertained.

Somewhere around the end of the Clinton presidency or the campaign of 2000, he changed. I couldn't put my finger exactly on when, but he stopped being funny. Part of his "charm," such as it was, was that his humor took the edge off of his ranting. As it stands now, all you have left is the ranting. He has, for the most part, forgotten that he is entertainment, and you can't really blame him. He has been put on a throne and anointed the King of the Angry White Men. He is the tail wagging the dog in right-wing political circles. He has given birth to all kinds of imitators, male and female, each vying in their own way to outdo the King in being more controversial, angrier, more pedantic, more reactionary, and more mean-spirited. He even spawned an imitator on the left in the form of the failing Air America. Al Franken was much more controlled, and much more cerebral than Rush. He's wasn't very funny either anymore, and often sounded half asleep, but he didn't spew the vitriol and hate that Rush does. He's taking his political career to the Senate in Minnesota. Ed Schultz *sounds* like Rush, but doesn't *hate* like him. Stephanie Miller is a comedienne, and while her liberal act gets monotonous at times, she is still funny. If there were a mirror image of Rush on Air America, it would probably have been Mike Malloy. That is no compliment, Mike. More recently, Keith Olbermann at MSNBC has become the Left's go-to ranter.

What Rush does is speak in an authoritarian way, not unlike a fundamentalist preacher, making people believe that his version of the truth is as unfailingly inerrant as the Bible itself. He uses every single tactic that he accuses his enemies of using to make his points. He is mean-spirited while accusing his opponents of being mean-spirited; he name-calls while accusing others of name-calling; he constantly accuses the other side of using inappropriate issues as political footballs, but that is exactly his *modus operandi*. What is telling is that the "other side" is getting larger and larger all of the time. By that I don't mean that there are more and more left-wingers running around these days. As Rush moves farther and farther out on the right limb, what he (and his fellow travelers) call "liberal" and "the left" just gets bigger and bigger. In Rush's world, even "moderate" is a dirty word. All those who even try to understand or come to any compromise with the people not out there on the right limb are viewed as weak, indecisive, and wrong. Viewed through Rush's coke-bottle lenses, an old, garden-variety conservative is a centrist—someone like George Bush Sr., or John Danforth. A Republican like John McCain borders on heresy, and is frequently cut down to size on Limbaugh's show.

As for everyone else, from the middle on over, forget about it. They are all tarred with the same brush: Liberals, left-wingers, Feminazis, environmentalist wackos, troublemakers, traitors, peaceniks, terrorist-lovers, appeasers, communists, and socialists. There is no middle in Limbaugh's world, and if you do happen to be a moderate, whether nominally a Democrat or Republican, watch out—Rush saves his some of his worst venom for you.

What I find so dangerous about Limbaugh is that so many people blindly buy into his shtick. From his lips to millions of peoples' mouths come his words. Rush claims that, unlike the "other" side, his listeners have been taught to be independent thinkers. Obviously, nothing could be further from the truth. They aren't called "Ditto-heads" for nothing, even if the original meaning (which was short-hand for all of the set-up phrases that callers use, like "first-time caller, long-time listener, love your show, you're the best," etc.) has been lost. For there is no one in the media—with the *possible* exception of Oprah Winfrey—that commands such a slavish following, ready to parrot his every word. I know this from experience—you see, my brother and many of my friends in the Christian music industry and at the church I worked at wouldn't think that I would listen to Rush, but I do, as much as I can stand. I then hear from their mouths the contents of what he has said that morning. Whatever the listeners of Rush Limbaugh think they are, they are *not* free thinkers. This is yet another example of Limbaugh claiming the exact opposite of the reality.

Every day, Rush says something that could be easily debunked, but does it in such a way that the Ditto-heads accept it as Gospel Truth. For example, as the Right went into "the best defense is a good offense" mode concerning the allegations that presidential advisor Karl Rove might have been the person who leaked the name of Ambassador Joseph Wilson's wife, CIA agent Valerie Plame (it has turned out that I. Lewis "Scooter" Libby, Vice President Dick Cheney's top advisor, has been indicted for perjury over this), Rush actually claimed that Ambassador Wilson and the Democrats hatched this whole scheme up—the phony Niger documents, the uranium story that I referred to in the Iraq chapter—as a conspiracy to discredit the president. This laughingly absurd idea sounds like something out of *The Onion*, except that it is a classic tactic of the Right. If you throw enough smoke out there, however absurd it is, it sows enough confusion among people that pretty soon you have people showing up around the water coolers saying, "Well I heard that the Democrats hatched the whole thing up!" or, "I heard that Valerie Plame was just a desk jockey and it didn't really matter that she was exposed." This is from the same group of people that managed to turn the comparison of a man with a distinguished war record (Kerry) versus a man who managed to skip the war (Bush) into an attack on the man with the distinguished war record! By the time the smoke had cleared on that one, the Right had managed to sow just enough doubt in people's minds to make a huge difference—people who only get their news in bits and pieces.

Rush Limbaugh is from a long line of hate-spewing radio dem-agogues, from Billy Sunday in the '20s, to Father Charles Coughlin and Gerald L.K. Smith in the '30s and '40s, to people like Senator Joseph McCarthy and George Wallace in the '50s, to Carl McIntire and Billy Hargis in the '60s, all in love with the sound of their own voices, all considered merely conservative in their moments of glory, but all eventually exposed for the bigots that they were.

While Rush could hardly be accused of anti-Semitism, and he is not a racist by most people's definition of the word (this chap-ter's epigraph notwithstanding), he is most certainly a bigot. After all, here are some synonyms for bigot from my handy (must be left-wing) dictionary: *biased, chauvinistic, dogmatic, intolerant, close-minded, narrow-minded, opinionated,* and *illiberal* (I like that one). The two antonyms for "bigot" are *humanitarian* and, guess what? *Liberal.* There is absolutely nothing remotely Christian about this man. His attitudes, which praise the wealthy at the expense of the poor, which called the horror of Abu Ghraib "frat hazing," which preach division and hatred of the classes while accusing others of doing the same, do not fall anywhere near any-thing Jesus ever said or did. And yet millions of Christians listen to this man, along with other similar hate-filled bigots like Michael Savage and Bill O'Reilly, with apparently no thought to the desecration he or they bring to the Cross. Jesus saved his strongest words for helping the poor, and for hypocrites; these men (and women) insult Jesus by celebrating the status quo in this country, by fighting against anything that reeks of leveling the playing field, while paying lip service to the "rugged individual-ism" of the American people. As soon as the issue of poverty in America is brought up to the Limbaughs, the O'Reillys, the Hannittys, the Coulters, or the Savages, one is immediately accused of promoting a class war. This is a classic device of the kind I named above, whereby these folks put people on the defensive by accusing someone of doing exactly what *they* are doing. For, in fact, there has been a class war in this country for a hundred years, and in the last 25 years, the rich, represented by these very same mouthpieces, have all but won. The rich in this country *are* getting richer, while the poor *are* getting poorer. This is not an opinion, it is a fact, by any set of reliable statistics you want to use.

There are so many examples of blatant contradictions in Limbaugh's aural résumé, that I could fill page after page, particularly if you are looking for examples of "what Jesus wouldn't do." The very morning of the horrible terrorist attacks on the transportation system in London, Rush wasn't talking about helping the victims—no, no, no. What he was doing was blasting the "Libs" in Congress for what he assumed they were going to say *two days from then*. He was *assuming* that the Democrats would find a way to politicize the bombings by tying them to the war in Iraq. He was doing *exactly* what he was accusing the "other" side of doing, politicizing a tragedy, only this time he had to pull it from the future.

On November 3rd, 2008, one day before the election, Rush was obviously not a happy camper. A woman called in, identified by Rush as a Chinese immigrant. She started accusing Barack Obama of being the Marxist vanguard of revolution that Solzhenitsyn warned America about in a speech in 1976. Even Rush wasn't swallowing this whopper, but it allowed him to segue into a contradictory rant. "Obama always talks about unity! I haven't seen any unity! These people are all about *hate*!! He has a wife that hates America, a pastor that hates America, he hates America!! It's all HATE!! HATE!!! *HATE!!!*" spluttered Limbaugh, with all the hate he could muster. "These people are the most *miserable* group of unifiers I have ever seen!!" said Limbaugh miserably. "This is a Balkanized country we have here, folks, and it's entirely the fault of the American Left!!"

This constant projection, accusing others of doing exactly what you are doing, is by no means confined to Limbaugh. Take this quote from Bill O'Reilly: "It makes me sick to see intellectually dishonest individuals hide behind the First Amendment to spread propaganda, libel and slander, but this is a growing trend in America, where the exchange of ideas often degenerates into a verbal wrestling with intent to injure." He couldn't have said that with a straight face.

I have noticed something very telling, though, in Limbaugh in the last year or so. As a long-time listener of the man, I could tell right away, before it was made public, when he had trouble with his hearing. It was evident in his delivery. I have heard something else lately. He stutters and splutters a great deal more than he ever has before, and this indicates to me that he has had to work a lot harder at justifying his positions, especially the glorious war in Iraq, that have been increasingly hard to justify. It is also part of the reason that he has gotten increasingly angry, bitter, and vitriolic. He has been forced to support increasingly unsupportable situations. If you ever heard Rush Limbaugh during the Clinton years (for example, the big deal he made about Clinton getting a haircut on the tarmac at LAX), you know without a doubt that if the Clinton administration had done one tenth of the lying about the situation leading up to the war in Iraq that the Bush administration has, Rush would have led the charge toward impeachment right from the beginning.

On the day after the 2008 election of Barack Obama, Rush was at his most self-righteous, pompous, worst. He called the President-elect a "Chicago thug," and a "radical leftist extremist," and cited "closing Gitmo (the torture prison at Guantanamo, Cuba)," and "ending the war in Iraq" as two of the three examples of this. The other was national healthcare. Please, call *me* a radical, leftist, extremist. He again, hatefully and miserably, called the American left, including Obama, hate-filled miserable people. He derided John McCain's beautifully elegant concession speech, saying, "His whole campaign was a concession speech!" He derided civility, graciousness, and being conciliatory as the further erosion of Conservative values. He claimed that the Republicans lost, in essence, because they played "too nice," and, were not *enough* like him.

The first caller to the Rush Limbaugh show on the day after the election said this, and I quote: "You, after God, are my refuge and my strength today, Rush." Christians, I urge you to listen to Rush Limbaugh with fresh ears. He has created an entire industry based on hate, and has done it with your backing. If you can find the principals and teachings of Jesus Christ in what Rush Limbaugh says, or what Bill O'Reilly says, or what Michael Savage says, or what Ann Coulter says, you must be using the special decoder ring they sent you. There is very little equivalence on the left, with the exception of the sorry Air America and a few others, and these sadly smack of the very worst kind of imitation. There is a perception in secular America, among the very people that Christians would hope to take the message of Christ, that Rush Limbaugh represents, in thought and in words, the average evangelical Christian. This, of course, represents stereotyping on their part, and whether it is actually true or not, perception is everything. As long as Christians walk around repeating their favorite Limbaugh quote of the day, and parroting whatever he is going off on, then Christianity itself will be associated with this bigotry. What am I saying? We already are. This is our image. I hope you like it.

Ann Coulter, In Her Own Words

I was going to do a whole chapter on Ann Coulter, but I'd prefer not to see her name at the head of a chapter. Instead, I'll just give a sample here. Notice the slimy rage that oozes out of her every pore as she attributes the same feeling to liberals: *"When contemplating college liberals, you really regret once again that John Walker (Lind) is not getting the death penalty. We need to execute people like John Walker in order to physically intimidate liberals, by making them realize that they can be killed, too. Otherwise, they will turn out to be outright traitors."* —CPAC convention, February 2002.

"My only regret with Timothy McVeigh is he did not go to the New York Times Building."
          —To George Gurley, *New York Observer,* August 21, 2002
(Looking for the New York vote on that one.)

"A central component of liberal hate speech is to make paranoid accusations based on their own neurotic impulses, such as calling Republicans angry, hate-filled, and mean."   —*Slander,* p.19
(That's a great one—hahaha...)

"Liberals don't try to win arguments, they seek to destroy their opponents and silence dissident opinions."   —*Slander,* p. 91

"Political debate with liberals is basically impossible in America because liberals are calling names while conservatives are trying to make arguments.... It's really all the same lie [that liberals tell], that conservatives are either stupid or scarily weird and therefore you don't have to deal with their ideas."   —Katie Couric Interview,
                                        Today Show, June 26, 2002
(The funny thing about Coulter is that *she* never says anything of substance—she just runs around making these types of hateful pronouncements about liberals making hateful pronouncements!)

"The swing voters—I like to refer to them as the idiot voters because they don't have set philosophical principles. You're either a liberal or you're a conservative if you have an IQ above a toaster. "
          —Beyond the News, FOX News Channel, June 4
(That's a thoughtful thing to say....)

"Progress cannot be made on serious issues because one side is making arguments and the other side is throwing eggs—both figuratively and literally. Prevarication and denigration are the hallmarks of liberal argument. Logic is not their métier. Blind religious faith is."
          —*Slander,* p. 2
(That one borders on the delusional....)

"...a cruise missile is more important than Head Start."
  —Nov. 2001 speech rebroadcast by C-Span in Jan. 2002
(...and she's a regular Maria Montessori!)

*"I think [women] should be armed but should not [be allowed to]
vote. No, they all have to give up their vote, not just, you know, the lady
clapping and me. The problem with women voting—and your
Communists will back me up on this—is that, you know, women have
no capacity to understand how money is earned. They have a lot of
ideas on how to spend it. And when they take these polls, it's always
more money on education, more money on child care, more money on
day care."*   —Politically Incorrect, Feb. 26, 2001
(Well...we wouldn't want any of that now, would we?)

"The thing I like about Bush is I think he hates liberals."
                    —Washington Post, August 1, 2000.
(Compassionate conservative that he is....)

*"[The] backbone of the Democratic Party [is a] typical fat, implaca-
ble welfare recipient."*   —syndicated column, October 29, 1999
(She called me implacable!)

*"My libertarian friends are probably getting a little upset now but I
think that's because they never appreciate the benefits of local fascism."*
                    —MSNBC, February 8, 1997
(Her true colors come out.)

Tell me, *please*...who on the left gets to go on mainstream TV, on
national news programs, and make outrageously, ridiculously
biased statements and comments like this? Who?

26 / presidents, religion, and credibility

He who digs a hole and scoops it out falls into the pit he has made.
The trouble he causes recoils on himself; his violence comes down on his
own head.   —Psalm 7:15-16

WHEN PRESIDENT BILL CLINTON WAS at the height of his
denial concerning his affair with Monica Lewinsky, pointing at the
TV camera and saying, "I...did...not...have...sex...with...that...
woman!" I don't know about you, but I was thinking that his own
history was not in his favor at that moment. Whether he was ever
actually caught red-handed or not, the sheer volume of previous
charges concerning his sexual behavior called his credibility on
sexual affairs into doubt, to say the least. Even if you buy into his
specious argument about the definition of "having sex," the fact
remained that President Clinton became harder and harder to
believe about *anything* because his credibility was so compro-
mised over *l'affaire Lewinsky*.

Bill Clinton seemed to me to represent the Fallen Man; caught in
his own web of lies in an affair with a younger woman, he had to
painfully come crawling back to his wife and child and ask forgiveness. The only thing that made this at all interesting is that it was
played out on the world stage, and he was, at the time, the most

powerful man on earth. By all accounts, Bill Clinton is a likable man, not unlike Ronald Reagan was, even to his political foes.

Also, not unlike Reagan and almost every other modern president save Jimmy Carter, Bill Clinton would invoke the name of God when it was appropriate, and considered himself a Christian, but could hardly have been called an evangelical Christian, at least by the definition that most people reading this book would accept. Most presidents, again with the exception of Carter, would give God His due without wearing their religion on their sleeves. (Richard Nixon was supposed to be a Quaker—isn't that ironic?) Until George W. Bush, Jimmy Carter was the most overt president in regards to his Christianity. I don't remember Carter being as up front about religion when he was in office as George W. was, but I think that is just a sign of the times.

Likable or not, while Bill Clinton's credibility with many of the people in his own nation was pretty well shot by 1997, much of the rest of the world shrugged. Heck, most of the men in power around the world were wondering what the big deal was, while the rest were sighing, "There but for the grace of God go I." When Richard Nixon was forced to resign over Watergate, many of the leaders around the world had a similar reaction.

When George W. Bush was elected in 2000, although I was not in favor of many of his policies, I was optimistic that the credibility of the Presidency would be restored. Being an unabashed evangelical Christian, Bush promised to bring decency and moral values (that slippery phrase), and, although he didn't use these words, a Christian world view to the White House. If what we were all looking for was a guy who doesn't cheat on his wife, then, although *nothing* is absolutely certain except death and taxes, I think we can pretty safely say that Dubya has been true to his word.

When you become a member of Alcoholics Anonymous, one of the reasons for anonymity, *especially* if you're famous, is that if you tell the world that you're in AA, and then you stand out on your front stoop waving a shotgun at the police with a bottle of Jack

Daniels in your other hand (which actually happened with a famous female rock singer), then you give the whole program a bad name and people think that it must not work. Unfortunately, this image hit home with many people around the world—our President metaphorically stood out on the front stoop of the White House with a Bible, and then waved "Shock and Awe'" in the world's face.

When George W. Bush became President and wore the evangelical Christian label on his sleeve, he took on a tremendous responsibility to uphold the faith while in office, a responsibility that proved too hard to bear. The Founding Fathers knew what they were doing when they separated Church from State. When one is waving the Cross as well as the Flag at people from other cultures and faiths, they are given twice as many reasons to want to blow you up. While Johnson, Nixon, Reagan, and Clinton may have done some things to make other countries mad, it is George W. who appeared unbelievably hypocritical by adopting a holier-than-thou righteousness about our cause, and then allowed his administration to act in this most un-Christ-like fashion. This has not only hurt our nation, it has set the faith back, too. The louder he barked about being a Christian, the more Christ-like he should have tried to be. This did not happened. He was all about revenge, and two-eyes-for-an-eye. He spent our money on guns rather than poverty. He's just an ol' fashioned Texas oilman, and if that were all he was, then no one would give him a second thought. But as the leader of the Free World, and an avowed Christian, he has done immense harm both to the prestige of the United States, and to the Christian religion. I'm not being overblown about this; look again at the percentages that didn't like George Bush's policies *among our allies and friends*. And this, following the overwhelming support our nation received in the aftermath of 9/11. That was The Moment. If George W. Bush could have risen to the occasion after 9/11 in a *truly* Christian way, with words evoking Martin Luther King, or C.S. Lewis, or Billy Graham, imagine the world's surprise. Instead we got the words of a cowboy out of the old West. *Vengeance is mine!* How un-Christ-like was the behavior of the Bush administration since 9/11. Once again, I know that governments are secular. That's fine if your rhetoric is secular. But George W. Bush invoked the power of Almighty God in our cause while arbitrarily changing international law as he saw fit. He claimed to pray while he detained prisoners without charging them with anything and allowed them to be tortured. While thumping his Bible, he invaded a sovereign nation without provocation, causing endless suffering and misery in an attempt to undo suffering and misery (destroying the village in order to save it), and he arbitrarily ignored the parts of the Constitution that he didn't care for.

Just as Bill Clinton's previous "bimbo eruptions" made it hard to believe his Monica Lewinsky explanations, the Bush administration, led by the President, had a real credibility problem when it came to anything they said about war, or anything else for that matter. When Vice President Dick Cheney said that the insurgency in Iraq was "in its last throes," this man lost his credibility. This is the same guy who said in 1992: "And the question in my mind is how many additional American casualties is Saddam worth?" Cheney said then in response to his own question, "And the answer is not very damned many. So I think we got it right, both when we decided to expel him from Kuwait, but also when the president made the decision that we'd achieved our objectives and we were not going to go get bogged down in the problems of trying to take over and govern Iraq." Continuing on, he then said, "All of a sudden you've got a battle you're fighting in a major built-up city, a lot of civilians are around, significant limitations on our ability to use our most effective technologies and techniques. Once we had rounded him up and gotten rid of his government, then the question is what do you put in its place? You know, you then have accepted the responsibility for governing Iraq." The end result, Cheney said in 1992, would be a messy, dangerous situation requiring a long-term presence by U.S. forces.

How about these Cheney quotes: "We will, in fact, be greeted as liberators (in Iraq)." (March 16, 2003, to Tim Russert on "Meet the Press.") On the same show: "We believe he (Saddam) has, in fact, reconstituted nuclear weapons. I think Mr. El Baradei (head of the UN Atomic Inspections Team) frankly is wrong." Or this, on August 26, 2002, at the national VFW Convention: "Simply stated, there is no doubt that Saddam Hussein now has weapons of mass destruction." Simply stated, frankly, in fact, in my mind, this man lost his credibility.

When Secretary of Defense Donald Rumsfeld insisted that we had just the right amount of troops in Iraq to complete the mission successfully, despite the repeated objections of the most senior military men on the ground, he had already shot his credibility. "I can't tell you if the use of force in Iraq today will last five days, five weeks or five months, but it won't last any longer than that." Donald Rumsfeld said that. He also said, "It is easier to get into something than to get out of it." That one, I agree with. He also said, "There are known knowns. These are things we know that we know. There are known unknowns. That is to say, there are things that we know we don't know. But there are also unknown unknowns. These are things we don't know we don't know." I don't even know what that means.

When the President of the United States, George W. Bush, stood up in the summer of 2005 and continued to link his adventure in Iraq to the tragedy of 9/11 despite *all evidence to the contrary*, people all over America began to tune out. He lost them. He went to the well one too many times. Even the die-hards had begun to throw up their hands. Without his credibility, a president will find it almost impossible to lead.

Be A Christian First

Even if one accepts the fact that our government, or any government for that matter, is a secular organism, with an almost Darwinian "survival-of-the-fittest" mentality and morality, I still believe it is incumbent upon us as Christ-centered people not to condone their bad behavior. As much as we pour our hearts and energies into the attempt to counter the secular culture here in our own country by offering the alternative of a life built around the precepts and divinity of Jesus Christ, we cannot ignore the damage that was done in our names and in *His* name around the world by the hostile, bent-on-revenge-and-world-domination folks we have had running this country. How many of our leaders, be it Democrat or Republican, are ready to stand on even the secular principles that Jesus brought forth: to love your neighbor as yourself, to turn the other cheek when someone strikes you, to wash the feet of your brother, and that the first shall be last and the last shall be first? These are the very definitions of a small "L" liberal, and no one wants to be caught dead running a political race based on these principals. So, we end up with Frick versus Frack, two politicians who spend most of their time raising the money they'll need to paint themselves at the farther end of each political spectrum for the Primaries, and then raising even more money to convince the public that they are not really at the far end of any spectrum after all, but solidly and unabashedly centrist. After the election, the winner can then return to wherever he really stood on the spectrum, counting on the short attention span of the electorate to forget any "distortions or misstatements" said candidate might have made along the road to being elected.

So what, then, are Christians supposed to do? If there is one point that I wish emphasized in this book, it is that we as Christians need to be Christians first, Americans second, and (Fill in your Party) third. We have a tremendous opportunity to be radicals for peace, and a truly decisive independent voice in this country, as long as we don't give that chance up by submitting meekly to whatever the conservative politicians and their mouthpieces in the media say. Your leader is Jesus the Christ, not James the Dobson, or Oliver the North, or Rush the Limbaugh, or even George W. Bush. If you voted Republican, then I urge you to hold your elected leaders responsible for their actions.

My two Senators in California are Barbara Boxer and Dianne Feinstein, two Democratic women whom I voted for the last time they came up for reelection. Of the two, Boxer is certainly known as a liberal Democrat; Feinstein is more centrist, but would probably be put in the liberal boat with Ms. Boxer nonetheless. I have let both Senators know that my vote in the next election is not a given; it is dependent upon how they use their political power. If they sit meekly on their hands with their lips buttoned in mortal fear of appearing "soft" on Defense, then I will vote for a third-party candidate who has the guts to stand for what is right. It must be said in fairness that the smaller candidates do have the freedom to say whatever they want because they know they won't be elected; the major candidates have to tread the fine line of being all things to all people, so they end up being "nothings" to anyone.

How can you vote for two people who are obviously so...pro-choice?
I say to you again, a life is a life is a life. If a politician that is pro-life comes out against the death penalty, and against imperialist wars in general and the war in Iraq in particular, then he/she most certainly will get my vote. If a politician who is pro-life takes a truly pro-life agenda on *all* world issues, then he/she's got me at hello. I think it is hypocritical to look at it any other way. If we are really pro-life, then we are going to support the politician that is going to try to save the most lives and kill the fewest, a politician who is going to view the earth as God's Creation and not ours to use up and destroy, regardless of his or her political affiliation. Again, *"There is none righteous; no, not one."*

27 / independent thinking

I AM NOT RECOMMENDING A DEMOCRATIC Party solution to the problems the nation is facing. The Democrats, when in power, have mainly shown only differences in style in regards to the way they conduct foreign policy. They have also foregone the spiritual side of politics to the extent that they have, in effect, ceded the field to the Republicans. What bothers me is that, just as African-Americans have long been seen to be "reliably" Democratic, evangelical Christians are assumed to be in the hip pocket of the Republican Party so securely that it is a given to the Republican leaders that these Christians are just going to go along with everything they do. A strong, independent Christian community committed to holding all politicians accountable for their policies as well as their actions in the name of our first love, Jesus Christ, would be truly a powerful force for change.

How do we become politically independent? How do you really know if you are or you aren't already an independent political thinker? Well, for starters, you can answer a couple of questions. When you see or hear a piece of news or information on Fox News or on the Rush Limbaugh radio show, do you apply the same criteria as to whether the information is valid, (i.e., where did they get their data, who are the sources, etc.) as you would from anyone else? Or, do you just assume that they must be correct? When you heard George W. Bush speak, did you judge the truthfulness of his words in the same way that you did Bill Clinton? When you read the things that I have written, are you naturally suspicious of the data or the sources? If so, why? How do you know what you know? This comes back to the issue of how we've learned our history, and what bits of it we've retained.

The journal *Sojourners*, an evangelical Christian publication, led a petition and an ad campaign entitled "God Is Not A Republican. Or A Democrat" during the 2004 election season. Among the many excellent beliefs espoused in this petition, this one really stood out to me:

"We will measure candidates by whether they enhance human life, human dignity, and human rights; whether they strengthen family life and protect children; whether they promote racial reconciliation and support gender equality; whether they serve peace and social justice; and whether they advance the common good rather than only individual, national, and special interests."

A lot of people grow up in families whose parents are so vocal about their political leanings that by kindergarten little Alex or little Sarah will say they're a Republican or Democrat without knowing the first thing about it. My wife grew up in a house of Roosevelt Democrats and as far back as she can remember "we were Democrats; Republicans lived in big houses and didn't care about the poor and basically were some kind of unknown evil." I grew up in a conservative Republican household and at least until I was ten or eleven, I remember hearing my father and grandfathers talk about Democrats like they were all big-city thieves; you always had to keep one hand on your wallet when you were around a Democrat.

The Vietnam War made things confusing because there was a Democratic president in Lyndon Johnson who was being hounded out of office mainly by young people who certainly weren't Republicans, and for the first time it may have entered the back of my brain that one might call oneself a member of a certain political party without necessarily being in favor of everything that party's leaders stood for. Democrats have always seemed more likely to fight about things within their own party than Republicans. Republicans, at least in the last twenty-five years, have been more adept at closing ranks and presenting a united front, which has been a large part of their success.

At some of the evangelical churches that I have attended, the political education must start early. I wonder if you polled kindergarteners, 1st graders, and 2nd graders at evangelical churches, how many of them would say they were Republicans? Why is this? If you were to have polled Southern kindergarteners, 1st graders, and 2nd graders before the 1960s, how many of them would say they didn't like the Coloreds? Why was that?

All right, now you've really gone too far. First it was Nazis, now it's racists. You're making a HUGE generalization and a slanderous comparison.

I'm just trying to make a point. Little Soviet kids grew up as atheists and communists. Little German kids grew up learning to hate Jews before they ever knew any. Little Southern kids learned to hate black kids before they knew any of them. Little Arab kids learn to hate Jews and Christians, and little Jewish kids learn to hate Arabs. Where did these children, by and large, learn these things? There's nothing in the Bible that I can find that urges us to train our children up to be Republicans. I would like evangelical Christians who call themselves conservative Republicans to question themselves as to why they think politically the way they do. Are you operating under long-held assumptions that square with the facts? Do they square with Jesus' words?

I heard a guy on the radio, Walter Williams, a conservative columnist who was subbing for Rush Limbaugh. I'm paraphrasing here, but anyone could probably look this up on Rush's website in June of 2005:

Williams (to caller): "There's two kinds of theft—illegal theft, and legal theft. Let's say I walk out of this building and stumble over an old person lying in a doorway. If I then go up to my friend and point a gun at him and say "give me $200" and then I turn around and give it to the old person in the doorway, is that legal or illegal?"

Caller: "That's illegal."

Williams: "That's right, that's illegal theft. Don't matter what I did with it, it's still illegal. Now let's say I have $200 in my pocket that I've worked hard to enjoy, and I'm planning with this $200 to buy a couple of bottles of Lafitte Rothschild Cabernet, and the Congress, by way of its agent, the IRS, says 'no, no, no, Mr. Williams, you have to give that money to us, and *we're* gonna give it to the old person lying in the doorway'—what is that? I'll tell you what it is—it's legal theft. Don't matter if it's legal or not—it's not morally right. Keep in mind what the Nazis did to the Jews, and what Stalin did to his people was considered legal in those countries. They have no more moral right to take that money from me and give it to another person than I did in holding up my friend for $200 and giving it to another person. I've been around for awhile, sixty-nine years, and I've never been able to find the moral reason for someone to take what is mine and give it to someone else."

First of all, I'm no apologist for the IRS. I would never cast the first stone concerning anything to do with collecting taxes, paying taxes, paying taxes on time, or trying to do all those little things one tries to do to pay less taxes. But this is just wrong on so many levels. First of all, nobody likes paying taxes, but how else is the government going to get the revenue it needs to build schools, fix roads and bridges, and feed the homeless and hungry...*in Iraq?* Secondly, geez, call me a sloppy sentimentalist, but if there's anything that would make me feel a little better about shelling out money for Uncle Sam, it would be knowing that my $200 went to some old person lying in a doorway, instead of paying for a screw on yet another 500-pound bomb destined to land on some foreign hut.

Mr. Williams, I wish everyone was as generous and philan-thropic as you seem to be, but I'm afraid that they're not. I know those two $100 bottles of wine would go to good use as you enjoy the "fruits" of your labor with that unfortunate person in the doorway (you were planning to share, weren't you Mr. Williams?). I know that you know better how to use your money than some bureaucrat in Washington, Mr. Williams. After all, how many dying old people in doorways get to sample a Lafitte Rothschild Cabernet? Not many, if my data is right. That's really putting the "compassionate" in the "conservative," Mr. Williams. What's that? Oh, you're *not* planning to share the Lafitte Rothschild Cabernet with the old person in the doorway? My mistake, Mr. Williams, but I can see where you've really staked out the high moral ground, sir. You are a true Mother Theresa, Mr. Williams.

Conservatives believe that helping one's fellow man is an indi-vidual discipline; that charity begins in the home and continues through faith-based or private giving. A government that takes money out of your pocket and gives it to others less fortunate is engaging in "Robin Hood-ism," or "legal theft." Oh, would that it were so. It is not all that different, if you think about it, from star-ry-eyed liberals imagining a world where everyone would just put down their guns and join in a big world hug.

Unfortunately, human nature being what it is, for every person who gives generously of what they have, whether it be time or money, to those who by accident of birth weren't as fortunately endowed, there are far more people who can't be bothered. It would be great if the top 10% wealthiest helped to pull the bot-tom 10% poorest out of their misery on their own, but it never seems to happen. Good, smart people have been grappling with wealth and poverty issues for thousands of years without a lasting solution. I do believe, though, that this is one more area that Christians can be out in the forefront, both in the public sector as well as the private.

This item is from the "Agape Press":

COURT SIDES WITH STUDENT ON RIGHT TO WEAR
SCRIPTURE-BEARING SHIRT

I'm thinking, "Right on, that's pretty cool, freedom of speech, etc."

A federal judge has told an Ohio school district it can no longer bar a middle school student from wearing a t-shirt with a Christian message.

I gotta say I'm with him here. I mean, kids can wear some of the most explicit, filthy things, or hear them on the radio, but the one thing you can't say is *Jesus.* Way to go, judge.

Judge George Smith has ruled that Sheridan Middle School in Thornville, Ohio, violated the constitutional rights of student (name withheld) by prohibiting him from wearing a t-shirt bearing a quote from the Bible verse John 14:6. The front of the shirt reads, "Jesus said, 'I am the Way, the Truth, and the Life.'"

Up until here, they totally have me. C'mon, PC crowd, don't you think you're taking this a little too far? However, the next line reads:

The back of the shirt contains the statements: "Homosexuality is sin. Islam is a lie. Abortion is murder."

Whoooaaaa, Nelly! Wha...

Although no complaints were filed over the t-shirt a few school officials—described by the boy's attorney as "overzealous"—deemed its message may be "offensive" to some individuals and "potentially disruptive," and thus could not be displayed.

I'll say! Why doesn't he just put "Kill the Niggas" on there, too, and "Send the Greasers back to Mexico" while he's at it?!

The attorney for the boy, James Nelson of the Orlando-based American Liberties Institute, says the decision has "broad, sweeping significance," especially for students in the southern district of Ohio, many of whom he says were watching for the outcome. "Other students and parents had been waiting for this decision to know whether their own children and students may now wear their shirts," Nelson shares.

There it is, Christian on the front, bigot on the back. I suppose the good folks at the American Liberties Institute will no doubt defend the right of a Muslim child to wear a shirt saying "Christianity is a lie," or "Christians are Murderers" to their middle school, and the wonderful Christian parents in that middle-American town of Thornville, Ohio will back the child's right to do so as well.

This is exactly the kind of situation in which we have to put our independent-minded hats on. There are free-speech issues here, as well as common sense and decency issues as well. As a Christian *first*, we look to Jesus for advice: "Do unto others as you would have them do unto you." The boy has the *right* to wear the t-shirt, but as an apparent Christian, he, as well as his parents— *especially his parents, for gosh sakes*—are going against Jesus' Golden Rule and should have the *common sense* not to.

28 / katrina

I WAS HESITANT ABOUT WRITING ANYTHING about the tragic events surrounding Hurricane Katrina because I wasn't sure I could be unbiased about it.

You haven't been unbiased about anything else—why start now?
I was born in New Orleans, as were four out of five of my brothers and sisters, both of my parents, all four of my grandparents, and all of my aunts, uncles, and cousins. One of my earliest memories was riding out Hurricane Betsy at my grandparent's house on my mother's side, because they lived in a part of New Orleans that was on slightly higher ground than us. As a six year-old, I remember that it was a little exciting, a little scary, and really fun to have to do that. When we returned to our home, we found that a giant tree had fallen in our back yard, but it had missed our house. Other than the mess of tree limbs in our yard, we were spared any major damage.

My mother's sister Dottie and my cousin Petey and his wife are my only close relatives left with houses in New Orleans. They left the city by car at 2:30 in the morning right before Hurricane Katrina hit. My aunt stayed for ten weeks at my parent's house in Dallas and my cousin went to his wife's relatives in Shreveport,

Louisiana. Neither of them had the slightest idea when they would be able to return to New Orleans, or what they would find when they got there. In the event, my aunt lost her house and everything in it, while my cousin's house was largely spared. They left New Orleans with one suitcase apiece. In many ways, though, they were fortunate—they had cash, credit cards, and a working car. For many in New Orleans, those three things were the difference in leaving and living, or staying and dealing with the severe consequences. Knowing a little about the geography of the city, I can speculate with reasonable accuracy that both the house that I grew up in and my grandparent's house on my father's side would have been under twenty feet of water. My other grandparent's house, the one that we stayed at during Hurricane Betsy, might have done slightly better, because it was near St. Charles Avenue around the corner from Tulane University, but the pictures I saw of Tulane didn't look good, either.

My father told me that he attended a lecture on the levees in New Orleans fifty years ago that closely predicted the conditions that we see today in the event of a hurricane of this magnitude. This is just to say that there is probably more blame to go around than there are fingers with which to point. New Orleans did not acquire its nickname "The Big Easy" because of its incorruptible standards of civil government. The state of Louisiana has come in for more than its fair share of corruption charges as well over the last hundred years. The city, already 12 to 24 feet under sea level, is sinking, along with its levees, due to fault lines that run underneath. The levees were built to withstand a Category 3 hurricane, and Hurricane Katrina was a high 4 when it came ashore.

There were nonetheless several striking things about this disaster that deserve mention. The first thing is how absolutely *partisan* every single bit of news has become in this country. One would think that a tragedy like this would unite the country in a way not unlike 9/11, but instead, it just brought to the surface all of the rage that the great class divide has wrought upon this nation. The rank-and-file citizenry showed once again that we are a nation of good people. The outpouring of money and help was a beautiful and encouraging thing to see. However, the underlying animosity towards the Bush administration threatened to tear this country apart. Katrina seemed to signal the ignominious end of the American people's trust with an ideological approach to government that never admitted the slightest error, believed in the smallest possible role for the federal government except when it came to its military adventures (who can forget this charming Grover Norquist quote: "My goal is to cut government in half in twenty-five years, to get it down to the size where we can drown it in the bathtub"), gave a tax cut to the wealthiest people in the country while maintaining record deficits, and appointed unqualified cronies to positions of major importance for the safety and security of this nation, all the while arrogantly failing to level with *we the people* about anything that they were doing.

In order to have embarked on the extremely costly regime change/nation-building/spreading capitalism/opening-new-markets-for-our-goods imperial strategy of invading Iraq, we needed to come up with several hundred billion dollars (and counting). This money, despite what many people think, doesn't fall from a tree. Despite the soaring budget deficits in part due to the Bush tax cuts, the money still had to be appropriated from a finite source. The bean counters in the administration knew that they couldn't just *add* $300 billion dollars to the budget—they had to try to cut a little bit from this program, a little more from that program, as in, "we don't *need* that food program for poor urban families," and "we can take some funds out the levee maintenance program—I mean, they've made it this long." It really makes one wonder what surprises are in store for us when we face the next disaster.

Now, the cleanup and resettling of 600,000 people has cost the American people about another war's worth of money—and where has this come from, now that we've spent so much on Iraq?

The spreading thin of our armed forces came back to haunt the Bush administration doubly when many National Guardsmen from the Gulf Coast states were unavailable to assist in hurricane recovery efforts due to being deployed in Iraq, thereby creating one of the factors in the delay of assistance. So, too, the spreading thin of available funds put a crimp in the Bush war plans, resulting in a more conciliatory tone in the following months toward Iran, Syria, and even North Korea while the administration dealt with the Katrina debacle.

In an item that could have come out of *The Onion*, ousted FEMA director Michael "Heckuva job" Brown announced following his removal that he had started a Disaster Consultancy Firm. Brown was the face of the administration's non-response to Hurricane Katrina, and also represented the worst kind of unqualified patronage imaginable.

As stated in the chapter on bias, the right wing has created such a cacophony of guttural hate in this country that it was only a matter of time before some people on the left sunk to this level of imitation. I happen to think that this "if you can't beat 'em, join 'em!" mentality is wrong on so many fronts.

The left has long prided itself on intellectual criticism. One of the things that I have discovered in my research is that criticism from the left tends to be detailed, long-winded, and polemical; its critiques tend toward policies more than personalities. Frankly, much of the left's material causes me to read and then re-read concepts that tend to go over my head on first reflection. When highly critical, the left tends toward highbrow, rapier slicing of a concept or person, somewhat like the late William Buckley on the right.

The right, on the other hand, intentionally goes straight into the gutter and right for the politics of personal destruction, all the while claiming that this is what the "other side" does. This is not my opinion; there are many quotes from right-wing gatekeepers that spell this strategy out in detail, as they apparently don't have any qualms about this aspect of what they do. I would urge you, as an experiment, to go into a local Borders and buy a copy of *The Nation*, a seminal left-wing weekly (you can probably get the bookseller to put it in a plain brown paper bag for you), and check out the *tone*. It really surprised me, after all that I had heard (but never actually checked out for myself) about this "pinko paper." It is an extremely well written journal; you may very well disagree with much of the content, but you will see that the criticism is grounded in civility.

Pick up almost any right-wing rag and you will find quite the opposite. They are filled with rumor, unsubstantiated gossip, and biased opinion of the basest kind masquerading as "journalism." Once again, this is a calculated strategy. If you read interviews with Rupert Murdoch, the owner of *The New York Post*, *HarperCollins Publishers*, *TV Guide*, and *FOX News Channel*, among others, or Sun Myung Moon, who owns *The Washington Times*, and *United Press International*, or Canadian media mogul Conrad Black, until recently owner of more than half the daily newspapers in Canada, along with *The Chicago Sun-Times*, *The London Daily Telegraph*, and *The Jerusalem Post*, you will very easily find out for yourself that they have self-consciously set out to take objectivity out of their media. None of them view their journals as anything less than a forum for their opinions, and any facts that get in the way of these opinions are quickly silenced. Don't take my word for it; do your own research and find out for yourself. (Sounds like a quote from Joe the Plumber.)

Until recently, the left held the higher ground in partisan criticism. Then there emerged a mirror image of right-wing hate in the form of much that was heard on Air America radio. The reason I bring this up is that Hurricane Katrina seemed to have brought out the worst in this monkey-see monkey-do bashing, and not only was it counter-productive, it was entirely unnecessary. The more intelligent members of the conservative press corps did the heavy lifting on this one, finally admitting that their fearless leaders went too far this time in their detachment from the reality that faces ordinary Americans. In the meantime, the right-wing hate machine wildly and desperately searched for anything and anyone else to blame—the Clintons, sadly for them, seemed to be unavailable for crucifying on this one—and were eventually hung on their own petards. It was not the time for the left to be copying the right's worst tendencies.

For example, suggestions of racism that came predictably from the Jesse Jackson/Al Sharpton wing, but also were echoed on Air America with regularity, were off target. To call it racism was a gross oversimplification; what we saw was the exposed underbelly of the class war that has been going on for around 35 years. The lid was sheared off in Hurricane Katrina; you and I weren't supposed to see this, but fortunately or unfortunately, Nature had other ideas. This little taste of "Third World America" exposed in our country the very dark side of the capitalism-at-all-costs mentality that the rest of the world has been subjected to for the last 30-plus years. The fact that around eighty percent of the people most affected by Hurricane Katrina's destruction were African-Americans was an economic condition, not an overtly racial one. Now, the fact that it *was* African-Americans mostly in this pitiable condition was turned into a racial issue faster than you could say "George Wallace," but the point is, the relief was not held up *because it was African-Americans who were suffering.* It is very important to get the criticism straight, and present it in a clear, civil manner.

There were those in certain corners of the fundamentalist Christian world that proclaimed that the city of New Orleans had it coming, that it was somehow a wicked place and God had sent His judgment upon its people. This was just bad theology. Jesus said in response to a similar statement concerning the Galileans whose blood Pilate had mixed with their sacrifices: "Do you suppose they were worse sinners than all others because they suffered such things? I tell you no; but unless you repent you will all likewise perish" (Luke 13:2-3).

President Bush delivered an address from the French Quarter that promised a virtual Marshall Plan for the Gulf Coast, a massive, federal government set of programs designed to completely rebuild the region. I thought the speech was well done. His problem came from the true conservatives in his own party, who viewed this gargantuan spending with great alarm. The President seemed to have been painted into an uncomfortable corner by the initial non-response of his administration to this disaster, and his subsequent poll numbers reflected an all-time low. The result of this was to have to produce over-the-top results in a Big Government way to prove that he really was the compassionate conservative that he claimed to be, and to regain a grip on the crisis leadership that was so much a part of his strength in the immediate aftermath of 9/11. This represented a sea change in ideology, methodology, and strategy that was bound to have an enormous impact not only on President Bush's legacy, but the 2006 and 2008 elections as well. By your deeds, Mr. President, by your deeds....

The outpouring of help from people all over the country and indeed, the world, gave us something to cheer about. It's as if people have this reservoir of giving and caring and compassion inside of them and they can't let it out within the confines of everyday life, but when there's a disaster, the top blows off and help flows like the rushing water through the broken levees.

One church, Second Baptist Church in Houston, pastored by Ed Young, became the hub of an interfaith army of volunteers almost 5000 strong, Christians, Muslims, Jews, Baha'i's, and many others, putting aside all conflicts of dogma to work together as God would wish all of His people to do in a time like this. There were hundreds of other, smaller stories of love and caring and of people of all faiths walking the walk and helping their fellow men and women in their time of need. A hopeful sign in a sad, sad story.

Meanwhile, the big three American oil behemoths announced record third quarter profits—this at a time when supposed shortages of oil and gas due to, among other things, the potent hurricane season, was allegedly supposed to be putting a real strain on their abilities to provide enough supply. There was a contemporaneous commercial on the radio from Chevron, but it could have well been from any of the others. It featured the CEO in a serious, "can we talk?" mode. He somberly stated that the recent hurricanes Katrina and Rita had put such a strain on supplies, that, unfortunately, gas prices had to rise to unprecedented levels. He then proceeded to implore motorists to "curtail unnecessary trips in the car," and, "drive 55 miles per hour rather than 65," and "to try not to accelerate too fast"; he then said something to the effect of "we're all in this together, and at Chevron, we're dedicated to do to everything blah blah blah...." Two days later record profits were announced. I wanted to put my fist through the radio.

29 / what i believe

I BELIEVE THAT WE SHOULD USE OUR enormous wealth and power to help those in the world less fortunate, by accident of birth, than we are. We must remember that we didn't have anything to do with where we were born, or under what economic or political conditions. Jesus said more about helping the poor than anything else, except maybe legalism. We must not buy into the lie that some people in the world are "beyond help" or are "born evil."

We must not shirk our responsibilities as the world's most powerful nation, but as such we must eschew violence in all but the most desperate of situations. For as we use violence, so will other nations model their violent behavior after ours. I believe that we should have a strong and powerful military, as befits the most powerful nation on earth, and should maintain enough strength to repel any attack from any two nations at the same time. I believe that our military should be centered on defense, and not on the capabilities to export our beliefs at the point of a gun. If a country is in need of our help militarily, they should request it through the proper international organizations. We should re-allocate "defense" spending to a greater vigilance of our borders and especially our ports. The huge volume of container shipping coming into our ports every day uninspected is one of the gravest threats Americans face.

I do not believe that simply throwing money at the poor (whether it is at home or abroad) is the solution to the problem of poverty. This was tried overseas in the 1970s and '80s and literally trillions of dollars were wasted on corrupt governments and dictators who simply squirreled the money away in Swiss or offshore banks. I agree with the decision of the Bush administration to tie loans and grants to Developing Nations to certain behavioral markers. We have that right as lenders. I do not, however, believe in "Tied Aid," which is the proviso that foreign aid to countries is contingent upon "buying American"; 70% of our foreign aid is tied aid. While this understandably helps out American business, it often puts aid workers in needy countries in the untenable position of either paying much more for a particular item, or trying to get their money elsewhere. Paying five times as much for an AIDS drug from an American pharmaceutical company as opposed to a generic version just means that five times fewer people will get the drug.

I believe that the American president should throw down the gauntlet to American industry and science to come up with an energy source that will make us independent of oil in ten years. This would be on the order of John F. Kennedy's pledge to land a man on the moon by the end of the 1960s.

I believe that we should rejoin the family of nations, and stop acting as if the United States owns the earth. There is a phrase in the entertainment industry, "You meet the same people on the way up that you do on the way down." If for no other reason, nations have memories, too. I believe that we are at a critical moment in the ecological life of our planet. It is up to the people of this and the next generation or two to reverse the terrible strain that unfettered industry and profligate energy use has put on the finite resources and mortal ecosystems of the earth. We cannot leave this problem for someone else.

I believe that Christians should release themselves from the clutches of the Religious Right, and become independent voters and thinkers, judging *all* issues on the moral teachings of Jesus Christ, and not just the narrow few offered by these groups, keeping in mind that Jesus said more about poverty and greed than he did about any other transgressions. I believe that "moral values" are not the property of the Republican Party, the Conservative Right, or Christian fundamentalists who happen to speak the loudest on this issue. Moral values represent a much larger spectrum of issues than these people even begin to approach.

I believe that I am not naive in thinking that there is a nonviolent way to resolve our problems internationally, and that it is not part of Jesus' teaching to kill an innocent person in order to save another innocent person. I believe that revenge, that most human of emotions, is not an option for Christians. I believe that the life of an Iraqi mother and her child is equal to the life of two New York stockbrokers, or two unborn fetuses. I believe that if politicians had to send their own children to war, there would be a lot less war.

I believe that the government should pay for elections, with each major candidate getting a set amount of money, and the campaign season running a set amount of weeks.

I believe the people of this country have done an incredible job within two generations in wiping out the social divide that existed between the white and the black races. There still remains a lot of work to be done to level the field economically. According to Internal Revenue Services statistics, the top one-tenth of one percent of Americans had more income in 2003 than the bottom one third of all Americans. Call me Red, but I don't think this is the least bit fair, or the least bit Christian.

I believe that people of other faiths around the world, whether misguided or not, believe in their faiths as much or more as we believe in ours, and for our political leaders to invoke the name of God in the righteousness of our cause only inflames tensions and hatred and turns what is a political problem into a clash of fundamentalisms.

I believe that the right to bear firearms, written into the Constitution when the country had less than two people per square mile and more dangerous wild animals than people, is dangerously and provably outdated, and causes more harm and misery than good. I believe that in the same way that you cannot yell "Fire!" in a crowded movie theater, companies mass-marketing violent video games to children (like the one that makes killing the most policemen the object of the game) should not be protected by freedom of speech laws. I believe that somewhere in the future, when historians and anthropologists are unraveling the details our culture, they will come to the conclusion that video games did much more harm to the progress of our society than anyone today can imagine.

I believe that the tragedy of 9/11 gave our nation a once-in-a-generation opportunity to lead the world by example and to model the qualities that once made our country the envy of the world; instead, they heard the rhetoric of the Old West, and saw the all too familiar "bomb early and bomb often" response that has sadly become our government's solution to resolving most conflicts. I believe that the United States can never be an honest broker in the Israeli-Palestinian tragedy because we are neither neutral nor impartial. I believe that Jerusalem should be an international city.

George W. Bush is counting on the "judgment of history"—a subject that he is woefully unfamiliar with—to retrieve his good standing from the dumpster of failed American presidents. He likens his predicament to Harry Truman, who ended his presidency with similar poll numbers but has been rehabilitated by more recent historians.

I believe that this will not happen to President Bush, and that history will render the judgment that he has been the worst president in the history of the United States of America.

31 / mr. negativity? nah...

WHAT, THEN AM I ADVOCATING? What do I want? Do I wish for our political system to come crashing down? Absolutely not! Do I want the United States to lose the war in Iraq? Absolutely not! I hear comments from people that insist that those of us who criticize the actions of our government would like to see its demise; that each loss of an American life in Iraq is cheered by those "anti-American" citizens in the same way that Jews who are critical of Israel are somehow glad to see innocent Israelis killed in a suicide bombing. In fact, nothing could be farther from the truth.

When the number of American military personnel killed in Iraq passed the 2000 mark, the 3000 mark, and then the 4000 mark, there were the typical blasts from the far right that this was a number that was bound to delight liberals, as if the death of American soldiers anywhere could possibly be a good thing. Not only is this insulting, but I think it is an opinion that has to be rebuffed and disposed of right now.

This has to be made very clear—to the extent that anyone who shares my beliefs could possibly wish any sort of defeat on our military is most certainly only doing so reluctantly for the express purpose of hoping for a quicker end to the involvement of our soldiers, and the swift returning of them home from a bad situation. I think there is a great deal of confusion and misunderstanding about this. There is room here for reasonable people to disagree.

Let me try an example: if you knew that in the course of a business deal gone terribly wrong that you could give up your car to save the life of your kids, I don't think anyone in their right mind would think twice about it. No one would accuse you of being anti-family in that situation. Reasonable people may argue over the terms of the original deal, but no one would begrudge you the wish for the safe return of your children. Likewise, a turn of events that might be viewed as a negative for our side in Iraq could therefore be viewed as a positive if it meant that our soldiers would be returning home sooner. I don't care if these soldiers volunteered or not; a great percentage of them didn't realize what they were signing up for, or in many cases they were led to believe something that turned out very differently in the event. It gets back to being able to support the troops without necessarily supporting the mission.

I've heard another analogy: If I was the passenger in a car that I was convinced was heading over a cliff, could I be accused of negativity for agitating for a change of course?

As a Christian, the decisions of my government have to square with my belief in the things that Jesus Christ lived and died for, or otherwise, I am going to have a problem with it. For me, being a Christian comes *before* being an American, and *way* before my declaration for a particular party. If this seems obvious, think of how you would have thought about this in, oh, say, 1997. Never mind the fact that the same people who supported the Bush administration's decisions until hell freezes over are the same people who were screaming the loudest at each and every misstep of Bill Clinton; there was precious little talk of patriotism and "supporting our leaders" then. Back then, it was all about the moral values of the man who inhabited the White House.

Conservative friends automatically assume that if I felt the way

I did about the Bush administration, then that must make me a *Hillary Clinton* fan (the words ooze out of their mouths, as they can hardly spit the name out), or a fan of some other Democrat; the truth is, I don't much like what I've heard from Ms. Clinton. I don't like the way she supported the war in Iraq, or the way she tries to out-hawk the male politicians. She also continues to give Israel a free pass no matter what they do. I have actually been a Barack Obama supporter from the day that he announced his candidacy for president.

My favorite politicians are the ones who are willing to take positions based on principle, not polls.

Name one.

Dennis Kucinich; Bernie Sanders; John McCain, until he ran for president in 2008.

Among the many sad things about politics these days is the almost slavish devotion of most politicians to stick their finger in the air to find out which way the political wind is blowing before venturing an opinion on anything.

John Murtha has been a Democratic congressman for thirty-two years. The burly Pennsylvanian has also been in the military for thirty-eight years. Murtha won two Purple Hearts, a Bronze Star with a Combat "V," and the Vietnamese Cross of Gallantry. Although a Democrat, the ex-Marine has always been known as a "hawk." Congressman Murtha initially supported the war in Iraq, as he did the 1st Gulf War, and conflicts in Central America. On November 17th, 2005, Murtha stunned the political world by calling for a pullout of troops from Iraq saying, "the troops have done all they can." Predictably, Republicans pounced all over John Murtha, calling him a coward and a traitor. Most of the "pouncers" never served in the military and wouldn't know bravery if it slapped them in the face. The sad attempt by Republicans to "swift-boat" Murtha, as they successfully did another war hero, 2004 Democratic nominee John Kerry, this time quickly crashed upon the rocks of its own absurdity. John Murtha looked deep

within his conscience, realized he had made a mistake in supporting the war, and was man enough to admit it.

I don't want my government to come crashing down; I just
want it to perform better. I want politicians to do the right thing
because it's the right thing to do, not because corporations paid
them to do it, or because it will help them get re-elected. The
Bush administration forced a quick vote on a war resolution just
before the 2002 mid-term elections, and most Democrats were
too afraid of being on the wrong side of the perception of patriotism to vote their consciences. Then, with the 2006 mid-term elections, we saw politician after politician, both Democrat and
Republican, jump off the war bandwagon. They demanded that
the troops come home, not because they thought the mission was
over, but because they didn't want to be on the wrong side of public opinion.

In Conclusion

I would like to see the citizens of our nation become more
engaged in what our elected officials are doing on their behalf in
this country and in the rest of the world. This necessarily involves
a trade-off of time in some way. Most people, to the extent that
they are even interested (and it never fails to surprise me when
people say they either never give what we do overseas much
thought, or they simply aren't interested), will complain that there
just isn't enough time in the day (or night) to spend on these
things. Heaven knows we're all too busy. Life in 21st-century
America, at least in my part of it, is seriously overbooked. Those
of you who have school-aged children know how complicated
just living life can be. The combination of affluence and fear has
turned our children's lives into a seemingly non-stop race from
one activity to the next; the days of sending your kids "out to
play" until dinnertime have long since past. Our nation's obses-
sion to turn out future technocrats has increased our children's
homework past the reasonable point in most households, with
many parents having to share the load.

If you have a job, chances are you work more than forty hours at it. If you want to stay healthy, you need to carve out time for whatever exercise you choose. If your town is anything like mine, you spend way too much time in your car. Add to this the stress for many of us of living right up to the edge of our means, and throw in some chronic sleep deprivation, and you have the formula by which so many Americans live. These are the problems of affluence.

Given all of this, where does one possibly find the time to even begin to get educated about the oftentimes arcane world of foreign policy, or the economic workings of our government? It's no wonder that most people think themselves doing well if they just catch the drift of what's going on in the world. This is why most news these days is disseminated in bite-sized bits; this is what gave rise to the sound-bite. Politicians have understood for quite some time that most Americans catch their news on the run, so they've tailored their messages to take advantage of this. In-depth analysis is becoming harder and harder to come by.

In this hectic and harried state of mind, we look to the Great American Culture Machine to take our minds off our problems and escape the drudgery of everyday life. I'm always amazed at surveys that reveal how much television we watch as a nation. I don't think most people would go on record to admit the truth about their TV viewing. We never stop and add it up. If we did, it might be a little embarrassing. True enough, the computer has carved into this time to a varying degree. The Internet has taken its place right along side of the television in its ability to provide endless hours of mind-numbing entertainment.

What we watch, to a greater or lesser degree, are shows about other people living their lives. We spend a tremendous amount of our down time watching actors depict so-called "regular" people doing either mundane things (shows like *Friends, Seinfeld, King of Queens, Will & Grace,* and *Everybody Loves Raymond*), or actors depicting regular people doing important or extraordinary things (all your *CSI's, Cold Case, The West Wing, ER, Law & Order, Lost,*

NYPD Blue, Alias, The X-Files, 24), or actors depicting regular people doing "bad" things (*The Sopranos, Desperate Housewives, Sex and the City*, most soap operas). We watch a whole lot of "regular" people do all sorts of things, from the stupid or dangerous (*Fear Factor, Survivor, Temptation Island, America's Funniest Home Videos, Crocodile Hunter, Cops, Jerry Springer, WifeSwap*), to the mundane (*Trading Spaces, Real World, Growing Up Gotti, Airline*, watching Poker on TV), to watching "regular" people strive to do things we wish we could do (*American Idol, Extreme Makeover, Who Wants To Be A Millionaire, The Amazing Race, The Apprentice, Making the Band*).[31] There is more than a little of what the Germans call *Schadenfruede*, or pleasure in other people's misfortune, in watching many of these programs. There is also a whole network devoted to what actors do when they're not acting and what celebrities do when they do what they do (E!). In fact, the whole industry of celebrity is built on the premise that you and I are on average more interested in the ups and downs of Brad Pitt and Angelina Jolie's relationship or Tom Cruise and Katie Holmes' spiritual choices, or Britney Spears and Lindsey Lohan's meltdowns, or where Paris Hilton is shopping, than the serious business of what is going on in the rest of the world. We haven't even touched on the viewing of sporting events, when sports may be the biggest thing of all that we watch other people do.

Believe it or not, the government (and here I am speaking of it in a broader sense than just this administration) hopes you are more interested in Tom and Katie, and Lindsey and Paris, too. They hope that you are so preoccupied with work, getting the kids to one activity after another, and then watching other people do things on TV, that you won't have time to even try to understand the finer points of NAFTA, or globalization in general, or pre-emptive strikes, or the Patriot act, or the Kyoto Accords, or global warming, or alternative and sustainable energies, or why we have over 700 military bases in over 90 countries, or Free Trade versus Fair Trade, or why *exactly* are we in Iraq again?, or any of the promises that politicians trot out every two, four, or six years when they have our attention around election time. The great national sedatives of television and celebrity do the job quite nicely, leaving Americans with little time or space left in their brains to ponder the larger issues of the day. When the whole country is more concerned with who gets kicked off of the island than what is going on in Iraq, or who gets the hook on *Idol* more than how we turned a multi-*trillion* dollar surplus into a multi-*trillion* dollar deficit, or who gets fired from *The Apprentice* more than the brutal effects of economic globalization, then the government has us just where they want us.

I know a popular response to what I have just written will be something like this: "I *do* work too much, spend *way* too long in my car, run a taxicab service for my kids, don't *even* have time to exercise, so when I finally have time to relax, the last thing I want to think about is starving kids in Malawi, or NAFTA, or WMD's." This is a point well taken, and to be honest, I feel the same way much of the time. In fact, until a few years ago, this would've been very close to my own response. This whole spiel doesn't even take into account the fact that many people have worthy hobbies, or go to Bible studies, or participate in sports, or practice a craft, or write in journals, or read books, or walk the dog, or just have quality family time in what spare time they have.

Paul says in Romans 12:2, "Do not be conformed to this world, but be transformed by the renewing of your mind, that you may prove what is that good and acceptable and perfect will of God." Does this mean that we can't relax? Or that we can't have some "veg" time? Of course not. God rested on the Sabbath. If we want to indulge ourselves in a little mindless entertainment once in awhile, this not only acceptable, but is probably a good thing. I think what Paul is trying to say here is that we don't want to become so enveloped by the things in the world, in this case, the living of our lives through others, that we forego the renewing of our own minds in the process.

So, in lieu of all of these counter arguments, I have to come up with a really compelling reason why it is so important to spend some of this "down" time learning about why it is we do the things as a country that we do. Hopefully, if you've gotten this far in the book, I've already more or less made that case.

If I am bold enough and humble enough to call myself a Christian, then how can I be anything *but* against war? Where is it that Jesus says it is okay to do unto others what I wouldn't want done to me? If I am rightfully appalled at the evil inflicted on innocent people at the World Trade Center and at the Pentagon, then shouldn't I be appalled at each and every civilian who is killed at the hands of our military? What sort of moral relativism gives me the right to accept these deaths? As an individual, I can't stop my government from perpetrating this violence in response to violence. I can only register my own dissent, and I can pray that God will give our leaders the wisdom to find solutions to their grievances in a more peaceful way. I can write my representatives in Congress, and write the administration. I can write letters to the editor of my local newspaper. I can voice my opinion in polls, as it is very important to let politicians know that Christians are on the side of peace. All these things are infinitely easier to do in the Age of the Internet. Never in history has violence cured violence. It has only led to more violence. Thomas Merton said, "When I pray for peace, I pray not only that the enemies of my country may cease to want war, but above all that my own country will cease to do the things that make war inevitable."

If I dare call myself a Christian then I must seek the Truth. The first truth is that I am a sinner. I must acknowledge that nothing in my life will truly get better if do not admit that I fall short of God's expectations. We've all known people who think they are always right. We don't consider this boasting to be a strength; on the contrary, it points out all too obviously this person's weakness. We've all had times in our lives when we've mistakenly thought we were right. I know I have. I also know that I have stubbornly clung to my convictions even in the face of overwhelming evidence to the contrary. Likewise, President Bush calls himself a Christian, and I believe him. He therefore must know how hypocritical it has been to never ever admit that he has made a mistake. I can only assume that he has felt as the leader of the most powerful nation on earth, it would be a sign of weakness to admit any sort of fallibility. The rest of the world views the constant bellowing of invincibility and infallibility as weakness of character. I believe it has planted the seeds of further conflict in the future. This macho yet childish position flies in the face of everything he must know about Jesus. I can't stop the President from embarrassing himself and endangering our country in this way. I can only register my dissent through the voting booth, and through writing him to say that as a Christian I am appalled by his behavior, and pray that God will show him the path towards truthfulness and humility. For these are signs of strength, not weakness.

If I am to bear the name "Christian," then I must be conscious of the tremendous gift of material prosperity that God has given me personally, and our country collectively, and the admonition that "to whom much is given, much will be required." This passage has local, as well as global significance. It is about service. Service is a word that is analogous to the hub of a wheel. There are as many ways to be of service as our imagination will allow ourselves to conceive. They are spelled out in detail in Romans 12:6-8. Paul could have spent many pages elaborating on this passage, and we can extend this list to include the needs of our community and the world that apply specifically to life in the twenty-first century. Being of service does *not* necessarily assume that you have to leave the comforts of your own home. This is a great barrier to some who cherish the time they have at home with their families, or some who, for a variety of reasons, are confined to their homes. If you have a computer and Internet service (an assumption of American affluence on my part), you can be of great service in the transmission of information, the rendering of opinion, and the furthering of all sorts of worthy causes. As the most powerful nation on earth, the United States has the tremendous opportunity to use this power for the betterment of mankind. They also have the capacity to abuse their power through economic bullying, unilateral military action, and ignoring international law. I can't change my government's position on free (fair) trade and the unfair aspects of globalization, but I can make my opinion known by registering my dissent through the writing of letters and emails both to my local Congressmen and women, and to the letters and forum sections of my local newspapers, and I can pray that God will help our leaders find more compassion for others less fortunate. I can pray that God will help our leaders turn our swords into plowshares, and our guns into butter. This would not be a sign of weakness, but a sign of strength.

I hope that my children don't grow up with the same misunderstanding of history that I had. I would like them to be aware of the idea that in any historical rendering, they are often getting only one side of the story. The winners get to write the history. Our schools have made progress over the last thirty years in starting to balance the scales. I would like to think that if our children are taught the whole truth about our country's history, both the good and the bad, they will be better equipped to make intelligent choices about their shared futures. If they are only presented the sanitized version, then they are apt to perpetuate and pass on the myths that are in some measure responsible for the chasm between the way we see ourselves, and the way the rest of the world sees us. While I certainly can't change history, and I can't do very much about the way most people learn history, I can register my opinion by sending letters and e-mails to people in positions of power, and by participating in school board meetings. I can also pray that God will allow the powers-that-be that decide what goes into our history textbooks to see the wisdom in telling the whole truth about our history so that our children will be equipped with the full knowledge they need to lead our country into the next fifty years.

As a child of God, I have been given a share of the stewardship and dominion over the earth and its living things. I need to respect these living things as God's creations, and not abuse the privilege so graciously given me. As the most powerful nation in the world, and the leading contributor of harmful greenhouse gases, the United States should be taking the lead in trying to slow down the environmental degradation that is resulting in global warming. Instead, in the face of overwhelming evidence, the Bush administration acted as though the entire science community is wrong and the whole global warming crisis is a creation of environmental wackos. I can't change my government's position on the environment except to vote them out of office, but I can make changes in my lifestyle that conserve energy and preserve the environment. I can also register my dissent from the environmental policies of this administration and pray that God will grant our new leaders the wisdom to make choices concerning the stewardship of this planet that will leave it in better, not worse shape than they found it.

I spent the first twenty-five years of my adult life basically taking up space. I could tell you *what* I believed on a variety of political issues, but my knowledge base was shallow. I couldn't tell you *why* I believed what I believed, except to parrot vague bits of things that I had heard. We all, as citizens of the United States of America, face the individual choice of whether we're even going to pay attention while *our* government tramples on the original ideals set out by the Founding Fathers. If we don't, then we have absolutely nothing to complain about. The Constitution is a great document, a much-copied model of representative democracy that is one of our greatest exports. However, it isn't perfect. It was a product of the time that it was conceived and of the men who wrote it. The failures to exclude slavery and the lack of voting rights for all Americans were only two prominent examples of issues that had to be tackled by various amendments and a Civil War. The only way to move the government in any great way is through mass activism. Abolition, the women's vote, the civil rights movement, and the opposition to the Vietnam War were all fueled by mass citizen action, and most of these history-changing events were led by what we would today call liberal Christians.

Voting is essential, but sadly, it is not on its own enough. Politicians need to know that their promises made during the election season need to be kept and that their actions between elections will be closely monitored.

The coalition of far-right conservatives and the evangelical movement led by the likes of Jerry Falwell and Pat Robertson understood these concepts very well. They created a mass movement based on the large databases collected from church rosters and viewers of their television programs whose energy and single-mindedness outflanked their opponents time and time again.[32] They learned that by deluging corporations, television stations, politicians, and the print media with letters, e-mails, and phone calls, they could have an impact that far exceeded their numbers. This coalition has reaped the benefits of an admirable work ethic with results that would have surprised even the most optimistic of them thirty years ago. But what is good for the far right wing has not proven to be good for the country, for reasons that I hope I have adequately elaborated on in this book.

For those of us who are followers of Jesus, there is even less excuse to sit idly by as our government engages in practices that are morally and ethically unacceptable. Despite the unholy alliance between the Far Right and a large swath of the evangelical Christian community, the ideological precepts of the right wing are not compatible with the concepts that Jesus taught and that He died for. Evangelicals—unfortunately many who are led by gullible pastors with questionable political instincts—have been practically brainwashed into believing that the only political choice they have is from the center-right to the far, far right. This is emphatically, biblically untrue. Any sober reading of the four Gospels, centering in on Jesus' words, tells a completely different story. I hope that I have shed enough light on this throughout the book as well.

We desperately need to change the face of Christianity back to Jesus'. Too many people in this world think of all sorts of unsavory and most definitely fallible human beings when the word

"Christian" is uttered. It is a dirty, unpleasant word for millions upon millions of people. Not that Jesus needs our help, but the only way for us to participate in changing these unfortunate perceptions is by taking Jesus back from the right-wing clique who hijacked him some thirty years ago. These people have acted since then as if Jesus was their personal property while almost completely ignoring the actual things that He said. The constant stream of negativity and ranting about anything that is not in their agenda has gone on for too long without an adequate response. I've had enough of it. That's why I wrote this book. I hope that I have presented an alternate view of how we should look at our American history and how to interpret both this history and the actions of our government through the only lens that matters: that of our Lord and Savior, Jesus Christ.

afterword: the election of barack obama

WHEN I STARTED WRITING THIS BOOK in the Spring of 2005, Barack Obama was barely on my political radar. I had been impressed by his Democratic Convention speech in 2004, and there was no doubt that he had a bright political future, but that future seemed eight to twelve years away. When I heard that he was running for president in 2008, I thought it was a trial run, not unlike John F. Kennedy in 1956—getting his feet wet, getting his name into the arena, but not to be taken too seriously yet.

The Democratic nomination for president in 2008 was Hillary Clinton's to lose. The Clintons were Democratic Party royalty. Despite large negative numbers from conservatives, there seemed to be no one else on the Democratic side with the organization in place, the ability to fundraise, and the charisma and experience that Hillary and her husband, former president Bill Clinton, had. The Iowa Caucus, held January 3rd, 2008, changed all of that.

Hillary Clinton found herself, out-organized, out-managed, and out-hustled by an inspired group of Obama supporters, and suddenly, the game was on.

By the time this book hits the shelves (or cyber-shelves), there will already be at least a half-dozen books by well-known authors and journalists recounting in minute detail the amazing and historic Campaign of 2008, in which the people of the United States of America elected the first (half) African-American as President. My goal in these last few pages is simply to find out, as a perfect bookend to the book, why this is such a happy event for me, and such an unhappy one for most evangelical Christians.

First of all, I know that the tragic and catastrophic events of the last four-to-eight years have left even many evangelicals scratching their heads and wondering if gay marriage is really a strong enough issue for them to endure four more years of this mess. The very people in which the Christian right invested so much of their support have run our country into the ground. For those Christians who have consistently made abortion the litmus test for any candidate to elective office, the last eight years have proven that being pro-life means much more than this single issue. We, as in "we the people," who put into power a regime that killed hundreds of thousands of people in a war that they lied to the country to fight, "we the people," who voted twice for a Christian president who went against sixty years of international law to allow torture of prisoners of war, "we the people," who voted not once, but twice, for an administration that has almost irreparably weakened our country both domestically and in the eyes of the rest of the world, "we" have gotten exactly what we deserved. And yet, here in my home state of California, with the economy falling apart, foreclosures rising beyond the unthinkable level, stores closing, and people being thrown out of work, evangelical Christians have succeeded in leading the way once again in trying to deny gays the legal right to marry. This narrow-minded, fear-based thinking is what gave us the presidency of George W. Bush, and his re-election in 2004 is what drove me to write this book.

On Election Night, John McCain made the most elegant, humble concession speech I have ever heard.[33] When he urged his supporters to unite behind the new President-elect, they booed. This represented a fitting picture of the two Americas that we currently live in.

I listen, watch, and read more right-wing media than is healthy for anyone, especially for one whose views are so diametrically opposed. I have long felt that it was a necessary function of being completely well informed, and that I needed to walk the talk of this book. To absorb the information masquerading as fact that is spewed each and every day by these media is to truly place oneself in an alternate universe. In this world, Barack Obama is an anti-American, terrorist, Muslim, socialist, whose election to president will mark the beginning of the United States of Socialist Amerika. This ugliness, particularly as it manifested itself in late campaign rallies of both Vice Presidential nominee Sarah Palin and John McCain, bordered on the truly dangerous, as it takes only one hyped up wing-nut with a rifle to put deed to words.

Even more disconcerting was the headline in a "Faith2Action" commentary by Janet Porter on WorldNetDaily.com: "You Cannot be a Christian and Vote for Obama." I will just quote the first sentence: "To all those who name the name of Christ who plan to willfully disobey Him by voting for Obama, take warning. Not only is our nation in grave danger, according to the Word of God, so are *you*." (Italics in the original.) Dr. James Dobson churlishly and childishly prayed for rain to come down on Barack Obama's outdoor acceptance speech at the Democratic Convention in his home state of Colorado, only to have the not-amused Man Upstairs deliver Hurricane Ike on the day of the opening of the Republican Convention. Dobson, who is second in prescient prophecy only to the Reverend Pat Robertson, wrote a sixteen-page "Letter from 2012 in Obama's America" that is a summation of every real or perceived fear that white evangelical America could possibly imagine short of Armageddon.

I honestly don't know where these Christians have been the last eight years. Using any metaphor you like, how far in the sand does one's head need to be buried, how far under the rug does one need to sweep the disaster that has befallen this country? People all over the world are now rejoicing! Our friends, allies, neutrals, and yes, some enemies. All these people, who *cannot be dismissed,* who are our neighbors in an ever-shrinking world, understand that something that has been treasured for so long and been most recently lost—that "something" being the Good that America stands for, the decency of our values and the greatness of our Constitution—has a chance to be renewed now that the long, dark shadow of arrogance and hubris and biggest-bully-on-the-block behavior has been finally shown the door. When the American people, led by the evangelical Christian right, voted *a second time* for George W. Bush in 2004, the people of the rest of the world began to stop delineating between the American government and the American people. *You* are *they*, was the logic.

Now, if only for a moment, our nation has reason to hold its collective head high. For there indeed is hope of a better relationship with the rest of the world, a chance to truly lead by example. Much of the world welcomes our leadership, as long as it is within the bounds of our Constitution and International Law. It seems funny to even have to write that, but after the last eight years, it sadly must be said. We *are* the leaders of the Free World, as long as we do unto others as we would have them do to us. We *are* the "bastion of freedom," as long as we don't expect a different set of rules for us than for the rest of the world. We *can* be again a nation that other nations want to model themselves after, but for the right reasons, reasons of true freedom, liberty, and democracy, not because we allow torture and create pre-emptive wars, and change international law as we deem fit.

Will President Barack Obama be perfect? Of course not! He has said as much already; he has said he will fail, a refreshing bit of humility not once broached in the last eight years. It will take quite awhile to turn this Titanic around. As a Christian, as a follower of Jesus Christ, I have hope that the secular principles that embody the definition of the word "liberal"—along with the spiritual principles—embody the words and deeds of Jesus, and will come together for the betterment of not only the United States of America, but for the whole world. I love my country, and tonight I will sleep better than I have in a long time.

notes

1   Reverend Jim Wallis has written several fine books, among them, are *The Soul of Politics: Beyond "Religious Right" and Secular Left"*, *Who Speaks for God?: An Alternative to the Religious Right—A New Politics*, and probably his best known work, *God's Politics: Why the Right Doesn't Get It and the Left Gets It Wrong*, while Rabbi Michael Lerner's best-known works include *The Politics of Meaning: Restoring Hope and Possibility in an Age of Cynicism*, *Healing Israel/Palestine: A Path to Peace and Reconciliation*, and *The Left Hand of God: Taking Back Our Country From the Religious Right*.

2   See Part One of Paul Johnson's *A History of Christianity* (Simon & Schuster, 1976) for more detail on the early battles over what constituted heresy.

3   For more on this, see Bruce Bawer's *Stealing Jesus: How Fundamentalism Betrays Christianity* (Three Rivers Press, 1997).

4   Called COINTELPRO, this FBI program, run from 1956 until 1971, was initially supposed to infiltrate communist groups in America, but eventually made its way into the Peace movement and the civil rights movement.

5   The list of right-wing talk show hosts that went on the trip
    included: Melanie Morgan (KSFO, San Francisco), Mark
    Williams (KFBK, Sacramento), Martha Zoller (WDUN,
    Atlanta), John Batchelor (WABC NY), Michael Graham
    (WMAL, DC), and Lt. Col. Buzz Patterson. The trip was from
    July 13–18, 2005.

6   I particularly enjoyed Tuchman's *The Proud Tower*, and *The
    March of Folly: From Troy to Vietnam*, Robert Massie's
    Dreadnought, *Castles of Steel*, and *Peter the Great*, David
    McCullough's *The Path Between the Seas*, and *Truman*, Stephen
    Ambrose's *Crazy Horse and Custer: The Parallel Lives of Two
    American Warriors*, and *Undaunted Courage: Meriwether Lewis,
    Thomas Jefferson, and the Owning of the American West*, and
    *Nothing Like it in the World: The Men Who Built the
    Transcontinental Railroad 1863-1869*, and I devoured every-
    thing Alison Weir wrote about Medieval England.

7   See *1421: The Year China Discovered America* (William Morrow,
    2003) by Gavin Menzies for more on this.

8   I got a lot of pertinent information about national myths, par-
    ticularly America's through the films of Hollywood, in
    American Dream/Global Nightmare (Icon Books, 2004), by
    Ziauddin Sardar and Merryl Wyn Davies.

9   These statistics were taken from The Program on
    International Policy Attitudes and GlobeScan Incorporated.
    PIPA is a joint program of the Center on Policy Attitudes and
    the Center for International and Security Studies at the
    University of Maryland. PIPA undertakes research on atti-
    tudes in both the public and in the policymaking communi-
    ty toward a variety of international and foreign policy issues.
    It seeks to disseminate its findings to members of govern-
    ment, the press, and the public as well as academia.
    GlobeScan is a global public opinion and stakeholder
    research firm with offices in Toronto, London, and

Washington. GlobeScan conducts custom research and annual tracking studies on global issues. With a research network spanning 40+ countries, GlobeScan works with global companies, multilateral agencies, national governments and non-government organizations to deliver research-based insights for successful strategies.

10 There is a great website www.globalissues.org that covers these and many similar issues related to spending on poverty, U.S. military spending, world health issues, conflicts in Africa, and a wealth of other topics.

11 For more on greedy Sub-Saharan dictators, read *The Fate of Africa: From the Hopes of Freedom to the Heart of Despair* (Perseus Books, 2005), by Martin Meredith.

12 There is a documentary film based around this address, called *Why We Fight*, which explains in detail the American military-industrial complex that Eisenhower warned about.

13 Much of the information in the next two chapters comes from the following books: *The End of Oil* (Houghton Mifflin, 2004), by Paul Roberts, *Blood and Oil* (Metropolitan Books, 2004), by Michael T. Klare, *Secrets of the Kingdom* (Random House, 2005), by Gerald Posner, and *Hatred's Kingdom* (Regnery Publishing, 2003).

14 While there is an absolute treasure trove of material from all sides of the Israeli/Palestinian conflict, one book I found extremely helpful was *Healing Israel/Palestine: A Path to Peace and Reconciliation* (Tikkun Books, 2003), by Rabbi Michael Lerner. Another is Motti Golani's *From Civil War to Interstate War and Back Again: The War Over Israel/Palestine 1945-2000*. For the Palestinian/Arab perspective, I would suggest Edward Said, Hanan Ashrawi, or the articles of journalist Rami Khouri. British journalist Robert Fisk has lived in Beirut, Lebanon, for over thirty years and has a fine-tuned sense of the pulse of the Middle East.

15 For more on the subject of the non-violence inside the Civil Rights movement, read Taylor Branch's epic three-part history of America in the Martin Luther King Years: *Parting the Waters, Pillars of Fire,* and *At Canaan's Edge* (Simon & Schuster, 1988, 1998, 2006), as well as *The Children* (Fawcett, 1998), by David Halberstam, *Walking With the Wind: A Memoir of the Movement* (Harvest Books, 1999), by John Lewis and Michael D'Orso, and *Voices in Our Blood* (Random House, 2001), edited by Jon Meacham.

16 There are so many books about the folly in Iraq; just the books written by former administration officials and ex-military and intelligence people are too many to list here. The unanimity of voices condemning this catastrophe is astounding. I have listed the books that were essential to my research in the bibliography.

17 James Bamford, "The Man Who Sold the War," *Rolling Stone Magazine,* November 17th, 2005.

18 A great read on the background of our adventure in Afghanistan is *Ghost Wars: The Secret History of the CIA, Afghanistan, and Bin Laden, From the Soviet Invasion to September 10th, 2001* (Penguin Books, 2004). Another is *America's Secret War: Inside the Hidden Worldwide Struggle between America and its Enemies* (Broadway Books, 2004) by George Friedman.

19 www.christianalliance.org

20 Seymour Hersh's book *Chain of Command: The Road from 9/11 to Abu Ghraib* (HarperCollins, 2004), is yet another devastating indictment of the Bush administration's hubris.

21 *Washington Post,* May 23rd, 2005, Josh White.

22 See *The Illusion of Victory* (Basic Books, 2003), by Thomas Fleming, for more on the Wilson government's curtailment of free speech during World War I.

23 Figure taken from the Center for Arms Control and Non-proliferation FY 2009 Pentagon Spending Request. http://www.armscontrolcenter.org/policy/securityspending/ar ticles/fy09_dod_request_global/. This is a great place to see how your tax dollars are being spent.

24 This idea has been widely disseminated by Rabbi Michael Lerner, most recently in his book, *The Left Hand of God: Taking Back Our Country From the Religious Right*, and is one the founding principles of the Network of Spiritual Progressives, of which Lerner is the co-founder.

25 The information about the Gablers comes largely from *With God on our Side: The Rise of the Religious Right in America* (Broadway Books, 1996), by William Martin.

26 The entire subject of the similarity of fundamentalist thought between the major religions and the dangers involved is covered beautifully by one of my favorite writers, Tariq Ali, in *The Clash of Fundamentalisms* (Verso Books, 2002).

27 A particularly good book on how Western hyper-capitalism affects the rest of the Developing world is *The No-Nonsense Guide to World Poverty* (New Internationalist Publications Ltd., 2003), by Jeremy Seabrook. In fact, there are a whole slew of "No-Nonsense" guides on a range of world problems. These books are small, full of facts, and well written, and I would highly recommend them. http://www.newint.org/pub-lications/no-nonsense-guides/ Another book that was helpful in this area was *Another World is Possible if...* (Verso, 2004), by Susan George.

28 Two books to recommend here are, *Globalization and its Discontents* (W.W Norton & Company, 2002), which won the Nobel Prize in Economics for its author, Joseph E. Stiglitz, and *The End of Poverty* (Penguin Books, 2005), by Jeffrey Sachs.

29 Three books that provided information in this chapter are: *The Republican Noise Machine* (Three Rivers Pres, 2004), by David Brock, *Big Lies* (Thomas Dunne Books, 2003), by Joe Conason, and *What Liberal Media?: The Truth About* BIAS *and the News* (Basic Books, 2003), by Eric Alterman. Also, the book that inspired Alterman's book, *BIAS* (Regnery Publishing, 1996), by Bernard Goldberg.

30 *The Way Things Aren't: Rush Limbaugh's Reign of Error* (The New Press, 1995), Steven Rendell, Jim Naureckas, and Jeff Cohen.

31 I admit that this list is out of date. I don't watch much TV at this point in my life, so I couldn't comment on the up-to-the-moment equivalents of these shows.

32 See *American Theocracy* (Viking, 2006), by Kevin Phillips, and *With God on our Side: The Rise of the Religious Right*, by William Martin.

33 This got me thinking about some recent losing presidential candidates. In 1996, Republican Bob Dole came across during the campaign as a cranky old man. Immediately following the election, starting with an appearance on David Letterman, he displayed a charming, self-deprecating sense of humor that would have been a real asset to his campaign. In 2000, Democrat Al Gore was seen as wooden, whiny, and excessively wonky, but in the years that followed, he displayed a vigorous passion not only for the environment, but also as one of the lone politicians with clout on either side of the aisle to consistently and forcefully oppose the war in Iraq. If he had been even half as passionate during the campaign, he almost certainly would have won what was the closest election in American history. And now, in 2008, John McCain apparently took the poisoned advice of the men who so viciously defeated him in the primaries of 2000, and became an angry, negative campaigner, more like the candidate Dole than the

maverick McCain. It seemed to bother him during the campaign, which would account for the lurching political movements that he displayed throughout. Finally released from the shackles of the race, John McCain on Election Night became again the man that so many people, including me, had admired for so long.

bibliography

Ali, Tariq, *The Clash Of Fundamentalisms*, Verso/New Left Books, 2002.

Ali, Tariq, *Bush in Babylonm*, Verso/New Left Books, 2003.

Ali, Tariq, & Barsamian, David, *Conversations With Tariq Ali: Speaking of Empire and   Resistance,* The New Press, 2005.

Alterman, Eric, *What Liberal Media?*, Basic Books, 2003.

Barsamian, David, *Louder Than Bombs*, South End Press, 2004.

Bawer, Bruce, *Stealing Jesus*, Three Rivers Press, 1997.

Beacon Anthology, *The Power of Nonviolence*, Beacon Press, 2002.

Bello, Walden, *The Dilemmas of Domination: The Unmaking of the American Empire*, Metropolitan Books, 2005.

Bergreen, Laurence, *Over the Edge of the World*, William Morrow/HarperCollins, 2003.

Berry, Wendell, & Duncan, David James, *Citizens Dissent,*

Blum, William, *Freeing the World To Death*, Common Courage Press, 2005.

Boal, Iaian, Clark, T.J., Matthews, Joseph, Watts, Michael, *Afflicted Powers*, Verso/New Left Books, 2005.

Branch, Taylor, *Parting The Waters, America In The King Years 1954-63*, Simon & Schuster, 1988.

Branch, Taylor, *Pillar Of Fire, America In The King Years 1963-65*, Simon & Schuster, 1998.

Brock, David, *The Republican Noise Machine*, Three Rivers Press, 2004.

Chomsky, Noam, *Imperial Ambitions: Conversations on the Post-9/11 World*, Metropolitan Books/Henry Holt and Company, 2005.

Chomsky, Noam, *Failed States: The Abuse of Power and the Assault on Democracy*, Metropolitan Books/Henry Holt and Company, 2006.

Coll, Steve, *Ghost Wars*, Penguin Books, 2004.

Conason, Joe, *Big Lies*, Thomas Dunne Books, 2003.

Cushman, Thomas, ed., *A Matter of Principle*, University of California Press, 2005.

Fallaci, Orianna, *The Rage and the Pride*, Rizzoli International Publications, 2001.

Ferguson, Niall, *Colossus*, The Penguin Press, 2004.

Fischer, David Hackett, *Historians' Fallacies*, HarperPerennial, 1970.

Fleming, Thomas, *The Illusion of Victory*, Basic Books, 2003.

Friedman, George, *America's Secret War*, Doubleday Books/Broadway Books, 2004.

Frank, Thomas, *What's the Matter With Kansas*, Henry Holt and Company, 2004.

Gardner, Lloyd C., and Marilyn Young, *The New American Empire*, The New Press, 2005.

Gareau, Frederick H., *State Terrorism and the United States*, Clarity Press, Inc./Zed Books, 2004.

George, Susan, *Another World Is Possible If...*, Verso, 2004.

Gladwell, Malcolm, *The Tipping Point*, Back Bay Books/Little, Brown and Company, 2000.

Glover, Jonathan, *Humanity: A Moral History of the Twentieth Century*, Yale Nota Bene, 2001.

Gold, Dore, *Hatred's Kingdom*, Regnery Publishing, 2003.

Gordon, Michael R., and General Bernard E. Trainor, *Cobra II: The Inside Story of the Invasion and Occupation of Iraq*, Pantheon Books, 2006.

Halberstam, David, *The Children*, Fawcett Books/Ballentine Publishing/Random House, 1998.

Hall, Anthony J., *The American Empire and the Fourth World*, McGill-Queen's University Press, 2003.

Halstead, Ted, ed., *The Real State of the Union*, Basic Books, 2004.

Hart, D.G., *Deconstructing Evangelism*, Baker Books, 2004.

Hersh, Seymour M., *Chain of Command*, HarperCollins, 2004.

Jensen, Derrick, *The Culture of Make Believe*, Chelsea Green Publishing Company, 2004.

Johnson, Chalmers, *Blowback: The Costs and Consequences of American Empire*, Metropolitan Books, 2002.

Johnson, Chalmers, *The Sorrows of Empire*, Henry Holt & Company, 2004.

Kick, Russ, ed., *You Are Being Lied To*, The Disinformation Company Ltd., 2001.

Kick, Russ, ed., *Everything You Know Is Wrong*, The Disinformation Company Ltd., 2002.

Kick, Russ, ed., *Abuse Your Illusions*, The Disinformation Company Ltd., 2003.

Klare, Michael T., *Blood and Oil*, Owl Books, Henry Holt & Co., 2004.

Krugman, Paul, *The Great Unraveling: Losing Our Way in the New Century*, W.W. Norton & Company, 2005.

Lakoff, George, *don't think of an elephant!*, Chelsea Green Publishing Company, 2004.

Lance, Peter, *1000 Years For Revenge*, ReganBooks/HarperCollins, 2003.

Laqueur, Walter, *No End To War*, Continuum International Publishing, 2003.

Lerner, Rabbi Michael, *The Politics of Meaning*, Addison-Wesley Publishing, 1996.

Lerner, Rabbi Michael, *Healing Israel/Palestine*, Tikkun Books/North Atlantic Books, 2003.

LeVine, Mark, *Why They Don't Hate Us: Lifting the Veil on the Axis of Evil*, Oneworld Publications Ltd., 2005.

Macmillan, Margaret, *Paris 1919*, Random House, 2003.

Mahajan, Rahul, *Full Spectrum Dominance*, Seven Stories Press, 2003.

Martin, William, *With God On Our Side*, Broadway Books, 1996.

McLaren, Brian D., *A Generous Orthodoxy*, Youth Specialty Books/Zondervan, 2004.

McCullough, David, *John Adams*, Simon & Schuster, 2001.

Menzies, Gavin, *1421 The Year China Discovered America*, William Morrow/HarperCollins, 2003.

Meredith, Martin, *The Fate of Africa: A History of Fifty Years of Independence,* Public Affairs, 2005.

Miller, Bruce J., with Diana Maio, *Take Them At Their Words*, Academy Chicago Publishers, 2004.

Nagler, Michael N., *The Search For A Nonviolent Future*, Inner Ocean Publishing, 2004.

Palast, Greg, *Armed Madhouse*, Dutton, 2006.

Pearse, Meic, *Why The Rest Hates The West*, InterVarsity Press, 2004.

Phillips, Kevin, *American Theocracy*, Viking, 2006.

Phillips, Peter, ed., *Censored 2005*, Seven Stories Press, 2004.

Pinker, Steven, *The Blank Slate: The Modern Denial of Human Nature*, Viking, 2002.

Posner, Gerald, *Secrets of the Kingdom: The Inside Story of the Saudi-U.S. Connection*, Random House, 2005.

Power, Samantha, *A Problem From Hell: America and the Age of Genocide*, Flamingo, 2002.

Prestowitz, Clyde, *Rogue Nation*, Basic Books, 2003.

Reid, T.R., *The United States of Europe*, Penguin Books, 2004.

Ricks, Thomas, *Fiasco,* The Penguin Press, 2006.

Roberts, Paul, *The End of Oil*, Houghton Mifflin Co., 2004.

Roth, John D., *Choosing Against War*, Good Books, 2002.

Roy, Arundhati, and Barsamian, David, *The Checkbook and the Cruise Missile*, South End Press, 2004.

Sachs, Jeffrey, *The End of Poverty: How We Can Make it Happen in our Lifetime,* Penguin Books, 2005.

Sands, Philippe, *Lawless World: America and the Making and Breaking of Global Rules,* Penguin Books Ltd., 2005.

Sardar, Ziauddin, & Merryl Wyn Davies, *American Dream/Global Nightmare*, Icon Books, 2004.

Schell, Jonathan, *The Unconquerable World*, Henry Holt and Company, 2003.

Schell, Jonathan, *The Jonathan Schell Reader*, Nation Books, 2004.

Scheuer, Michael, *Imperial Hubris*, Potomac Books, Inc., 2004-2005.

Seabrook, Jeremy, *The No-Nonsense Guide to World Poverty*, New Internationalist Publishing/Verso Books, 2003.

Sifry, Micah L., & Cerf, Christopher, eds., *The Iraq War Reader*, Touchstone/Simon & Schuster, 2003.

Stiglitz, Joseph, E., *Globalization and its Discontents*, W.W. Norton & Company, 2002.

Vanden Heuvel, Katrina, ed., *A Just Response*, Thunder's Mouth Press/Nation Books, 2002.

Wallis, Jim, *God's Politics*, HarperCollins, 2005.

West, Cornell, *Democracy Matters,* The Penguin Press, 2004.

Woodward, Bob, *Bush at War*, Simon & Schuster, 2002.

Woodward, Bob, *Plan of Attack*, Simon & Schuster, 2004.

Woodward, Bob, *State of Denial,* Simon & Schuster, 2006.

Wright, Lawrence, *The Looming Tower: Al-Qaeda and the Road to 9/11*, Vintage Books, 2006.

Young-Bruehl, Elisabeth, *Hanna Arendt: For the Love of the World*, Yale University Press, 1982, 2004.

Zakaria, Fareed, *The Future of Freedom*, W.W. Norton & Company, 2003.

Zelikow & Kean, *The 9/11 Commission Report*, W.W. Norton & Company, 2003.

Printed in the United States
220816BV00001B/3/P

9 781933 993744